WOMEN AND THE BIRTH OF RUSSIAN CAPITALISM

WOMEN AND THE BIRTH OF RUSSIAN CAPITALISM

A HISTORY OF THE SHUTTLE TRADE

IRINA MUKHINA

NIU PRESS *DeKalb, IL*

© 2014 by Northern Illinois University Press

Published by the Northern Illinois University Press, DeKalb, Illinois   60115

Manufactured in the United States using acid-free paper.

All Rights Reserved

Design by Yuni Dorr

Library of Congress Cataloging-in-Publication Data

Mukhina, Irina, 1979–

Women and the birth of Russian capitalism : a history of the shuttle trade / Irina Mukhina.

   pages cm

Includes bibliographical references and index.

ISBN 978-0-87580-480-4 (cloth) — ISBN 978-1-60909-152-1 (e-book)

1. Soviet Union—Commerce—History. 2. Women merchants—Soviet Union—History. 3. Business-women—Soviet Union—History. 4. Small business—Soviet Union—History. 5. Black market—Soviet Union—History. 6. Capitalism—Soviet Union—History. I. Title.

HF3626.5.M844 2014

382.082'0947—dc23

2014002306

Contents

List of Figures, Tables, and Graphs   vii

Acknowledgments   ix

Mystery Women: An Introduction   3

1—Origins of the Shuttle Trade, 1987–91   18

2—The "Golden Age" of the Shuttle Trade and Its Structure   40

3—Women Traders: Success in Numbers   72

4—The Price of Success   98

5—Where Did All the Women Go?   124

Notes   145

Bibliography   157

Index   169

List of Figures, Tables, and Graphs

Figure 1.1: A monument to shuttle traders in Yekaterinburg, Russia 2
Figure 1.2: A monument to shuttle traders in Blagoveshchensk, Russia 2
Figure 2.1: Traders' plaid bags at a train station 59
Figure 4.1: Merchandise on display in one of Moscow's stalls 102

Table 1.1: Crude oil prices in relation to Soviet GDP, 1984–87 23
Table 1.2: State revenues from alcohol production and sales, 1985–87 25
Table 1.3: Evaluation of economic situation in the country, workplace, personal life, 1989 35
Table 2.1: Consumer goods that did not meet quality requirements 52
Table 2.2: Number of Russian citizens who traveled abroad in 1995 53
Table 2.3: Economic situation in Russia, 1994–97 70
Table 3.1: Educational levels of traders 77
Table 3.2: Age distribution among traders, as of 1996 78
Table 3.3: Trading as a share of overall employment, as of 1996 78

Graph 2.1: Turkey's shuttle trade exports 63
Graph 2.2: Various actors in the shuttle trade 64
Graphs 3.1a and b: In your opinion, are [were] shuttle traders richer, poorer, or as well-off as most people in Russia? 80
Graph 3.2: Have shuttle traders become rich? 81
Graph 3.3: Do traders do their jobs willingly? 81
Graph 5.1: The exchange rate of the US dollar to the Russian ruble, 1998 126
Graph 5.2: Russian GDP 127
Graph 5.3: Patterns in acquisition of goods 130
Graph 5.4: Share of domestic goods on the markets 131
Graph 5.5: Assessment of the shuttle trade by the population of the Russian Federation 134

Acknowledgments

My intellectual and institutional debts run deep with this project. I would like to express sincere gratitude to my own institution, Assumption College, for appreciating and understanding the challenges and limitations of our workplace and for awarding me three faculty development grants for this project (during the summers of 2008, 2010, and 2012). These grants allowed me to travel to many places in Russia and Eastern Europe for fieldwork and to complete the project in a timely manner. The help and friendly advice from my colleagues as well as their unfailing support have been instrumental to this project. I am especially grateful to Carlo Marco Belfanti of Dipartimento di Studi sociali, Università degli Studi di Brescia, Italy; Liubov Denisova of the Russian Academy of Sciences; Dariusz Stola of the Institute of Political Studies of the Polish Academy of Sciences; Kate Transchel of California State University at Chico; and Christopher J. Ward of Clayton State University. I am also grateful to many scholars who have offered their advice at numerous conferences worldwide and who have reviewed the various sections and drafts of this manuscript. I have always found their advice insightful, and it challenged me to think of my work in new ways and from different perspectives. I would like to thank my colleagues in the department for their collegiality and their sense of humor. Last but not least, my family has been my support group from day one, and I am forever grateful for their patience and love.

WOMEN AND THE BIRTH OF RUSSIAN CAPITALISM

Figure 1.1 A monument to shuttle traders in Yekaterinburg, Russia, depicting two female traders, a former teacher and a former engineer. *Source:* ekmap.ru (Open Source).

Figure 1.2. A monument commemorating the hard labor of shuttle traders, Blagoveshchensk, Russia. *Source:* Photo taken by Alexander V. Solomin, 2012, Wikimedia Commons (Open Source).

Mystery Women

An Introduction

> There should be no movies made about criminal gangs and racketeers.
> They, vultures, did not invent anything but came for everything ready:
> [these criminals] killed and kicked owners out of their own businesses.
> And now they have everything. [Despite many movies made about
> them,] these gangsters are not the heroes of our times. But women are;
> those who in the early 1990s waited in lines with cargo bags at border
> crossings. It was they who built capitalism and taught Russians to trade.
>
> —From an interview with a trader, Khabarovsk, 2007

When I show my friends and colleagues images from Russia of statues of men and women with huge bags, they often ask me: "Who are the people commemorated by these statues?" "Shuttle traders," I say. Yet even after I tell them that these people represented up to a third of the population of post-Soviet Russia in the mid-1990s and that these people are commemorated by five different statues in different towns across Russia, my friends often still have no clue who these people are. And they are not alone. Even though we commonly use terms like economic depression, economic revival, birth of capitalism, free market economy, private enterprise, and a wide range of other catchy words to describe the post-Soviet states, little is known, acknowledged, or studied about one of the major manifestations of entrepreneurship in the 1990s: the shuttle trade. For most people, except a limited group of scholars and people of the post-Soviet space, the term itself—"shuttle trade"—is either incomprehensible or appears to be too narrow in scope. After all, shuttle traders with bulging bags traveled abroad ten or more times a year to bring home for resale only as many goods as they could personally carry in their enormous suitcases. The amount of each transaction was indeed miniscule. But the phenomenon hidden behind the term "shuttle trade" was by no means insignificant, small in scale, or too well researched to be forgotten.

The economic, social, and political reforms of *perestroika* in the USSR gave rise to a form of international trade called "shuttle trading," "suitcase trade," or "trading tourism."[1] Individual traders who were involved in these activities purchased merchandise abroad in small quantities and sold it back home in local, mostly open-air markets.[2] Though this form of trade became commonplace after 1990, it originated in the midst of the Soviet transition from a socialist to a capitalist economy in 1987. The progressive unraveling of the centrally planned economy facilitated new forms of international trade. By the late 1980s, the economic demands of the Soviet population, fueled by greater openness under *glasnost*, suddenly escalated. Due to the growing influx of information about the living standards of people in Western European nations and the United States, the Soviet people became increasingly consumer conscious at a time when the inefficiency of the Soviet economy and its growing inability to provide even basic consumer goods had become obvious to everyone. Distortions and inefficiencies in the supply system that were exacerbated by the liberalization and restructuring of the Soviet economic system in the late 1980s frustrated and aggravated Soviet consumers who saw, instead of jeans and color television sets in the stores, only endless queues for basic necessities and, in some places, the reversion to rationing. Simultaneously, the legalization of private enterprises and self-employment in 1987 minimized legal restrictions on the type of activities pursued individually by Soviet citizens. The lifting of travel restrictions and simplification of visa requirements for trips to socialist countries, especially after 1989, allowed many Soviet people to cross the border easily. Finally, the ambiguity or nonexistence of regulations concerning goods in small quantities that crossed the border left many legal loopholes through which both people and goods could and did pass.[3]

Though it was small at first, this peddling came to attract as many as three million would-be entrepreneurs by the time the economy of post-Soviet Russia began to progressively collapse under Boris Yeltsin in the early 1990s.[4] By the mid-1990s, nearly 30 million people were directly involved in the shuttle trade, which had come to provide 75 percent of all the consumer goods in the Russian market.[5] In 1995 to 1996, shuttle traders supplied the Russian market with 70 percent of all clothing and fabrics, 30 percent of imported fish and processed and raw meat, 50 percent of color TV sets, and 80 percent of VCR players. The volume of trade was estimated to be 15 billion US dollars annually, with the Ankara-Moscow route as the most profitable, providing a sizeable cash flow of $8 billion annually by 1997.[6] Estimates for the scale of this trade abound, but precise numbers have been hard to come by, as no official records were kept. Although the shuttle trade had come to constitute the backbone of Russian consumer trade, this sort of business remained semilegal. Presumably, shuttle traders legally brought various items in small quantities into Russia. But they claimed illegally that these items were not intended for resale but for personal use and consistently failed to pay customs duties and income taxes on this trade. Because of this chronic tax evasion and the near impossibility of controlling the low-scale trade, estimates for the trade turnover in the shuttle trade reached 20 billion US dollars annually nationwide,[7] yet this figure remained only an estimate.

Though the illicit nature of the shuttle trade made it a fascinating subject to study, the most intriguing feature of the trade was simultaneously its most obvious aspect and its best hidden secret. Uniquely, approximately 80 percent of the participants in the shuttle trade in the mid-1990s were women.[8] The exact numbers constantly changed along with the trade itself, but for the duration of its existence, the trade remained largely a gendered phenomenon. It is this discovery and realization that prompted the study of the trade, and thus emerged the multifaceted goal of this work: to tell its gendered story, to assess the motivations of those involved in this trade, and to discuss the range of personal experiences of female shuttle traders and the social impact of women's involvement in this sort of economic activity. By analyzing the social and gendered dimensions of the shuttle trade, we can begin to understand more broadly how gender shaped the "transition" period associated with the end of Communist regimes in Eastern Europe.[9] At the very least, the experience of women traders sheds some light on their work experiences in the transition period, the processes of large-scale social transformation, and the shaping of women's identities in relation to their family and social status that took place in the post-Soviet space.

Thus, the book provides both a public discourse and a personal narrative of the trade and the era of emerging market capitalism. It aims to highlight both the rupture and the continuity of the two social orders, i.e., socialism and capitalism, that marked the lived experiences of these traders and especially women. The traders had to unlearn the socialist ways of working and living, yet they bitterly resented the demise of the social-welfare system that could have provided for their children. Some of these women were forced into the trade by the abysmal economy of post-Soviet life. But many others entered the trade in hopes of giving their children not just the bare essentials but also private education and luxury vacations abroad. All of these complex motifs and all of those great possibilities and great tragedies form the core of the book.

Women's participation in this illicit business had important consequences for their self-perception and for our understanding of a woman's position during Russia's transition. Though women traders relate to their past experiences through the prism of their present-day situation, they nearly universally acknowledge that the trade allowed them to earn enough to survive and even prosper at a time when many were on the verge of starvation and when their own employment was questionable at best. Yet the scale of the trade and its semilegal position had important consequences for obscuring economic data on women's employment patterns. What these women did and, most important, how they did it and how much they earned in the process have a significant impact on our understanding of wages and employment patterns in the 1990s. While the official record of registered unemployment in Russia was, as in many other places, one "with a female face," and while women earned only 40 percent of men's wages,[10] these numbers represent only an imperfect official dataset that was accumulated at the time. Among the "unemployed" women, many were involved in trading and earned decent profits that often outweighed the earnings that their husbands received from their jobs.

Women's participation in the labor force and market economy, as well as their predominance in peddling, was not without precedence both in the Soviet context and in the global perspective. The participation of women in the labor force in the Soviet Union, including in private trade and especially in the sale of home-produced foods, was not new in the 1990s. Neither was private trade itself, which flourished during the New Economic Policy (NEP) era of the Soviet 1920s. Almost from the very inception of the NEP in the early 1920s, small-scale peddling and other small-scale entrepreneurial activities were highly gendered. Mostly women sold domestic goods and food in the open markets of the early Soviet days.[11] Private trade of the Stalinist period was also heavily feminized,[12] and even in the late Soviet period, there was a significant amount of female participation in the black market.[13]

Yet such parallels might mask the true scale of the shuttle trade of the 1980s and 1990s and many of its unique features. To name just a few: unlike in previous years, women traders of the 1990s traveled abroad rather than domestically and resold merchandise that they did not produce at home. Moreover, most of them had not previously been involved in the Soviet shadow economy, and they even described Soviet-era profiteers (*spekulianty*) in derogatory terms. For these and other reasons, many of which will be discussed later, the shuttle trade can hardly qualify as a mere extension of previously existing Russian or Soviet practices. As Caroline Humphrey pointed out when she described the shuttle trade in the 1990s, "Russia does not appear to be reverting to its prerevolutionary combination of family merchant houses and great periodic fairs. In fact, Russians seem surprised by what is happening with their trade."[14]

At the same time the shuttle trade was not unique to the Soviet Union and the Newly Independent States (NIS); indeed, it existed in most countries of the (former) Soviet Bloc in the 1980s and even prior to that.[15] For example, Poland's experience of shuttle trading dates back to 1972, which was the year that saw the liberalization of travel between Poland and East Germany. The so-called Borders of Friendship project allowed nationals of both countries to cross the border easily without a visa and even without a passport. Though the official purpose of this gesture was to allow for broader lines of communication of "international proletarianism," it was widely understood as an attempt to raise living standards on both sides by creating additional possibilities to access goods that were in short supply domestically. East Germany, in other words, was expected to become Poland's "shopping Mecca." Czechoslovakia signed similar agreements with Hungary and later Poland, East Germany, and Romania shortly thereafter.[16] But the Polish-German shuttle trade was short-lived. Dissatisfied with the trade imbalance and the shortage of some previously abundant goods, the German government imposed bans that began as early as 1972 and then progressed through the 1970s, effectively curbing the trade. The flow of goods was stopped with the reclosing of borders in 1980. Though the trade allowed for some flow of images (fashions) and new modes of consumption in Poland, it turned out to be too problematic for both sides to accept.[17]

Female predominance in the peddling of goods was not unique even to Eurasia. There has been ample research demonstrating that women assumed leading roles in the marketplaces, especially in the sale of domestic products and food, in places ranging geographically from Peru to West Africa to Taiwan.[18] But once again, the case of post-Soviet Russia appears unique due to the scale of the shuttle trade; it has been estimated that nearly 41 percent of Russia's working population was directly or indirectly engaged in the trade in 1996, the year that it peaked.[19] Moreover, on nearly all occasions the number of traders from Central European countries and other members of the NIS was so insignificant in proportion to the numbers of (former) Soviet people engaged in the trade that scholars nearly universally acknowledge that the shuttle trade of the late 1980s and the 1990s was indeed a massive (post-) Soviet experience and not a Central European or Asian phenomenon.[20]

If we were to look for global links and connections, they would be found not in drawing parallels or discovering replicas elsewhere but in acknowledging, as several researchers have done, that the shuttle traders in many ways promoted globalization and the westernization of the desires and demands of the former Soviet people in the post-Soviet states. Shuttle traders brought not only new goods but new lifestyles to their customers.[21] At the same time, such traders influenced the image-making process in supplier countries (like Turkey and China) that sought to market their goods to post-Soviet consumers as "Western." Many supplier factories abroad embraced styles and goods that could be marketed as "Made in Italy" in the NIS, where customers craved symbols of westernization. As a result, as Deniz Yükseker has argued, globalization was not a top-down process with its origins in large corporate headquarters. In a more complex way, "the mobility of 'ordinary' people across borders facilitated the flow of signs and images. Moreover, Western images and fashions got remolded and acquired new meanings in the process of circulation."[22]

Moreover, some scholars argued that the shuttle trade became a new form of globalization as it created "patterns of interdependence that are qualitatively different from those produced during previous episodes of globalization." Specifically, it linked various regions in the chain of relations that were informal yet vast, unregulated yet transformative in their potency and scale. It irrevocably tied various regions as trading partners in an informal alliance of major economic significance. Because of the scale and intensity of such trade networks, the shuttle trade is "illustrative of a novel aspect of contemporary globalization with important implications for a host of domestic factors ranging from regulatory regimes to social change."[23] Indeed, precisely the two factors mentioned in the latter part of the statement, with a special emphasis on social—and gendered—change, are at the core of this study. The government's attempt to codify a de facto market within a regulatory, and thus controllable, base and the social implications of the massive female engagement in the shuttle trade collided to highlight the monumental importance of this phenomenon for the transformation of the post-Soviet space.

Yet with all of this said, the role of gender still remains underrepresented and understudied in the process of reshaping and reconstructing the social space of post-Soviet existence. Female participation in this trade has yet to receive its due attention. Thus, with the goal to illuminate the role of female traders in mind, I aim to present a discussion of the reasons for female predominance in this trade and the major problems that women shuttle traders faced while pursuing their business. This is a story of the shuttle trade from a social and gendered perspective, the story of the role of women in peddling international consumer goods that coexisted with the collapse of the Soviet Union.[24]

White? Black? Gray!

The ambiguity of the shuttle trade firmly placed it in the framework of the so-called gray market. As such, it is challenging and might be misleading to evaluate these peddling activities solely as a form of private entrepreneurship that constitutes an integral part of all market economies (and the one that was emerging in post-Soviet space as well).[25] Various chapters of the book return to this question of whether the shuttle trade should be assessed as a form of necessity entrepreneurship, an emerging genuine entrepreneurship, or something else altogether, to address it more fully. Whatever the final verdict, we need to keep in mind that the shuttle trade of the 1990s did not have any formal or legal features of an established business.[26] Though the informal transaction costs of such trading could be high (for example, given the need to bribe border guards to ensure safe border passage), most traders never aspired to make permanent or legal arrangements, and very few obtained even a most rudimentary license to trade.[27] In trying to assess peddling and its links to private enterprise, Jeffrey Hass has argued, for example, that the failure to fully understand the post-Soviet market creation stems from the limited available data and the radical nature of the transformation, but primarily from erroneous frameworks adopted by both neoclassical economics (stressing costs, benefits, and rational action) and new institutional economics (encapsulating rational action in law) in evaluating various *pseudo*-entrepreneurial endeavors like the shuttle trade.[28] Though the range of definitions adopted for the term "entrepreneur" is wide and less than perfectly coherent, most scholars of the shuttle trade accept that the genuine entrepreneurship that was emerging in post-Soviet Russia involved getting a license, registrations, and some foundational documents (codes, etc.). Thus, shuttle traders were labeled as "would-be entrepreneurs" for their early potential to build up a new sector of the economy and later "pseudo-entrepreneurs" for failing to pursue any business opportunities. To some, these people could be called "necessity entrepreneurs" because they were pushed into trading by the economic instability of their lives, though we need to keep in mind that they always had other options for employment.[29]

Moreover, because of the cultural constraints, the shuttle trade can hardly qualify as a simple modification of anything that had formerly existed in the Soviet Union. From a gradualist perspective, the revolutionary nature of the communist collapse did not result in an immediate change in individual behavior. Instead, people of Russia and Eastern Europe could easily learn small-scale trading, but the process of learning-by-doing and acquisition of genuine entrepreneurial knowledge was more gradual and did not happen overnight. Since the process of introducing capitalism is complex, multifaceted, and characterized by various other factors like institution-building, structural adjustment, informational (a)symmetry, and of course, behavioral change,[30] international peddling burst out as a spontaneous manifestation of the people's craving to satisfy their immediate needs. It was not until post-1998 that the trade acquired some features of a small business and required a new mentality from its participants.[31] In a way, it might be helpful to think of the trade in the early to mid-1990s as akin to children selling homemade lemonade to passersby. These children have an immediate goal of making some profit; they do not pay taxes, and more often than not they prosper relative to their peers (by having some pocket change). Do they learn the basic workings of capitalism? Possibly. But are they entrepreneurs? Does their act represent the origins of a small-scale private enterprise? I'll leave it to the readers to decide.

The semilegality of trading also made shuttling problematic for the government to control. Most attempts to regulate the shuttle trade had little to do with regulating private businesses or creating a more business-conducive environment. Instead, the government of Russia sought to improve border controls in order to make the borders "hard" and stabilize the economy enough to encourage people to look for jobs in non-trading sectors of the economy. None of the measures adopted by the government, however, were able to contain this trade of the 1990s.[32] The government's failure to regulate the shuttle trade also makes studying the development of the "suitcase business" difficult.

In the late 1980s, the main feature of the trade was its ad hoc nature; there were no more than mere hints at rules and regulations to govern it. Initially, the government was willing to "look the other way" or even support such trade as a way of providing for the collapsing consumer market in Russia. Yet the government drastically underestimated the vast numbers of people that the trade would attract and its subsequent scale and longevity. By the end of 1993 and then progressively through the mid-1990s, the government aimed to bring this highly problematic aspect of the emerging market under its control, at first mostly by improving border control in order to make the borders "hard." Crucially, most government regulations in the mid-1990s were remedial and did not appear in a timely manner that could have structured the trade from the start. Moreover, enforcement of any regulation, no matter how effective and precise its content, proved to be challenging if not impossible and resulted in ample opportunities for subjectivity and corruption among bureaucrats and state agents. Many of the early changes took place in response to the acquisition of knowledge and statistical data on the volume and nature of trade. Decision makers collected raw data about border crossings and the scale of the trade and utilized these statistics to create regulatory measures that attempted to shape both the border control and customs regulations, and eventually the emerging free market space of post-Soviet Russia.

Though the trade affected the new administrative order that was emerging in post-Soviet Russia, data accumulation and border crossing regulations were of paramount importance. By analyzing the administrative acts in relation to the shuttle trade as well as many intrinsic features like social welfare, one can better understand the difficulty of using these trade networks for creating a permanent and collective market. Rather, the shuttle trade was shaped by the particularistic, material and mundane individual goals of those who participated in it. Thus, this niche of the illicit trade could hardly be celebrated as an example of viable and vibrant entrepreneurship that could have blossomed into a new entrepreneurial sector of small businesses, nor could it be turned into such by rigorous regulations and formalization. As is explained in chapter 5, most traders left the business after 1998, and very few used it as a platform for developing small-, middle-, or large-scale businesses of their own.

Traders facilitated the transition to the market economy in Russia but did so mostly by offering consumer goods in high demand to a society starved of basic necessities. The difficulties that these traders faced highlighted the gap between the rhetoric of free market economy and actual market practices. These traders had to create and shape the physical (i.e., open-space) market for their goods without the basic legislative and other provisions and protections of market economies. The shuttle trade thus could only be understood as "market without market." In its early years, the state became a midwife of this informal economy, though it simultaneously aimed to create a de jure market out of a de facto market. Yet the transformation of the shuttle trade was assured by its very fragility, especially vis-à-vis economic crisis situations, more than by specific legislative acts passed by the government.

Where Are You, My Friends?

The default of Russian foreign debts and the collapse of the ruble in August 1998 were devastating to shuttle traders because all transactions depended on the exchange rate of USD. Many shuttle traders suffered such massive losses that they never recouped; others reported that their profits dropped from at least 100 percent or more prior to 1998 to at most 30 percent after the default. For this reason many scholars treat the year 1998 as a turning point in the dynamics of the shuttle trade, citing a much smaller number of traders in the 2000s compared to the 1990s. Moreover, in 2006, in an attempt to control revenues and bring the trade out of the underground, the Russian government lowered the duty-free allowance for individual travelers from 50 to 35 kilograms. This change in customs regulations prompted an avalanche of short articles that claimed the death of the shuttle trade and the miserable failure of the traders. But the authors of these articles missed the fact that the shuttle trade had already undergone a considerable transformation since 1998 and was already dead (i.e., in the form that had existed from 1987 to 1998) by the time the new customs regulations were put in place.

The shuttle trade experienced a split in two directions after 1998. Though most traders abandoned their occupation after 1998 and either retired or found alternative ways to make a living, those who remained went one of two ways. On one hand were the few who managed to turn their peddling into medium-sized businesses. These new entrepreneurs no longer travel abroad constantly and carry goods on their backs; instead, they arrange to deliver large quantities of merchandise via cargo carriers. They also do not stand in retail booths; instead, they hire workers to sell their items. Official statistics confirm that even though the number of traders has declined, the monetary volume of the trade had more than doubled by 2004. On the other hand, the traders who never managed to succeed and develop their trade beyond their suitcases, turned into "internal" traders who either resell domestic goods (which now constitute 40 percent of all retail items) or buy imported goods in bulk locally to make profits on retail sale, most often from people in the first category.

Even though the shuttle trade no longer exists in the form that it did in the 1990s, both this form of female activity and the underlying question of women's role in post-communist transition economies remain highly relevant to understanding the transformation of the social space in post-Soviet Russia. Even though capitalism had an appeal and a promise of a new radiant future, the actual lived experiences of the first few years were different and hardly coincided with the promises and expectations that accompanied the transformation of the post-Soviet economy. The shuttle trade, or this "market without market," became an avenue of female suffering but also of survival and even empowerment during the time that most Russians now call "the wild 1990s."

Methodological Labyrinths

If it was difficult for the government to regulate this illicit trade, it was even more challenging to find reliable economic data or a "perfect" methodology for its study and analysis. The source base of this gray market is limited and at times elusive, and on occasion when I was trying to locate sources I reminded myself of my own students who wanted to write research papers that exposed and unveiled the secrets of the KGB. But in order for the study to happen, I realized that I needed to find a *workable* methodology instead of a *perfect* one. Thus, I have combined scholarly works and statistical reports on the scope and evolution of the shuttle trade with firsthand accounts of traders themselves. Most firsthand accounts come from extensive oral history fieldwork conducted predominantly, but not exclusively, in Moscow, Khabarovsk, and Krasnodar.[33] In addition, I have accumulated a collection of written testimonies, personal statements, and life stories that appeared in various sources ranging from newspapers to published autobiographies to random conversations. Although the number of formal interviews was limited, the number of various short statements counted into hundreds.[34] Though the interviews on which this study rests are inevitably only a limited and somewhat personal representation of the broader pattern, they nonetheless reveal several common themes and tendencies that are also supported by data available from other sources. At times, the "hard data" to supplement the oral history fieldwork was simply insufficient; hence it is the lack of such data, not the lack of research, that makes some of my arguments more speculative than definitive.

Finding people to interview seemed to be as easy as it gets. Anyone who traveled to Russia in the 1990s knows that traders were almost omnipresent, and it looked like everyone was in the business at the time. The same goes for finding people who had some experience in trading. They are no longer in the markets; I systematically failed to find traders of the 1990s in various open or covered markets at the present day. All the interviews that I conducted there revealed that a new group of people offered consumers the products of their choice. On the upside, everyone seemed to know someone who had participated in the business in the 1990s. Informal conversations and kitchen talks were enjoyed by all, even if some details were omitted or avoided by the respondents. However, chronic tax evasion, endemic corruption, less than flattering popular attitudes to traders, fear of envy by neighbors, or to the contrary, unwillingness to share their own failures all had an impact on the kind of information that was "forgotten" and the kind that was shared and revealed. Stories of intimate relationships were eagerly shared, whereas information on profits and capital was not. Equally, nearly all interviewees wanted to remain anonymous if their stories were to appear in a published work.

Moreover, while shuttle trading and specifically its gendered dimensions are a matter of my *historical* research, the recent nature of this phenomenon necessitates a heavy reliance on a wide range of social-science techniques and research methodologies. Because the trading affected social, economic, and legal spheres of Soviet and post-Soviet life as well as gender relations, on occasion I attempted to bind together methodologies and studies that belong to such diverse disciplines as cultural anthropology, economics, sociology, history, and psychology. I do not claim to have an expertise in these fields; the very thought of such a claim would appear horrendously arrogant to me. This remains true even when I consider multidisciplinary links and reference multidisciplinary methodology throughout the book.

A few aspects deserve to be separately addressed here. As mentioned above, economic theory and sociological research have found their way into the research and discussion of the shuttle trade. They have proven to be invaluable additions to the study and have allowed a historian by training to gain insights into the shuttle trade that might otherwise have been lacking. Yet the challenges of multidisciplinarity remained predictable at best. In reading a study by an economist about gender earning differentials in Russia, which is a topic that I believed I was familiar with through my work on gendered divisions of labor and income discrepancies in the Soviet Union, I reached my limits when I read that the gender wage differential was (reproduced here to the best of my abilities):

$$ln W_m - ln W_f = X'_m B_m - X'_f B_f.$$

In this formula, "W_m and W_f are log wages of men and women respectively, X_m and X_f are vectors of mean productivity-related characteristics of men and women, and B_m and B_f are coefficient estimates in the OLS regression equations for men and women."[35] I would applaud anyone who can meaningfully utilize or criticize the above-mentioned equation. Yet to a humble historian with very little exposure to economics, I have to admit that this appeared to be gibberish. Even if I were to untangle all the signs and understand the importance of this formula, I would have been very unlikely to apply it to my own work. I realized at this point that even though I risk being accused of failing to engage with other disciplines sufficiently, I primarily want to avoid the most pervasive pitfalls of multidisciplinary research. As historian Glennys Young listed in his work, these pitfalls "include tendencies to accept uncritically the conventional wisdom in another discipline, to ignore internal debates, and to harvest tidbits without exploring their relationship." Since few, if any, can be experts in all disciplines at once, Young pointed out that, as we (historians) "engage in dialogue with other disciplines, we have rarely subjected to rigorous critique what we have borrowed and assimilated."[36]

Indeed, this has been the case for most studies that I came to utilize and even for data that seemed rather uncontroversial. For example, public opinion studies too have been under scrutiny and a subject of debate for over a decade or longer. In their study of sociology and public opinion, Osborne and Rose cited various scholars who argued that the "'scientificity' of a discipline can be measured by the extent to which that discipline is creative of new phenomena ... [and thus] specificity of a science is not just reducible to a question of exactitude, epistemology or methodology but also relates to the material and technical factors that lead to such a creation of phenomena."[37] Though typically this argument would extend to the natural sciences, Osborne and Rose suggest that sociology should be a part of this discourse, especially when it comes to the phenomenon of public opinion. Even if the kind of creativity and the temporality of change in sociology are not equal to these two factors in the natural sciences, social science research can produce quantifiable change and thus work as a creator of the phenomenon. In the context of my research, this argument demonstrated that public opinion studies exposed the heightened sensitivity of the population to a particular topic (e.g., the shuttle trade) only as it was *created* by a researcher or a team of researchers of that topic. Thus, such studies do not validate or accurately demonstrate the scope or the scale of public engagement with a given theme.

To me, it became more important to acknowledge and internalize the value of "understanding [the] economic life as a set of social and cultural practices"[38] than to borrow selectively from the many disciplines that cared to write about the Soviet demise. Yet this did not resolve the issues of how to combine the methodologies and findings of various disciplines effectively. Hence, I apologize in advance to all specialists in economic and human geography, sociology, anthropology, economics, political economy, and any other relevant fields for failing to authoritatively use research findings from these disciplines to supplement my own.

The book is divided into five chapters with multiple themes in each. Chapter 1 analyzes the unraveling of the Soviet economy and presents a thorough analysis of the early stages of the fledging shuttle trade. It specifically addresses the relationship of the trade to legal changes, including the Law on Individual Labor Activity, the emergence of cooperatives and their role in shaping international peddling, Komsomol (Communist Youth) international exchange programs, and economic challenges of the later Soviet era. Chapter 2 covers four fundamental questions that help readers to appreciate the scale and uniqueness of the trade. By analyzing interviews and popular notions of women's roles and supplementing these with official statistics, the first part of this chapter identifies a range of factors that can help explain the prevalence of women in this gender-specific business. The second part deals with governmental attempts to regulate the trade. Various regulatory measures were introduced in order to make the trade easier to control, yet their enforcement was a different matter altogether. Furthermore, it is impossible to appreciate the scale and complexity of this trade network, which bonded millions of women in the transition economy, without acknowledging the broad geography of the trade. Spanning from socialist Poland in the late 1980s to China and Turkey and to a lesser extent India and the United Arab Emirates by the mid-1990s, the shuttle trade became truly global to include dozens of destinations, explored in the third part of the chapter. Last but not least, chapter 2 addresses by far the most complex and disputable question of the economic impact of the shuttle trade on the Russian economy and its share of all imports in the Russian Federation.

Chapters 3 and 4 deal directly with gender-specific aspects of the trade. Chapter 3 begins by presenting a social portrait of the so-called typical trader. Such insight is crucial to gender analysis, and the discussion of interviews and life stories might help readers relate to these women and understand them better. The chapter also addresses the role that these traders played in changing consumption patterns in post-Soviet Russia. If the consumption of foreign goods was deeply sacramental to most Soviet people (who, for example, saw jeans as a symbol of westernization), the massive influx of foreign goods made possible by traders rendered such notions less relevant. Brands meant everything at first, but little by little consumption became non-sacramental when people stopped caring for the products' intrinsic value. Chapter 4 analyzes the positive outcomes and negative consequences of the shuttle trade for female traders. For women, the shuttle business assured their survival and even relative financial prosperity, at least for the short term. Some women saw it as an avenue of empowerment and were able to start large genuine businesses that now include significant capital investment and dozens of employees. On the other hand, the business produced a cohort of problems: persistent tax evasion excluded women traders from many social welfare benefits, the need to conduct business unofficially fostered corruption, and the increase in the volume of trade directly corresponded to a rise in the number of divorces, abortions, and sexually transmitted diseases among female traders.

Chapter 5 analyzes the final phase of the shuttle trade. The default of Russian foreign debts and the collapse of the ruble in August 1998 were devastating to shuttle traders, and in many ways the financial crisis exposed the instability of this gray market and shaped it much more than any provision adopted by the state. Though retail markets are still commonplace in Russia, the shuttle trade of today would be unrecognizable to most of its participants of the 1990s. To them, the shuttle trade was a momentous opportunity that disappeared in 1998, yet it was an opportunity that shaped both their lives and the social and economic space of post-Soviet Russia.

1

Origins of the Shuttle Trade, 1987–91

The harsh reality of life destroyed all romantic aspirations. Perestroika
scared us. The mass conscience was soon overburdened by yet another
historical, typical for Russia, incompatibility of ideals and desire to eat.
This wave [of enthusiasm for perestroika] retreated like a tsunami in
the Indian Ocean, leaving behind heaps of corpses, ruins of an empire,
and an abandoned faith in a brighter future.

—From an interview with a resident of St. Petersburg, 2005

The specific origins of international peddling are complex and even
disputable, yet the birthdate of the trading is much easier to pinpoint.
Shuttle trading—more of a trading tourism, at the time—was born in 1987,
in the midst of the reforms that swept across the Soviet Union after 1985
and that eventually led to its demise. The shuttle trade was born in the process of transition from a socialist to a capitalist economy, though its origins
were not nearly as spectacular or grandiose as the shuttle trade that emerged
by the mid-1990s. This is one of the most often overlooked social aspects
of perestroika, and it is one of the most powerful, transformative, and far-
reaching social developments of the reform era.

The dynamic of unraveling of the centrally planned economy facilitated
or even bore the shuttle trade. The conditions during the era of perestroika
and later, during the demise of the Soviet Union, were just right to allow
the semilegal shuttle trade to blossom. To begin with, the demands of the
population, fueled by the era of greater openness during glasnost and the resulting influx of information about the living standards of people in various
Western European countries and the United States, were becoming increasingly complex and consumer-conscious. Many of the consumer goods that

were manufactured in the Soviet Union no longer satisfied people's demand for fashionable and high-quality clothing, cosmetics, and food. Not just any pair of pants, but specifically Wrangler jeans, became a commodity of choice. Yet this growth of consumer demand was coupled with the growth in inefficiency in the production system and its inability to provide even basic goods during perestroika. Though the specific role that the traders played in globalizing consumer tastes will be discussed separately, the chronic shortages of all consumer goods, coupled with greater aspirations for achieving "Western" standards of living, combined to create a significant push factor for early peddlers.

Legal changes promoted during the Gorbachev era were also of major significance. Trade had long been treated as an illegal or at least highly suspicious activity. But legalization of private enterprises in general and trade in particular in the second half of the 1980s, though failing to transform people's attitudes to trading overnight, lifted legal restrictions on the type of activities pursued individually by Soviet citizens. The lifting of travel restrictions and the simplification of visa requirements in the late 1980s allowed many people to easily cross the border, and the ambiguity or nonexistence of regulations concerning goods that crossed the border in small quantities left many legal loopholes by means of which both people and goods could pass.

The unique and different paths that former socialist countries followed during the period of transition also created many discrepancies concerning the goods available in each country and the prices for those goods. The ruble remained an unconvertible and rather useless currency for early shuttle traders. Yet during the early transformation era of 1988–91, stockpiles of goods such as cameras and watches were available at fixed prices in the Soviet Union but were priced much higher and were in demand in various countries of the socialist bloc. On the other hand, the availability of cheap items such as nail polish in Poland, and the high demand for these items back in the Soviet Union, assured sky-high profits for traders. High profits turned out to be unsustainable at the late-1980s level in later years. Yet they were sufficient to attract many Soviet people as the economy of the Soviet Union started to progressively collapse. This collapse of the economy in the post-Soviet space forced many people to seek alternative incomes, and many people felt that shuttle trade was the only way to make a living. Still, mass involvement in the trade did not come until 1990 or even 1991, and hence this story belongs to a different era.

In retrospect, the rise of Mikhail Gorbachev to the top of Soviet political leadership in March 1985 was not as revolutionary as many observers like to believe. After the deaths of numerous political leaders and a rapid succession of aged men in top political positions, there seemed to be no real alternative to Gorbachev. Moreover, both the people at large and those close to power were tired of the rapid changes and uncertainties that accompanied each passing of power. Everyone seemed ready for more stability and a positive change, and the new, young leader appeared to be capable of delivering on this promise. As Nikolai Ryzhkov remembered, "the country was tired of burying its leaders; [people] wanted to believe that the new leader was serious and here [to stay] for a long while and they wanted to know what to expect of him."[1] Most Politburo members supported the opinion of Nikolai Tikhonov, then-chairman of the Council of Ministers, that "the very logic of life led us to these decisions. ... We simply did not have an alternative candidate."[2] Gorbachev's coming to power in March 1985 was accompanied by a new leadership of the party at large. Andrei Gromyko was appointed Chairman of the Presidium of the Supreme Soviet of the USSR and Tikhonov was replaced by Nikolai Ryzhkov in the position of Chairman of the Council of Ministers in the fall of 1985.

Immediately, the new leadership initiated a campaign to revive and restructure socialism. From Gorbachev's perspective, the key component of this revitalization, along with some changes in favor of greater democratization, was the strategy of accelerating the economic performance of the Soviet Union. The acceleration campaign was officially announced at the Plenum of the Central Committee of the Communist Party in April 1985 and was ratified at the XXVIIth Party Congress in 1986. The reformers, including Gorbachev, did not excessively emphasize the shortcomings of the economy but, rather, underlined the need to integrate the national economy into a larger and more affluent global economy. According to Gorbachev's team, four main factors shaped the need to accelerate the economy: (a) the need to address the old and unresolved social problems, especially in terms of improving food consumption, housing, and health care for the masses; (b) the danger of overcommitments from the Cold War era and the inability to maintain parity with the United States; (c) the nation's desire to achieve complete independence from the need to import consumer goods from the so-called Western (i.e., non-socialist) countries; and (d) the need to maintain the image of an ideal socioeconomic system, something that was becoming increasingly challenging to do without providing people with more and better consumer goods.

Acceleration was understood above all else as an increase in the norms of production and economic growth; to Gorbachev, this implied GDP growth of at least 4 percent in 1986–87 and beyond. But acceleration also implied a new qualitative approach. Gorbachev proposed "to activate the human factor" by using the human potential of the country to the fullest. He aspired to do so by offering greater financial incentives for quality work, by encouraging private initiative, and by building upon the solid educational base of the society. Not least, the program recognized a need to put a new and greater emphasis on social welfare, which included Gorbachev's campaign to provide a separate apartment for each family by the turn of the century.

In 1987 the Soviet policy of economic acceleration was replaced by the policy of economic rebuilding, or perestroika, which allowed for even greater liberalization of economic policies. State planning was replaced with state orders, and now state orders controlled only 85 percent of all production and output, unlike state planning's universal control of all industrial output. Now state enterprises were entitled to the remaining 15 percent of their output and were allowed to sell it for profit. Ideally, the profits were to be used to subsidize the development of local infrastructure, to increase wages for employees, to invest in production technology, and to improve profitability overall. But as a result, managers of many factories and various enterprises, seeing a possibility for personal control of produce and profits, started to barter produce to minimize production "on paper," i.e., officially registered and thus controllable production. Oftentimes, managers saw an opportunity to sell off what their factories produced. Many people echoed the words of one worker that "managers rushed to steal [from their factories]; not to develop production but to grab whatever was at hand. Theft was the basis of most successful business. And this was all because of perestroika."[3]

In many different ways, none of the reforms worked out as planned. The main problem that the Soviet government faced in the mid-1980s was the decline in revenues from the export of natural resources (mainly oil and gas) and from the sale of liquor during Gorbachev's anti-drinking campaign. Directly linked to these processes and simultaneous to them was the growing deficit in all consumer goods that, in combination with liberalization of travel and new laws on private labor initiative (as will be discussed below), pushed many Soviet people to look for alternative means of income and a new source of consumer goods, both of which were found in the shuttle trade.

One of the main challenges for the Soviet Union in the mid-1980s was the decline in world oil prices, paralleled by a rapid increase in prices of products such as grain and various crops imported by the Soviet Union. If in 1980 a barrel of oil was sold for an average of $37.42 and the prices remained stable well into 1984, then in 1985 a barrel of crude oil went down in price to $26.92. By 1986, the price for crude oil nearly collapsed; that year a barrel of crude oil was sold on average at $14.44. The low prices, though with minor fluctuations, continued throughout the demise of the Soviet Union, and adjusted for inflation, the 1980 price for crude oil was not reached again until 2008 (or 2004 in absolute numbers).[4]

For the Soviet Union, such fluctuations in the world oil prices meant that its import and export balance of trade changed dramatically in a very short term, creating the so-called outside shock. Countries that do not have a single dominant item of export are often safeguarded from such drastic changes; a price fluctuation for one particular item is often balanced out by stability or an increase in prices for many other export commodities. Yet the situation of the Soviet Union was different because of its reliance on petrodollars: its main exports were crude oil and natural gas. Commonly, single-export countries might compensate for the changing market by importing less of what they used to buy abroad or by turning to different items as imports. But such a policy was hardly an option for the Soviet Union. The Soviet situation was complicated by the fact that the country depended on the import of specific quantities of specific foods, primarily grain. This is not to say that the government failed to recognize the challenges; it in fact attempted to stabilize the situation by writing off *kolkhoz* debts and subsidizing agricultural production. Typically, such measures should have gone hand-in-hand with increased retail prices. This is precisely what the Soviet government tried to avoid at all costs: cheap and accessible food was the main staple, the proverbial banner, of the socialist economy. The Soviet leadership decided to freeze prices artificially by offering subsidies. As a result, in 1989 alone, bread was subsidized at 20 percent, meat at 74 percent, butter at 72 percent, milk at 61 percent, and so on.[5]

The country's budget could have survived such a pricey commitment to suppressing inflation only if it raised additional revenues, but this goal was impossible in light of declining oil prices in the world market. Excellent harvests in 1986 and 1987 at least partially offset the declining oil prices by allowing for less import of grain. The year 1988, with its mediocre harvest, brought all the problems back to the surface.

Though Gorbachev employed a team of professional economists as early as 1985, neither he personally nor his team had a clear program of action at this point. In 1987, some two years after becoming head of state, Gorbachev acknowledged that the economic problems faced by the Soviet Union ran much deeper than he had anticipated.[6] As early as 1985, Gorbachev's attention was drawn to the fact that the volume of oil extraction had declined in recent years in West Siberia. Also, various problems related to the development of new mines and improving miners' working conditions had not been solved. The fall in oil prices and the decline in extraction created an even deeper problem.

Table 1.1: Crude oil prices in relation to Soviet GDP, 1984–87

	1984	1985	1986	1987
Crude oil sale incomes, billions in rubles	30.9	28.2	22.5	22.8
…of the sales above, outside the socialist bloc	13.6	10.6	5.5	7.1
GDP %, export of crude oil	4.04%	3.63%	2.82%	2.76%

Source: E. Gaidar, "O blagikh namereniiakh" (reprint of official data), *Pravda*, June 24, 1990.

By August 1986 Gorbachev was speaking of the need to increase oil extraction to offset the increase in the price of imports such as grain and the decline in oil prices.[7] The decision to tap into such massive oil deposits as Samotlor, though crucially important, did not on its own solve the problem of falling state revenues. Many untapped megadeposits were flooded or otherwise poorly prepared for tapping, whereas easily available or well-developed mines were near exhaustion. Hence the price of oil extraction and the need to invest more capital increased disproportionately with the price of oil or the scale of production. Thus, various leading officials reported to Gorbachev that in 1986, it took 30 percent more state resources and capital investment to tap the same amount of oil as in any year from 1981 to 1985, and three times more than in 1971–75. Both proverbially and literally, the oil was no longer at the surface. In terms of state expenditure, the share of investment in oil production increased from 14 percent in the early 1970s to 23 percent in the late 1980s.[8]

Ironically, though Gorbachev and everyone around him seemed to understand the challenges of the emerging oil market and the Soviet oil export crisis, other economic measures undertaken at the same time seemed to contradict this knowledge and to run counter to any logic of anti-crisis campaigning. Nowhere was this more obvious than in the case of the anti-drinking campaign. Gorbachev and his team later claimed that the initiative to pursue an anti-drinking campaign belonged to the people and not to any single political leader. Ryzhkov remembered that "the country was drinking insanely; [people] drank everywhere … before work, after work, instead of work; in party cells, construction zones and factories; in the offices and at home, just everywhere."[9] To curb the widespread abuse of hard liquor, the

Central Committee of the Communist Party issued a decree on "Measures to Overcome Drunkenness and Alcoholism" that limited the sale of liquor, at first by 50 percent. It was expected that the decrease in the volume of sales would be compensated for by increased prices on the remaining liquor.[10]

Prior warnings and concerns about this causing an imbalance in the state budget were dismissed as overly pessimistic. For example, N. K. Baibakov, the Chairman of the State Planning Committee, which was responsible for issuing production plans, warned that revenues on the production and sale of liquor accounted for nearly 24 percent of all retail revenues; hence any measures that drastically cut these revenues would bring massive negative consequences for the state budget. Yet such warnings were dismissed; instead, the deadline for the 50 percent cut in sales of liquor was moved from 1990 to 1987, the 70th anniversary of the October Revolution.[11]

The results were predictable, to say the least. In 1985–88, the budget fell short by 67 billion rubles because of the anti-drinking campaign. This was yet another massive blow to the Soviet economy, so much so that Gorbachev's team had to abandon the program for the sake of saving the state budget. In 1989, the revenues from the production and sale of liquor exceeded those of 1984. Yet the damage that had already been done to the economy was irreparable.[12]

The anti-drinking campaign was damaging to the Soviet economy for several reasons. In addition to undermining state revenues and unbalancing state budgets, it took resources away from importation of consumer goods. The retail sale of imported consumer goods fell from 27.1 billion rubles in 1984 to 24.8 billion rubles in 1987 and 22.0 billion rubles in 1988.[13] The resulting deficit and the overall shortage of consumer goods were perpetuated by a rising demand for goods such as sugar, which could be used in the production of homemade liquor, and other goods that could be used as a substitute for hard liquor (such as aftershaves and perfumes).[14] For example, the production of *samogon*, a homemade equivalent of vodka, increased sixfold by the fall of 1988 in comparison with 1984. In terms of consumption, this increase compensated for the shortage of hard liquor for sale; yet it implied a sixfold increase in the consumption of sugar.[15] Even excessive borrowing and debt, which reached 400 billion rubles or 44 percent of GDP in 1989, could not compensate for the deficit in the budget or pay to maintain sufficient imports of consumer goods.[16] The report submitted by Ryzhkov, the Chairman of the Soviet of Ministers, in September 1989 clearly demonstrated the problem:

Table 1.2: State revenues from alcohol production and sales, 1985–87

	1984	1985	1986	1987
Revenues raised on the sale of alcohol, in billions of rubles	36.7	33.3	27.0	29.1
Revenues from the sale of alcohol, in % of GDP	4.8%	4.3%	3.4%	3.5%
Volume of alcohol trade, in billions of rubles	52.8	47.7	37.0	36.6

Source: S. G. Sinel'nikov, *Biudzhetnyi krizis v Rossii: 1985–1995* (Moscow: Evrasiia, 1995).

A significant part of the population saved a lot of money on purchasing fewer alcoholic beverages. [As a result], many of them switched their interest and financial resources to other consumer products like various foods, clothing, shoes, and domestics. In the second half of 1986, the sales of sugar, candy, fruit juices, tomato paste and some other items that are often used in home-production of spirits increased dramatically. According to the State Statistical Committee, in 1987 1.4 million tons of sugar were used for *samogon,* which is roughly equal to 140–150 million liters of *samogon* and which practically compensates for limiting the production and sale of vodka and other alcoholic beverages.[17]

As a result of these various factors, the shortage of consumer goods became a pandemic by late 1988. By the end of 1988, of 989 items on the list of basic goods for an average consumer, only 11 percent were "available at most times."[18] Nearly everything was on the list of deficit items, from lightbulbs to detergent to toothpaste. Items such as TV sets, refrigerators, and furniture were nearly impossible to buy, and even previously overabundant items such as school notebooks and pencils were hard to come by. The rationing of certain goods did not help significantly in solving the problem. For example, among the first and most common items to be rationed were accessories for newborns, including baby soap, light cloth for cloth diapers, strollers, cribs, bottles, and swaddling cloth. Coupons that authorized the purchase of these items, however, were often realized years after the child was born due to the lack of these deficit items in any, even specialty, stores. Many people complained to press organs: "We lack too many things. At times we cannot buy a new T-shirt for a year or more and the same goes for dress shirts, let alone suits or anything else. We even cannot buy such basic necessities as cloth for towels, men's and women's socks, underwear, hats, and there is no children's clothing, women's scarves, or dishes whatsoever."[19]

Many other people echoed such complaints: "Why aren't there any dishes, pots and pans in the stores? We had to resort to cooking food in buckets [for water]. ... It has been six months since we had soap. ... We wash [clothing] with coal and ashes. ... Sometimes there is no salt for months at a time ... the stores are empty."[20] In such a situation, hoarding goods became commonplace. Many people purchased items that they had no use for or in quantities that far exceeded their lifetime need. Some purchased 40 identical handkerchiefs; others bought dozens of towels—at times 50 or 60. If some items such as towels were at least durable, others like cosmetics and detergents were purchased in massive quantities, even disregarding their expiration date.[21] Such hoarding perpetuated shortages, and these shortages also fed people's appetites for consumer goods and the need to search for alternative avenues to assure the supply of various consumer items.

Hence the dynamics of the Soviet economic collapse in many ways prompted the rise of the semilegal private trade. It was in the context of these changes and challenges that, for the first time since the NEP in the 1920s, the government considered the need for an alternative, nongovernment-controlled and private sphere of the economy. In August 1986 the Soviet of Ministers issued a resolution to organize cooperatives for waste management and recycling. On a grander scale, the same August resolution allowed 20 ministries and 60 state enterprises to independently enter the international market and negotiate their import and export strategies. Though these changes were first steps in the liberalization of the Soviet economy, the Law on Individual Labor Activity of November 1986 was of far greater importance to ordinary people. This law legalized the existence of a private sector and self-employment in the context of the socialist economy. The documents of the June 1987 Plenum of the Central Committee (most of which were signed into law in 1988) further legalized several diverse outlets for individual business initiative, mostly in the form of cooperatives. These cooperatives produced directly for the market and for individual consumers and set their own goals and production norms rather than using state plans and quotas. These new cooperatives were the first step on the way to a market economy.

As many contemporaries and later researchers noted, it took "people who had more individual initiative, [who were] more entrepreneurial, and, as a rule, better qualified and trained than most" to venture into this new and daring field of cooperation.[22] As a rule, almost half of all registered cooperatives in the early years of Soviet cooperation failed to take off. But their numbers increased dramatically, even from 1987 to 1988. By the end of 1987, nearly 23,000 cooperatives were registered in the Soviet Union, though only 13,600 of them were operational. Their number increased elevenfold to 135,600 in 1988, even if once again only 77,500, or about half of those, were conducting any business. These early cooperatives offered a wide range of goods and services in an effort to fill the gaps in the existing system and to satisfy the demands of the population. A quarter of them (25.1% as of January 1988) were in the fast-food service or restaurant business; another 22.4 percent were in the service sector, which offered services ranging from hairstyling to elder care. Only 25.9 percent dealt with trade, either as importers of consumer goods, retailers, or even manufacturers. The rest belonged to constructing and building businesses (14%) and other types of cooperatives (12.4%).[23]

Few, if any, of these early cooperatives of 1987–88 were directly related to the fledgling shuttle trade, which was yet to gain momentum. But it is significant that the most profitable cooperatives were those in the sphere of trade and retail, which earned on average nearly six times more than cooperatives offering medical care services, and those in the entertainment sphere, which earned three to five times more than cooperatives in the restaurant business—and even more than construction and remodeling firms, the next leader in earned incomes and profits.[24] Thus the era of early cooperatives at the turn of 1987–88 started to shatter the old Soviet perception of trade as something less than ideal and even immoral. Even though most Soviet people continued to treat private cooperatives with skepticism, and these establishments did not necessarily provide an example to immediately emulate,[25] the profits made by the early trade cooperatives were at the very least enviable. It is also worth pointing out that eventually, as the number of shuttle traders grew, the number of retail- and trade-related cooperatives declined to 8.7 percent by January 1989.[26] But in the second half of the 1980s, it took more than a drive for a better life to push people into peddling and small-scale trade.

First Wave of the Shuttle Trade, 1987–88

Here, roughly in 1987–88, begins the first stage of the shuttle trade, or its fledgling moments. The first wave of the traders went to "near abroad" (i.e., socialist countries bordering the Soviet Union) in 1987–88, even before the law of November 1989, which gave Soviet citizens a right to travel abroad and to emigrate. This first wave of trading had many peculiar characteristics that were hardly noticeable or were outright absent in the later, second wave of 1989–90 and in the third and main wave in the 1990s. Like a chick, it barely resembled a mother bird in either its size or its appearance.

To begin with, in this early stage, only a very small number of people were involved in the trade. Most of them managed to combine their full-time employment and the shuttle trade, and for most, trading was possible only because of their employment or certain job-related advantages. Though precise data is unavailable, most early traders could be classified into two groups. The first group consisted of those fortunate few who had the money and "connections" to buy first tours to socialist countries like Poland. These tourists indeed enjoyed sightseeing, and they normally went to see numerous tourist attractions. But all tour operators also made stops at local markets where tourists had a chance to sell goods that they had brought from home and to buy something in return. In a typical scenario, such a tourist sold two watches and purchased two or three pairs of jeans (or similar items), of which at least one was for personal use. The other one or two pairs, however, was sold at home to cover the expense of the trip and even bring some profit. Such tourist-traders were not only small in number in 1988, they also stayed abroad only for a few days before returning home to their everyday lives and their jobs. Their experiences generated the myth of wondrous riches to be found abroad; as one respondent remembered, it created the myth that "just by going somewhere [people] would make piles of money … and a miracle would happen and they would become rich."[27]

The second group emerged from circles that for one reason or another had advantages in terms of traveling abroad. By far the most common were Komsomol (Communist Youth Organization) leaders. Resolution No. 721 of the Central Committee of the Communist Party and the Council of Ministers, issued on July 6, 1988, "On the Expansion of the Foreign Economic Activities of the [Komsomol]" and the subsequent Resolution No. 956 of August 4, 1988, "On Supporting the Economic Activities of the [Komsomol]," created unprecedented opportunities for the Komsomol leaders. As a result, various new initiatives and foreign exchange programs under different banners, such as the "Center for Creative Youth," multiplied in the late 1980s in the Komsomol cells. These new "activity circles," to use the jargon of the day, were universally aimed at either traveling abroad or receiving various advantages for starting early cooperatives at home. Thus, one respondent remembers that he received an excellent facility free of charge "to show movies to Komsomol youth." Using this facility, the respondent invested 2,000 rubles in purchasing a VHS player, a novelty for the Soviet public, and charged an admission fee to watch videotapes there. The returns were so significant that in the first few months the respondent recouped his 2,000-ruble investment and made another 3,000 rubles in profit, a fortune by Soviet standards.[28]

Yet Komsomol officials who aimed to go abroad were more instrumental in creating not the trade itself but the image of marvelous wealth to be made abroad. A common scenario included a "cultural exchange program" between two towns or youth leagues, one in the Soviet Union and one in any of the socialist countries. Typically, Soviet citizens went abroad as a part of a cultural exchange delegation and traveled to what was called a "sister town" or a "sister organization." Then at a later time, usually within two or three months, the Komsomol cell that sent the delegation received a foreign cultural delegation from the place the Soviets had previously visited. Part of the exchange group usually consisted of school-age performers from dance clubs, schools for performing arts, and music schools. However, most seats on the bus for such trips were sold "under the table" to relatives, friends, and friends of friends of Komsomol organizers. The cost was insignificant compared to the profit to be made on the trip, so in the end it came down to "knowing the right people" for those who wanted to partake in these foreign-exchange trips. Travel with a Komsomol group had another important advantage. According to Soviet laws, every Soviet citizen had to possess an internal passport for the purposes of registering their place of residence, their marital status, and other vital information. Soviet citizens had a separate, international passport for the purposes of traveling abroad. Citizens who went to socialist countries on tours in the late 1980s received a tourist passport and thus were subject to regular customs inspection. Yet through a glitch in the system—or rather the inability of the legislature to catch up with the changes of the time—Soviet citizens who traveled abroad with various Komsomol and Communist Party groups received "work-related" (business) international passports which de facto had the status of a diplomatic passport, with certain protections vested in the bearer of the passport. As a result, most travelers with this type of international passport were not searched at all (and hence, for example, paid no bribes for bringing goods for resale) or were searched only superficially. Once again, most of these people kept their old jobs and traveled abroad part-time or only occasionally.[29]

Regardless of the chosen way of travel, those few who managed to go abroad made significant profits that were never again replicated. These marvelous profits were another unique feature of the first wave of the trade. Nearly universally, respondents reported profits of 200–300 percent on sales of small quantities of goods, such as a purse full of nail polish or a pair of jeans. For example, the resale of a single box of Marlboro cigarettes (50 blocks of 20 individual packs each) covered all travel expenses and brought profits of about 200 percent. In 1988 a box of Marlboro cigarettes cost less than 100 rubles in the countries in the Soviet Bloc but was sold at over 300 rubles in Novosibirsk and 400 rubles in Kazakhstan. By comparison, a monthly wage stood at approximately 120–250 rubles. Equally profitable were women's tights and Snickers chocolate bars.[30]

Somewhat ironically, in this wave of marvelous profits, money, or currency, was irrelevant. The ruble was nonconvertible and had no purchasing power in Central Europe in 1988. US dollars had not yet made their appearance in this trade, simply because they could not be bought or sold anywhere in the Soviet space. So all the trading depended on barter of goods or a quick sale and purchase in local currency, as well as the inequality of prices and shortages of certain goods in various locations. Though some items that Soviet traders brought to Central Europe were "borrowed" from factories where traders worked ("I have what I guard," as the Soviet joke went), many items were simply underpriced and widely available in the Soviet Union but not in transitioning Hungary, Poland, and Czechoslovakia. Most commonly, Soviet citizens brought with them tools, clocks, watches, select electrical goods, and cameras. These were often of low quality but also of low price. In return, Soviet citizens commonly purchased ladies' tights, condoms, and cosmetics, although cigarettes, electronics such as VHS players, and clothing were also popular.[31] Once again, this reliance on barter and the lack of hard currency were unique to the earliest wave of the trade, which was replicated neither in the second wave of 1989–90 nor during the main wave of 1991–98.

Second Wave of International Peddling, 1989–90

The appearance of cooperatives and early initiatives to go abroad on a quest for merchandise were, without doubt, crucial in stimulating the suitcase trade. Yet it would take a further exacerbation of Soviet economic and political problems; a greater liberalization of and later complete transformation of legislature in regard to travel and individual enterprise; and a change in people's mentality, their attitudes toward the state and their individual lives to see the trade grow in scale and reach its 1990s proportions.

Once again, as was the case in 1985–87, one of the main challenges faced by the progressively collapsing Soviet economy was import-export imbalance. By 1989–90 grain prices were even higher than in previous years. The economic crisis was deepened not only by the Soviet trade imbalance (which was not new to 1989) but also by the record poor harvest for various types of grain in many grain-producing areas of the world. The resulting price increase was especially pronounced for wheat, one of the main Soviet staples. But as the import of grain became more problematic, or at least much more expensive, its consumption in the Soviet Union actually increased—people could not afford to buy pricier foods like meat and were increasingly relying on bread as their main source of caloric intake. The consumption of bread increased nationally by 8 percent in 1989 alone, reaching in some regions an increase of 35 percent. It is little surprising, then, that shortages of flour and bread worsened.[32]

At the same time, the price of crude oil continued at its lowest. In addition, the extraction of oil shrank even further, from 624.3 million tons in 1988 to 515.8 million in 1991, largely because of poor accessibility and insufficient investment in tapping oil.[33] The Soviet Union could no longer rely on borrowing from the West to compensate for the weak prices of oil and its trade imbalance. By the late 1980s, the Soviet Union's position as a reliable payee was also shaken. In early 1990, investment and risk-assessment managers from 300 leading international banks concluded that the benefits of private lending to the Soviet Union no longer justified the risks. Any further credit would be available only from the governments of various countries and not individual private banks. These experts also emphasized the need for market-oriented reforms of the centrally planned economy. In response, Gorbachev announced that the Soviet Union might "prolong or slightly postpone" its repayment of debts, which market analysts took to mean a default on payments. Predictably, this made any further borrowing highly problematic, and the final option left for Gorbachev was to borrow against the gold reserves of the country.[34]

Simultaneously, in 1989 most socialist countries failed to make interest payments on credit loaned by the Soviet Union. The nonpayment was indeed significant because, as of January 1, 1989, the socialist countries of the Soviet Bloc owed the USSR as much as 61 billion rubles. But, lacking sufficient financial resources, these countries preferred to make payments on their outstanding balances to Western European and other lenders outside the bloc, arguing that they would always "find a compromise" with the Soviet government.[35] The Soviet Union's ability to secure loans worsened in 1990, to the point where it was no longer asking for loans but, rather, for uncompensated aid in medication and food. For example, the Soviet government asked West Germany to ship 415 million deutsche marks' worth of consumer goods to the Soviet Union either without any compensation or by accepting Soviet exports in 1995 or later as a substitute for payments.[36]

As the trade imbalance and credit situation worsened, so did Soviet industrial production and the state budget. The Soviet industrial growth rate shifted from minimal (approximately 1% in 1989) to a negative growth rate of –1.2 percent in 1990, though some experts cited an even worse figure. In the same year the Soviet state budget fell short by 40 percent of all contributions that were expected from the Soviet republics and were a normal part of the state budget. The overall shortage in the state budget was over 10 percent, and the revenues in certain industrial spheres such as coal, oil, and textile production shrank by 25 percent.[37]

The economic slowdown and the subsequent economic decline led to mass decline in living standards. In 1990 alone the inflation rate was at least 25 percent, though the prices for select consumer goods went up by 40–50 percent. In 1991 inflation was already at 5–10 percent monthly. Wages could not catch up with such a rate of inflation.[38] The government's decision to begin money emission only exacerbated the problem. The rate of emission was 4.3 billion rubles in 1986; it increased to 5.6 billion in 1987, 12 billion in 1988, 17.9 in 1989; and it reached 26.6 billion in 1990.[39]

By late 1980–early 1990, shortages had reached epidemic proportions; of 1,200 consumer goods considered essential, 1,150 were listed as deficit items.[40] In 1990, the volume of imports had declined by 17 percent by the third quarter of the year. By mid-1990, of 160 items for everyday household use such as detergent and soap, *none* was commonly available for purchase. The shortages, hoarding, and economic dismantling became evidently irreversible.[41] Hoarding worsened the supply situation even further. For example, the Chairman of the State Planning Committee reported to the Council of Ministers that imports of soap and detergents increased by 20 percent in 1989 against 1988; yet the shortage of these goods became more severe, and in most regions a rationing system for soap had to be introduced for the first time since World War II. The same tendency of an escalating crisis was evident for most consumer items, again including sugar, tea, flour, shoes, tights, school notebooks, and so on.[42] Many stories of hoarding were sadly ironic. For example, Liudmila N. remembered how she spent several hours in pouring rain waiting in line to get into a store, but once her turn came, the products she was interested in were no longer available. So she purchased in bulk everything that was available, including several pairs of size 35 slippers (US size 5) in the hope of later bartering them for something she might need or could use.[43]

Economic shortages were not the only factor that allowed the shuttle trade to take off in 1989–90 and go into its second wave. There was also a change in perception and mentality. Although many people became desperate enough to try anything and everything in order to make money, Soviet people were also becoming progressively more willing to venture into unknown avenues such as trading, because they were beginning to see the benefits of such endeavors and to meet people who had managed to reap these benefits. Yet this change did not come easily and did not happen overnight, and some stereotypes persisted for several years. In 1989, for example, 54.2 percent of employed women thought that they were likely to lose their jobs in the future, whereas only 28 percent were sure that it would not happen to them. But in comparison, only 20 percent of respondents believed that Soviet economic restructuring could potentially improve their financial lives, whereas three times as many women thought they stood to lose out as a result of the more liberal market economy and wanted to keep the *ancien regime.*[44]

Another opinion poll reflected that people had a poor understanding of the totality of change and dynamics of the free market. Thus, by 1990 more than half of respondents thought that free market economy was necessary for the Soviet Union; yet, of the same number of respondents, 58 percent believed that unemployment was not acceptable at any rate, that the government had to regulate employment and assure its security for people, and that the liberalization of prices (when controlled by a supply–demand dynamic) was to be avoided at all cost. Hence the poll clearly revealed just how poorly Soviet people understood the market economy after three generations of socialist experience and how much needed to change in people's understanding of the new economic reality.[45]

The same discrepancy was also evident at the state level. Thus, in January 1991 the Supreme Council of the USSR simultaneously acknowledged the miserable condition of the Soviet economy, largely in shambles by this stage, *and* adopted a massive increase in state subsidies to such groups as single mothers and pensioners; in stipends to students; in wages for people employed in education, cultural venues, and health care; in better state-sponsored health care plans, which included extensive preventive care coverage; and in a variety of other benefits that were either expanded or had not previously existed.[46] No one found any contradiction in increasing state support at a time of state budget deficits, and no one questioned where the money for these added expenses would come from.

This idiosyncratic understanding of the economic changes was reflected in most people's actions. For example, one of the leading political figures of the time, L. Abalkin, remembered that he regularly received delegations of workers and voluminous petitions from workers demanding the state plan be lowered and greater or even complete freedom be allowed for them to market the merchandise produced at their respective factories and control all its profits. Self-management overall was high on the list of demands. Yet simultaneously, the same petitioners demanded that the government increase its investment in technology and equipment, guarantee the supply of raw resources, and provide all social benefits including guaranteed lifetime employment. It never occurred to these workers that such demands were contradictory.[47]

Similarly, reflecting on the Soviet economy at large in 1989, most respondents evaluated the overall economic situation negatively. But when it came to their workplace, most respondents saw either no changes or even an improvement, despite the poor state of the economy (as Table 1.3 indicates). Partially, this sentiment could be explained by the increase in wages. Wages increased by 8 percent nationally in 1988 and 13 percent in 1989 and were expected to go up by another 15 percent in 1990.[48] But it also demonstrates that, though greater freedoms of choice and self-control were widely appreciated at the microeconomic level, few people linked the problems of macroeconomy (e.g. shortages, inflation, etc.) to microchanges.

This discrepancy in the popular perception of the micro- and macro-economy initially led to a peculiar conclusion. Workers, who judged their performance by their wages, emphasized that they worked hard and did everything "the right way," yet the economy at large was still falling apart. Most state employees (almost all the employed population) concluded then that the fault was not with the system itself nor with workers' productivity or modes of production but, rather, with their bosses, who wasted or stole resources and money. So instead of searching for an optimal solution to their problems and learning about the market economy, the first and initial reaction of many working people was to blame others, primarily officials, for failing to improve economic performance for the sake of working people.[49]

People's outlook on the Soviet economy changed from mildly to outright pessimistic in 1990. The Russian Center for Public Opinion reported in 1990 that even though 56 percent of those who took the poll supported the transition to a market economy, 60 percent thought that such a transition would create problems rather than solve them, at least in the near future. The same number of respondents (60%) also believed that the transition to a free-market economy would prompt a massive political crisis and eventual political realliances.[50] Furthermore, 56 percent evaluated the economic situation as critical and an additional 37 percent as largely negative. In responding to the question of what they believed awaited the Soviet Union in the future, 70 percent predicted that the economic situation would worsen, 54

Table 1.3: Evaluation of economic situation in the country, workplace, personal life, 1989

The situation changed	For the better	Did not change	For the worse
… in the country's economy	4.6%	41.9%	31.6%*
… in respondent's own life	13%	58.4%	27.2%
… economically, at work	19.5%	51.9%	6.7%

* Numbers add up to less than 100%; the remaining respondents were in a "do not know" group.

Source: G. N. Sokolova, "Stali li my zhit' luchshe?" *Sotsiologicheskie issledovaniia*, no. 1 (1990): 20–21.

percent envisioned an economic catastrophe in 1991, 49 percent expected mass unemployment in 1991, 42 percent anticipated famine or food shortages, and 51 percent expected electric blackouts. More than 70 percent believed that they had suffered financially in the last two years, and the main concern by far was the shortage of food and clothing.[51] When questioned about the promise of economic improvement and recovery, 45 percent of respondents believed that only by the year 2000 would the economy begin to get better, and 12 percent saw no future improvement at all.[52]

In evaluating the economic situation in the country, many Soviet citizens blamed early cooperatives for various aspects of economic malfunctioning, from shortages of consumer goods to a failure to successfully restructure the system overall. The active development of cooperatives created, at first, a sense of apprehension among many people. Cooperatives as a rule were offered incentives such as the right to buy raw resources at state prices and the right to sell finished products at self-regulating prices. As a result, most items produced or offered for sale by cooperatives were priced two to three times higher than equivalent goods with state-regulated prices. But facing chronic shortages of goods in state stores, many people felt that they had no option but to pay the steep cooperative price. Hence there built a widespread sense of resentment. Wages in such cooperatives were also significantly higher than in state enterprises, and although the state attempted to regulate incomes by introducing substantial income taxes for cooperative employees (reaching 65% in some years), most cooperatives quickly learned to do double bookkeeping in order to avoid paying them; alternatively, some cooperatives were registered as partly under the cover of state enterprises, thus changing the tax brackets for their workers' incomes.[53]

It is unsurprising, then, that high wages and decent profits in the time of economic desperation made less fortunate people "hate these profiteers and robber barons, who grew rich on the misery and suffering of a common consumer."[54] Yet the profits made in cooperatives simultaneously stimulated among people a new interest in getting involved in "dishonest activities" like trading, for example. This seeming discrepancy in attitudes and the role that the cooperatives played in creating a new mentality was duly reflected in various opinion polls. In 1989, only 2.5 percent of respondents in one such poll perceived the actions of cooperatives or even their mere existence as beneficial to the state, economy, or people, yet of the same group of respondents, 22.4 percent, or nearly ten times the number in the first category, wanted to get involved in cooperatives or at least some sort of private activity.[55] Although most people used derogatory terms to describe early entrepreneurs and although trading was socially and morally stigmatized, nonetheless many were lured by opportunities to make more money.[56]

It was a combination of the economic collapse, especially in terms of supplying consumer goods and assuring decent wages, and examples of success in private enterprises such as cooperatives that prompted further interest in international peddling. Yet the last part of the changing tide of suitcase trading came with the Law of November 1989. According to this law, the Soviet government recognized the right of Soviet citizens to travel abroad and emigrate, thus facilitating people's ability to cross borders and travel to neighboring countries. Here the second phase of shuttle trading opened, which lasted from November 1989 to late 1990–early 1991.

Overall, the trading was still organized privately rather than through the shop-tours of later years, and most participants travelled irregularly as a way to supplement rather than replace their wages. Yet for the first time there emerged a group of peddlers who pursued shuttle trading as their main source of income. The goods that crossed the border also changed. As the demand for Soviet-era cameras and watches declined, gold, antiques, spare parts for cars, and at times even large machinery became the second wave's common commodities for sale in Central Europe. Finally, money made an appearance in the trading, as most transactions now involved some type of currency exchange, most commonly in US dollars.[57]

At this still early point, few traders treated their activities as their main job, though an increasing number of interviewees mentioned that either they or their friends were prompted by significant profits to think of trading as a full-time occupation. Not all goods imported by traders were sold on open markets; bulkier items such as furniture and TV sets often found their way into consignment shops, or *komissionki,* that legally existed in the

Soviet Union. These shops were created for secondhand resale but rarely functioned as such. Instead, they were commonly used by those who had deficit items (i.e., goods in short supply but high demand) to offer but who shunned the black market.

Yet the main feature of the trade at this point was neither the growing number of its participants nor the appearance of first professional peddlers: rather, it was its ad hoc nature. Although some sort of a structure started to emerge that would later crystallize into a well-functioning machine with its own rules and regulations, there were no more than hints of such rules and regulations in 1989. For example, open-air markets had no sections as of yet dedicated to different products, and spare auto parts were sold next to food, and food next to clothing. The division into sectors would emerge only during the golden age of the shuttle trade, in 1992 and later. Similarly, though traders started to rely progressively on US dollars as the currency of choice, various other options still existed. Some peddlers still relied on barter, while others preferred local currency as the token of exchange. Even the attitudes to trade varied; one respondent stated that there was no commonly shared shame in trading at this moment—he, for example, felt more excited about experimenting with trading on a part-time basis than ashamed of being "a speculator." He even compared his experiences to trying his first cigarette as a teenager. Teenagers know that smoking is bad and that they are not supposed to do it, but "trying it just once" makes them feel thrilled and even empowered.

Finally, the same ad hoc quality applied to criminal activities like racketeering. This started to emerge alongside trade itself but was then only manifest in select areas of trade, or only irregularly. The most profitable goods, such as medication, attracted the attention of organized criminal groups first. One of the key factors for both the boom in international peddling and corruption was the growing shortage of medical supplies. While other consumer goods such as refrigerators or clothing could be used for years, the lack of medication created a real pressing stimulus for people to search for other avenues of supply. The Soviet medical industry satisfied approximately 45 percent of all Soviet demand for drugs, with the rest imported from various countries.[58] But with the disintegration of production and the worsening of the credit situation, the supply of medication became problematic. By 1990 at least a third of all drugs had become deficit items. Both Soviet and international economists and other experts perceived the supply of drugs as of paramount importance and as potentially the greatest problem for the Soviet economy. But this recognition did not solve the deficit in medication. Thus began trips to Poland (mainly) to purchase drugs. Most of the traders who did business in the sale of medication at this early stage were women, often with some medical training, often with relatives who needed medication for their personal use. In a typical response, one of the women, formerly a medical researcher at a research institute, remembered:

> I left my [research] institute before they laid me off (it seemed that everyone was being laid off at the time) and started my trips to Poland. It did not take me long to find suppliers [necessary people, *neobhodimye liudi*]; since I already had poly-arthritis at the age of 40, I knew a lot about medication and prices from personal experience. I brought some medication for retail sale and some on demand once the order was placed. I earned all right and even bought a car, *Zhiguli* though [Soviet model]. But then it became too dangerous because of mafia involvement so I had to stop it and trade something else.[59]

Despite these bleak comments, there was still no sense of organization or predictability when it came to trading or racketeering; most traders, in fact, delivered their goods without ever encountering the "Mafia people." After all, the scale of trade was still insignificant in comparison with the proportions that it would assume in 1992 and thereafter, and the criminal gangs were experiencing a "fledging" of their own alongside the international peddling itself.

In late 1990 and early 1991, the economy, no matter how poorly it was performing, was progressively being overshadowed by pressing political concerns, especially on the subject of the survival of the Soviet Union and subsequent power struggles and power sharing.[60] In this era came the commonly known challenges and struggles, such as the declaration of Russian sovereignty (June 12, 1990), followed by those of Ukraine, Belorussia, and Armenia; the Yeltsin–Gorbachev confrontation; the "500 Days" program of economic restructuring, and the eventual liberalization of prices. It was also in 1991–92 that the new era of trading began. The golden age of international peddling would last until 1998. It was also in this period of 1991–98 that the trade would manifest all of its main features, primarily its "gendered" nature and its wide geography of trade.

There were many complex reasons as to why the trade became "gendered," and all of them will be discussed in detail in subsequent chapters. Among the leading causes was massive female unemployment that pushed many women into trade. By the early 1990s, unemployment had truly become a problem "with a woman's face." The average age of an unemployed woman was 34–35 years old; most had some professional training and post-secondary education; and more than half had children under the age of 18. Two-thirds of these women (63%) lost their jobs because they were laid off from unprofitable formerly state-owned factories that were now closing down. As a result, 53 percent of these women and their families survived under the official poverty line.[61] Although objective economic factors and financial stimulus were of crucial importance for the boom of international peddling, more nuanced and subjective gender stereotypes and legal loopholes also explained the predominance of women in the trade in the 1990s.

2

The "Golden Age" of the Shuttle Trade and Its Structure

I hoped for a good business, something that would be both enjoyable and profitable. My hopes were fulfilled [in the shuttle trade]. I made enough for a good life, not just for the bread but butter and even caviar. It did not feel like a boring job; I worked with pleasure, and I made good money. We made enough to afford a nice vacation and everything that a person might need, within reasonable limits. Well, actually, I made enough for more or less everything I wanted: a car, a flat, nice clothing. ... Now I have moved on to other things, and I also do something that I like, but it is different now. Now I belong to a different profession. [The shuttle trade] in Russia is already gone; it belongs to the past.

—Elena, aged 42, from an interview conducted in Khabarovsk in 2008[1]

The question of the massive female predominance in the trade might never be satisfactorily answered. Women dominated the trade, and at times they constituted 80 percent of its labor force.[2] Yet just why there were so many female participants in this business remains more speculative than definite because objective economic data, primarily centered on female unemployment, is obscured by the illegality of the trade. Moreover, unemployment statistics of the 1990s can offer only a partial explanation as to why women entered this business. Often it was not only the lack of a job and financial security but also a variety of gender stereotypes that prompted women to get involved in the trade. Characteristics such as the "natural" female roles of caregivers and negotiators and women's interest in fashion are cited as the cause of the male–female imbalance in the business. Nevertheless, by analyzing interviews and popular notions of women's roles and supplementing these with official statistics, we can identify a range of factors that help explain the prevalence of women in this gender-specific business.

Women's employment in the Soviet Union was a more complex issue than the wage differentiation and employment patterns might suggest. By the end of the Soviet era, Soviet economic growth and social expectations ensured that women were nearly universally employed outside their homes and contributing their wages to family incomes. Beginning in the 1920s, the percentage of women in the Soviet labor force grew continuously, even if with some predictable variations over time. During the New Economic Policy era of the 1920s, in the immediate post–World War II period, and during the Kosygin reforms of the mid-1960s, women's share of the labor force declined relative to that of previous years. Yet it grew rapidly in the 1930s during the industrialization push, again in the war years, and especially in the 1970s and 1980s.[3] As a result, the high rate of female employment that was achieved by the late 1960s and early 1970s, when 84–85 percent of all women worked outside the home, remained steady for the rest of the Soviet period. In addition, some 8 percent of women of working age were attending vocational schools, colleges, and universities on a full-time basis. Thus, the combined level of female involvement in gainful employment and the public sphere reached 91–92 percent in the 1970s and 1980s.[4]

Work for wages and resulting financial responsibilities were an integral part of a Soviet woman's life. Women of working age in the Soviet Union were universally doing just that, working. Moreover, women had no other choice but to work full-time for at least 40 hours a week. Various studies have demonstrated that in the late 1980s only 1 percent of all female employees worked less than a full working week (between 10 and 30 hours a week), though many women expressed a preference for part-time work under "ideal circumstances."[5] Yet the circumstances were never ideal for 99 percent of them, and at least 80 percent of all women considered their income crucial for the financial well-being of their families.[6]

On the one hand, despite years of gender equality propaganda, women continued to earn 30 percent less on average than men.[7] Yet on the other hand, a wide range of social services and price assurance on most consumer goods at least partially compensated for the difference in wages. The cost of public transportation and utilities was kept artificially low, and inflation of the basic staples of life was suppressed. Education and health care was free and universally available in the 1980s, and other services like child care, after-school programs, and passes to spas and resorts were available for only a nominal fee. There was no doubt that the system had deep-seated problems; nonetheless, this social service sector helps explain why, despite the wage discrepancy, two-thirds of all women were pleased with what they earned, and many women added that gainful employment boosted their self-esteem and gave them a sense of purpose in life. Financial and emotional factors were closely intertwined to create a situation that most women found acceptable.[8] By the late 1980s only 8 percent of women did not like their jobs, a third found their jobs acceptable, and over half of all women were satisfied with what they had in the workplace.[9] Hence it seems reasonable to say that Soviet women en masse felt no urge or craving to change their jobs or jump into the new avenues of employment solely based on their Soviet occupation patterns. The demise of the Soviet system and the resultant unemployment were far more important than workplace dissatisfaction in prompting women to look for income elsewhere.

The high rate of female involvement in the shuttle business can be at least partially explained by the economics of the Soviet collapse. What seemed like a massive economic crisis in 1990–91 was followed by an even more devastating economic collapse and the so-called Great Russian Depression, marked by hyperinflation and negative economic growth nationwide. Jobs, employment safety, and social provisions were among the first casualties of this economic disintegration. By the late 1980s, and then progressively in the early 1990s, Soviet citizens en masse either lost their jobs or were not paid for months at a time. Some salaries were in arrears for six months or more. And the majority of those who lost their jobs were women.[10] Abundant research has shown that the transition years from planned to market economy were marked by "unemployment with a woman's face." Various sources have indicated that by the mid-1990s between two-thirds and 85 percent of the post-Soviet unemployed were female.[11] Yet these statistics might be misrepresentative for at least two reasons. First, some sources maintain that "women's unemployment in Russia is even more acute than official data suggest, given the growing problem of 'hidden unemployment.'"[12] Hidden unemployment refers to the fact that a significant number of women remained officially registered as employed in order to maintain access to basic social services like day care and medical care while they received no pay and performed no work. This was especially true of many women with children under the age of three, as their employers usually kept such women registered as employed to assure their eventual access to day-care facilities. On the other hand, the unofficially employed, who constituted as many as 30 million people, paid income taxes rarely, incompletely, or never and were considered as unemployed. Thus, as a result of chronic tax evasion in Russia, individual income taxes in 1996 accounted annually for only 2.1 percent of government revenues instead of the anticipated 30 percent.[13]

Though the exact numbers changed from year to year in the 1990s, the unemployment rate for women has been estimated at between 22.5 percent and 33.5 percent of the working-age female population. In selected industries the unemployment rate for women was even higher; for example, the number of women employed by scientific research institutions declined by more than half, from 1.5 million in 1990 to 645,000 in 1998. As a result, by 2001 48 percent of all women who claimed to have any income were self-employed.[14] In the 1990s the average age of an unemployed woman was 34–35 years; most of them had some professional training and post-secondary education, while more than half had children under the age of 18. Two-thirds of these women (63%) lost their jobs because they were laid off from unprofitable, formerly state-owned factories that were closing down. As a result, 53 percent of unemployed women and their families survived on incomes below the official poverty line.[15]

Even when women kept their jobs, many respondents believed that it was less of a risk to lose a wife's income than to lose a husband's income, as women were generally paid less than men. This was not so much because of explicit gender discrimination but because women, due to their greater family responsibilities and constraints, were unable to assume key leading positions with high pay. Even though the male–female income imbalance had always existed in the Soviet Union despite years of propaganda about the equality of the sexes and the high rate of education and professional training among women, the difference was "leveled out" by the number of social services available to women in late Soviet times.[16] As stated above, regardless of their social status or income, by the 1980s Soviet women universally had access to extensive paid maternity leave, nearly free day-care facilities, summer camps, and after-school activities and lessons for their children as well as free medical services and vacations for themselves. But when the social sphere started to progressively disintegrate at the end of the Soviet era, those who were most affected by the loss of the social safety net were elderly women, women with small children, and though to a lesser extent, all women. Hence overall, lower incomes among women than men in combination with the poor availability of social welfare and a high rate of female unemployment "pushed" many women into seeking alternative incomes in "non-traditional" spheres, like trade.[17]

Moreover, women were less likely than men to find a new job, and they remained unemployed for longer periods of time. Aside from official data, which registered that it took women on average from 6 to 7.5 months to find employment, various studies reported that managers hiring staff preferred men to women as potential employees. A third of all employers admitted in the 1990s that they chose male job candidates over females with equal or even better credentials. This was done despite the fact that the law specifically prohibited sex-based discrimination.[18] Later in life, many shuttle traders recalled that unemployment and fear of unemployment was a massive psychological stress for people who had been used to guaranteed lifetime employment and state-secured incomes. The very existence of unemployment seemed inexplicable, and unemployment on a large scale was absolutely beyond comprehension. "I do not even want to recall that time," said one shuttle trader when referring to the early 1990s. She added:

> And if I do think about those days, I think it did not happen to us but to someone else. How could it possibly happen that industries and research facilities along with all their excellent and sometimes less than perfect employees became worthless overnight; neither the government nor labor unions cared for anything. I still do not understand the reasons for this total collapse. … The stress of uncertainty was so immense that some of my friends drank themselves to death. We constantly phoned each other to ask the same question: What do we do? What happens next? We have earned our better lives the hard way [speaking of incomes made in the shuttle trade], and the unemployment and the fear of it made us stronger.[19]

Indeed, many shuttle traders have made comments that are remarkably similar to the one above.

The massive transformation of the female labor force was also affected by the high divorce rate and the common Soviet and post-Soviet practice of leaving children with their mothers. It was nearly impossible for a man to acquire full custody of his children (and few men wanted to do so) because a mother was considered "naturally" better suited to care for her children regardless of her objective financial and emotional condition or even her substance-abuse problems. The percentage of children who remained in the full custody of mothers after divorce was (and continues to be) over 99 percent, while a fifth of all divorced fathers never see (or have seen) their children after the divorce. Only 20 percent of child-support payments extracted from fathers are at the state rate of the basic value of the consumer basket of a child, and only 2 percent of divorced fathers pay (or have paid) enough child support to improve the financial well-being of their sons or daughters. These statistics, of course, exclude 25 percent of all children born in the 1990s, because they were born out of wedlock and never had any legal rights to claim child support.[20] If we consider that, in the 1990s, 50 percent of all marriages ended in divorce and about one in every four women at this time was either divorced with children or was a single mother,[21] it is not surprising that a significant number of women found themselves displaced by the demise of the Soviet Union (along with its social-welfare system and guaranteed employment) and were forcefully pushed into the new international marketplace in order to provide for their children.

This grim economic reality set the stage for the massive expansion of the shuttle trade. If nothing else, millions of working-age women were in the process of actively seeking new ways to make a living, and the rapidly shrinking labor market was oversaturated with the labor force. Simultaneously, the chronic shortages of consumer goods, as discussed earlier, were further exacerbated by the collapse of the Soviet Union. The thirst for a decent livelihood combined with the collapse of the Soviet social infrastructure became a potent force in prompting the new post-Soviet people to consider engaging in activities that until recently had been considered a criminal offense. Few knew about the trade, and even fewer shed their notions that "speculating" was a borderline activity, one that was between illegality, or at least informality, and a legitimate source of income. But the ground was ripe for a change and for embarking on a slow process of learning to live in the new realities of market capitalism.

Even if the grim realities of the post-Soviet economic collapse formed the primary background to this massive movement of people and goods across the border in the informal economy that bound the entire post-socialist space, these factors did not by default qualify shuttle traders as "necessity entrepreneurs."[22] Though many people were desperate, all had some, even if limited, freedom of choice. As we are going to see later, especially in our discussion of the shuttle traders' social profile, women did have alternative means of income and alternative avenues of survival. It is possible that none of those alternative ways was perfect, easy, or financially or otherwise satisfactory. Those women who grew vegetables in their garden plots and later sold those products as street vendors, along with an endless string of petty vendors who sold anything from handmade crafts to old clothing or homemade sweets, would better suit the description of entrepreneurs by necessity. Moreover, there was a rapidly expanding job market for women who could provide child or elder care, as well as house cleaning and a wide range of other domestic services. Hence the shuttle traders could only be one group among many "would-be entrepreneurs," and at least financially, they often became the better-off group. Even if they were pushed into the trade in order to mitigate the harsh realities of their lives, those who did not fail on the very first trip transitioned into willing and eager participants in the business. Among other options available at that moment, future shuttle traders chose what seemed to them to be the most lucrative path, and that was the path to the "marvelous riches found abroad."[23]

In addition to various economic factors, we can identify a wide range of subjective factors related to commonly perceived gender roles that help explain the high rate of female participation in the shuttle trade. At the onset of the trade, the Soviet people's attitudes toward private business in general and resale in particular was negative, and the traders who started off in this business in the 1980s almost universally acknowledged that they feared being recognized by their neighbors and friends. "At first, when I saw people who knew me," recollects Elena Semienova, a former philologist, "I literally dived under the counter."[24] It was considered shameful to stand on the street or in the marketplace and sell goods, as most people who lived during the Soviet times were brought up feeling that trading was something akin to cheating or stealing or an act of extreme desperation similar to begging. Opinion polls revealed that, at the onset of the shuttle trade, people had very negative attitudes to private businesses and businessmen: the labels "cheater," "criminal," and "privateer" were used as close synonyms, and the notion of private business and terms like privateer "for some time carried connotations of marginality, and … were often used in a disparaging manner."[25] In this social environment, it was commonly believed that few men wanted to lose their status as respected workers and join the circles of dishonest cooperators, while women were not as ashamed of standing on the street, or at least they were willing to deal with this sort of shame. When the choice was between a husband and a wife, it most often fell to the wife to take on this unpleasant aspect of the business, if not the entire business itself.[26]

Social scientists have explained the female willingness to step into the unknown by the fact that Soviet women had broader boundaries of self-identity than men. Thus, men who went to work were identified as breadwinners while women were caretakers, mothers, and also workers.[27] Furthermore, men were commonly excluded from domestic life in the Soviet Union. The Soviet system implied women's dependency and reliance on various social services that facilitated their child-care responsibilities and freed them for public employment. But when most of the household chores were done by public services in public institutions (almost universally children were involved in day care starting at the age of one or earlier, affordable and nutritious meals were served in local eateries in each factory and office, and so on), men's roles in child rearing and domestic affairs became minimal, thus relegating men exclusively to the sphere of public employment and assuring their self-identification with work as being at the core of their masculinity.[28] But women were already accustomed to playing multiple roles, and hence it was women who had to sacrifice their pride and rely on that "broader identity."

At the same time, the popular early post-Soviet notion of traders as dishonest and aggressive was more readily applied to men than women. After all, women were seen as caring, supporting, and just more honest than men. Or, in people's words, women were moral, while men were profit-hungry. Many consumers believed that

> men, especially if from the southern regions [of the former Soviet Union], are out to make a profit at the expense of ordinary people and therefore contribute to the undermining of the Russian process of regeneration. ... Women, on the other hand, have probably been driven onto the street by the need to support their family, pay for their children's education and livelihood or other such morally laudable motivation.[29]

Needless to say, customers chose deprived mothers over deceiving men and commonly preferred to buy clothing and household items from female traders, if there was any choice.

Other gender stereotypes prevalent in the Soviet society further reinforced the belief that women were better suited for this sort of business than men. Thus, women were considered better able to deal with the semiofficial, unofficial, or illegal aspects of the trade, from begging with customs agents to allow them to bring their goods into the country, giving bribes, avoiding prosecution on legitimate or fraudulent charges, and preventing physical assaults on their persons by racketeers. Many shuttle traders mentioned that in the early stages of the shuttle trade, when the system of bribes and "protection" payments was not yet well established and codified, women could successfully rely on normative gender roles when facing officials by claiming to be weak, unprotected, unfortunate single or abandoned mothers forced into business to mitigate the harsh circumstances of life.[30] Women remembered that they often cried out, "Fear God! What are you doing?" and shed tears when they heard the amounts of the bribes demanded by the customs officials. This tactic of begging and crying could decrease the bribe demanded from \$70 for men to \$50 for women.[31] The same "female vulnerability" discourse applied to other situations as well. For example, in the early years of the trade, some men feared prosecution based on Article 154 of the Criminal Code of the USSR, "On Speculation," which was not officially revoked until December 1991 and required prison terms of between two and seven years for speculation (broadly defined). Though this law was not enforced after 1987, common belief maintained that unemployed men involved in the shuttle trade were perceived as "speculators" and could be prosecuted, but women were treated as victims of domestic instability.[32]

Finally, women maintained that they had no trust in men when it came to choosing the products for resale. As the popular wisdom of the day had it, only women knew about fashions, what was in demand, and how to pick good clothing. Since most traders relied on a very narrow range of goods, the right selection of merchandise could make or break the life of a shuttle trader. Of course, not all women were skillful—or lucky—enough to pick the best products. One woman talked about her experiences, with her anger aimed at more successful traders:

> and you look at [other] sellers: what do people buy? But in your soul there is a boiling female envy. Take Liuba: no looks, no body [*ni rozhi, ni figury*], [she] can't say two words coherently, and [she] was kicked out of a vocational school for failing classes [*za dvoiki*]. And you are a beauty with a university degree. But your swimsuits do not sell while hers, of the same design but different color, sell like mad. And you feel so sorry for yourself![33]

But most traders were willing to believe that women were less prone than men to make mistakes when it came to choosing brands, designs, and even the color of their goods. Nearly all respondents made a comment similar to Galina's: "Men are not meant to do this; women understand fashions and sell clothing better; [this trade] is not a man's job."[34]

Thus, the gendered division of labor on the Russian job market was not merely an economic phenomenon dictated by the economic realities of the time. Instead, it included the socially constructed and effectively manipulated—consciously or otherwise—normative gender roles that had been prescribed as "natural" by Soviet and post-Soviet society. Gender segregation in the labor market became a defining, if not central and essential, feature of the work order that emerged in the process of creating market capitalism in post-Soviet Russia.[35]

Regulating the Trade

If the economic crisis, massive unemployment, and a shortage of nearly all consumer goods were some of the key explanations for the eventual boom of the shuttle trade, the legislative changes of the post-Soviet era assured its further explosion into a truly massive phenomenon. In addition to massive transformation of the labor market in light of the Great Economic Depression, shortages of nearly all essential daily goods, changing consumer tastes, the gendered realities of the labor force, and a slow process of departure from Soviet-era practices and mentality, the ease of border crossing and currency exchange, along with the surplus of cheap consumer goods in neighboring countries came to be of paramount importance in shaping the shuttle trade.

Much of the massive expansion of the trade and its blossoming between 1992 and 1998, the so-called golden age of international peddling, had to do with the legal provisions that existed (or more often, were lacking) at the time. The first post-Soviet regulatory act that would remain the sole legal provision for the trade for nearly two years was signed by President Boris Yeltsin on January 29, 1992. The "Freedom of Trade" Decree, No. 65, set as its goal the rapid development of the consumer trade and the stimulation of competitive market relations in the context of the liberalization of prices and the rapid transition to a market economy. To ensure that this goal was met, the decree allowed all companies and individuals to carry out wholesale or retail trading without *any* licenses or permissions, with the exception of the sale of drugs, weapons, radioactive elements, and similar items. Further, "all goods that were imported to the Russian Federation … were not subject to *any* customs duty or *any* taxes." All businesses and individuals were allowed "to trade (from hands, cars, or in retail booths) in any place they find comfortable." Police force and administration were stripped of any right to regulate the trade and were "forbidden to delay or confiscate any goods carried by cargo transporters or individuals; nor [were they allowed] to ask for any documentation for such cargo and/or goods." Instead, local administration was expected "to take measures to organize wholesale bazaars." The decree only marginally indicated that it was the intention of the government of the Russian Federation to raise the question of taxation on such activities in the Supreme Soviet at some point in the foreseeable future.[36]

This liberalization of trade and border crossing did not mean, of course, that there were no attempts to regulate the import of various good into Russia. For example, Yeltsin's government was eager to promote measures that would support the WTO's GATT Article VII on customs valuation that would demonstrate Russia's overall willingness to change its policy in favor of a greater approximation to WTO standards. Various regulations on temporary and then permanent import tariffs and valuation procedures were adopted from June 4, 1992, and thereafter.[37] However, none of the regulations had an adverse effect on shuttle traders. A number of factors worked to the traders' advantage. First, because of the imperfectability of the new regulations, nearly all early customs procedures were applied only to vehicles and large-scale machinery. Second, regulations between June 1992 and December 1993 typically excluded the control of all individuals who claimed to bring in goods for personal consumption and did not engage in trading in cars, pharmaceuticals, and other high-profile commodities. Finally, the Freedom of Trade decree was still taken as the supreme regulatory measure that stood above all other normative acts and regulations. Thus, with the full recognition of the government, the system created loopholes that allowed the shuttle traders to have virtually unlimited freedom in their activities from January 1992 to late 1993.[38]

The only limitation was the $5,000 limit set on all imported goods. But no system existed to effectively assess the value of goods and to regulate the trade, and hence this regulation was nearly unenforceable and easy to avoid. Besides, this amount was astronomical for the turnover at a time when most traders did business with capital of only a few hundred dollars; also, many products were underpriced and undervalued even when their value should have exceeded this limit. As a consequence, as various sociological studies conducted post-1993 revealed, during the "honeymoon phase" of the trade in 1992–93, it was possible to bring wagonloads of goods to Russia without paying a single ruble in taxes or fees. It was especially easy to cross the border if a trader had a notarized letter from a third party that authorized the trader to buy goods "for the personal consumption" of the third party. In this scheme, a trader could claim that five kitchen furniture sets or ten TV sets were for the personal consumption of friends and the friends of friends.

But over the course of two years, the shuttle trade assumed proportions that were unprecedented even by comparison with international peddling in other post-socialist countries.[39] It is worth repeating here that by the mid-1990s nearly 30 million people, or approximately 41 percent of the working population of Russia, were directly or indirectly involved in the shuttle trade, which had come to provide 70 percent of all the consumer goods in the Russian market.[40] The unprecedented scale of the trade became obvious even with no reliable data to confirm its exact scope, and the lack of state revenues became a major concern for the government.

Also problematic yet urgent was the question of regulating the quality of goods that reached open-air markets. While poor-quality clothing was unfortunate but not dangerous, imported foods created a serious health hazard due to improper refrigeration and the falsification of the expiry dates, and poisonings from spoiled imported foods were reported daily in the press. The State Committee on Statistics conducted a study in 1993–94, trying to assess the socioeconomic situation in Russia over the two years. Among its many findings it reported that the Russian Trade Commission had attempted to implement quality control for consumer goods by the selective sampling of goods. Traders with goods that did not meet the minimal required quality standards were subsequently fined. Even this sampling revealed troubling patterns that are evident from Table 2.1. As much as a quarter of all goods was of substandard quality and posed health risks for consumers.

Even traders admitted that they sold poor-quality produce. One trader, for example, shared a typical—and indicative—anecdote with the interviewer:

> I started to sell sausages, cheese, [and] pickled herring. This was the kind of merchandise that spoils easily, but refrigerators, especially when it was hot, constantly broke down. But I had to sell everything to the last gram. At first this did not work; my conscience did not let me sell spoiled food to people. But then I learned the tricks, I started to wipe the rotten sausage and cheese with vinegar to make them look fresh again.[41]

Finally, Russian light industry experienced a complete collapse, which happened at least partially because it produced consumer goods that could not compete with goods made in Turkey or China, especially when it came to styles and affordability.

But because of the illicit nature of the business, unsurprisingly, the accumulation of data and any reliable quantitative information was extremely problematic and at times impossible. Most traders, even if confronted about their business, refused to answer questions on the volume of their trade, patterns of travel, and revenues.[42] Only in the mid-1990s did interviews and sampling techniques allow reasonable estimates of the nature and scale of the trade to be made based on the uniform probability distribution method. The method assumed that any random sampling of a select group of tourists, for example, would reveal a general pattern of how much border crossing and "tourism" was for shuttle trading and how much of it was for "pure" tourism. The summary of estimates is presented in Table 2.2.

Some of the research was carried out by the "receiving" side as well. For example, in 1996 the Turkish Central Bank used a quantitative research method technique called "self-completion method" to estimate the volume and revenues of the trade. The research was completed by distributing self-

Table 2.1: Consumer goods that did not meet quality requirements (post-expiration date, spoiled, damaged, etc.), as reported for 1994

Type of goods	% in relation to all inspected goods
Poultry	25
Processed meats	20
Dairy products	12
Butter	19
Vegetable oils	13
Eggs	29
Sugar	15
Textiles (clothing)	36
Socks	29
Shoes	26
Electronics	33

Source: Gosudarstvennyi Komitet Rossiiskoi Federatsii po Statistike, "Sotsial'no-ekonomicheskoe polozhenie Rossii, 1993–1994 gg," (Moscow, 1994): 166–67.

completion surveys to tourists from the former Soviet Union who came to Turkey. Though the primary goal of the research was to estimate the purchase and sale price of goods, transportation costs, and personal expenses in order to approximate revenues, the method also revealed that at least 64 percent of all "tourists" (of approximately one million) were shuttle traders who came to Turkey to participate in the trade. This number was similar to Russian estimates that anywhere from 65 to 80 percent of all tourists to Turkey were traders.[43]

This slow accumulation of reliable information explains why the process of enacting and later enforcing various policy measures as applicable to border crossing was gradual as well. After almost two years of a near-complete freedom of trade, Resolution No. 1322, signed by the Council of Ministers on December 23, 1993, attempted to set quotas on the volume of imported goods that were exempt from custom duties. Individual travelers were allowed to bring in to the Russian Federation duty-free goods valued at less than $2,000. It further stipulated that in the current regulation it was permitted to "determine the value of goods ... in a simplified manner," mainly at

Table 2.2: Number of Russian citizens who traveled abroad in 1995, in thousands

Countries*	Overall	Purpose of the trip***		
		Tourism	Business	Private
Overall	8,396	2,555	1,696	2,925
Estonia	1,750	1	4	1,700
Lithuania	1,082	114	298	509
Turkey	764	538	31	83
Finland	641	223	190	105
Poland	479	385	50	25
Germany**	443	52	178	131
China	343	239	38	6
Latvia	233	22	96	104
UAE	211	163	9	4
Japan	152	5	17	2
Italy	145	74	39	6
Mongolia	142	9	79	48
Spain	135	94	23	4
Greece	130	92	11	8
France	127	45	60	7
Bulgaria	125	66	25	20
Great Britain	117	17	69	8
Cypress	109	88	13	2
United States**	165	13	92	41
Republic of Korea	92	24	17	4
Israel**	78	15	14	40

* Statistics for India and Pakistan are not provided.
** United States, Germany, and Israel are estimated to be the exception in the rule where "tourism" normally implies sightseeing rather than trade.
*** Excluding "other" and undeclared.
Source: *Rossiiskii statisticheskii ezhegodnik* (Moscow, 1996). *Note*: Estimat ed 80% of tourists to highlighted countries are shuttle traders; estimates to other countries vary significantly.

the personal discretion of the customs officials who were granted authority to decide what was for personal consumption and what was not. All possessions and/or cash in excess of $2,000 were subject to duty and import fees.[44]

The implementation of this regulation became immediately problematic. First, in 1994 two traders submitted an appeal to the Constitutional Court of the Russian Federation. The two plaintiffs challenged the unconstitutional implementation of Resolution No. 1322. The resolution, which stipulated that it should be put into effect immediately, was applied by customs officials starting on January 1, 1994. However, this resolution did not become public knowledge until its publication in the *Rossiiskaia gazeta* on January 15, 1994, or two weeks after it became effective. Thus it gave traders no chance to make necessary adjustments to accommodate the new policy. Yet it created ample grounds for abuse by officials. The process of implementing a regulation without making it publically available contravened the Constitution of the Russian Federation of 1993.[45]

But the discourse on Resolution No. 1322 also touched upon a sensitive issue of widespread corruption and the abuse of authority and position by customs officials, and the various regulations only seemed to reinforce this problem. Every person crossing the border could be searched in cases when customs officers suspected that travelers were carrying contraband items like drugs, large amounts of cash, and/or merchandise in excess of the legal duty-free allowance. Some officials were only doing their duty, but others painstakingly searched through traders' bags in the hope of confiscating excess merchandise or cash. Though much of the confiscation was legal, it was commonly recognized that customs officials illegally kept the confiscated items for personal use. In many ways, it became a perverted game of who could outsmart whom, especially when it came to cash. Shuttle traders hid money in the soles of their shoes and between layers of cardboard in boxes. They made homemade false-bottomed bags to conceal their cash. They hid it in their hairstyles, in mattresses, and in makeup bags. The bravest even tried to carry cash in their pockets, hoping that the best hidden thing is sometimes placed in the most obvious spot. As one shuttle trader put it:

> the main problem encountered en route is the customs. At that time, ... everyone had to be resourceful. The most inventive hid their money in cans of food. [We] cut out the bottom of a tin, put money rolled in plastic bags there, and soldered up the can. But this method did not always work. Once a customs official confiscated such a tin, saying that he wanted to try out our canned sprats. It was probably the most valuable can of sprats ever![46]

On other occasions, bottles of vodka were taped to traders' bodies; special pockets hid packs of cigarettes in jacket sleeves; and special belts held hanging bottles secure under women's skirts. Traders knew all the customs officials stationed on "their" border crossings and gave them different nicknames that reflected each official's character traits or their preferences for bribes. Popular nicknames "*Vezdekhod*" (a four-wheel drive, or literally "go everywhere"), "Hitler," and "Don Juan" are quite suggestive. Some officials took bribes in cash, others in drink or merchandise, while others were incorruptible for anything less than "payments in kind," that is, sexual favors. But all the preparation and setup had to be done before customs officials conducted an inspection. If the traders hesitated or made a public display of offering bribes (or committed other "sins" in this tense relationship), officials had to search the offenders, and after conducting a thorough body search, they could usually discover bottles of liquor taped to women's bodies like an ammunition belt under their breasts. All such hidden merchandise was confiscated "for private use" by customs officials.[47] In the most extreme cases, some female traders bluntly explained that it was possible to cross the border with merchandise that exceeded the allowed norm only "by spending 20 minutes with a border official in a sleeping wagon compartment behind the closed doors."[48] Though most traders never experienced any sexual offenses and these urban legends were half fiction, they were also half true in that they exposed the level of corruption that was commonplace at the time. Time and again, traders depended more than anything else on their ability to bribe officials and even just cry their eyes out and beg for mercy.

Some officials also became accomplices in criminal and near-criminal activities. In some cases they chose to ignore violations of regulations, while in others they actively took part in the process and the profits of this semilegal process. For example, in Irkutsk customs officials approached a man in the waiting zone of the airport who earned his living by protecting shuttle traders. A quick look revealed that the man was armed with an AK-47 assault rifle! Because such protection was indeed necessary at a time when mass murders and armed robbery were commonplace and because of the sufficient "fee" paid to the officials, the man was let free.[49] In more extreme cases, criminal groups organized illegal crossings of the border for traders with merchandise, usually following a route to the traders' hometown from a market to some remote river on the border that was crossed on a raft made of tires. Many border officials knew about these "rafting expeditions." These officials did not take bribes at work; instead, they chose to share in the criminals' profits rather than enforce rules that they upheld in public. Commonly, customs officials and the transportation gang members "charged" traders 50 percent of their profits. These traders complained that the merchandise they purchased abroad and were hoping to resell later "was as easy to get to as the headquarters of NASA."[50]

Even racketeers started to use this common knowledge of corruption and abuse of authority in their schemes. Sometimes criminals pretended to be government employees by falsifying documents and demanded that traders pay them bribes in cash, goods, or even in private cell phones to prevent "authorities" from charging traders with drug smuggling and other heinous criminal activities. No trader who participated in such semilegal activities dared to double-check the policemen's IDs or complain to state authorities, and nearly every trader believed that she or he got the better end of the deal by paying a small fee to "officials," as opposed to facing charges of fraud or smuggling merchandise for resale. Most often, the victims of such crimes were women, because they were believed to put up the least resistance and to pay the most when threatened with "official measures."[51]

These are only a few of many examples that expose the problems of the trade. But most of the information on the functioning of the trade, its revenues, and its abuses was anecdotal, and it came from journalists' accounts or was collected by social scientists who conducted interviews and case studies in various parts of Russia. The shuttle trade was omnipresent in Russian life at the time, yet reliable information about its volume and scale was nowhere to be found. And the lack of reliable data was slowly but surely beginning to attract attention. As a consequence of this lack of data, all subsequent government measures became remedial as they aimed to curtail the abuse of authority and set out some guidelines—progressively stricter—on how to conduct customs valuations and border control.

Already in August 1994, a new government regulation on the border crossings and customs tariffs set as its main principle the accumulation of data. Even though it addressed some previous shortcomings (e.g., the resolution was to be published in *Rossiiskie vesti* immediately), most of its articles required customs and border-protection centers to collect and analyze information on the current estimated volume of trading. Specifically, thirty customs and border-protection centers were required to gather data and to propose to the central administration specific measures on how to monitor and regulate the trade. It was believed that on-the-spot knowledge of local conditions would be the best research tool for creating an effective means of controlling the flow of goods. After receiving this information, the Central Organization for the Customs Control was required to synthesize all the data and provide its findings to the Chief of the Customs Control, the Ministry of Finance, and the State Trade Committee.[52]

Only in mid-1996 did this knowledge result in a new measure. On July 18, 1996, the government of the Russian Federation issued Resolution No. 808, which dealt with the small-scale passing of goods across the border. The resolution limited the duty-free value of goods to $1,000. But to avoid any further confusion, minimize the arbitrary use of power, and set a precise and nonnegotiable limit, the value of goods was made less relevant than its weight. Now the total weight of all possessions, even if under the $1,000 limit, could not exceed 50 kilograms (or approximately 110 pounds).[53] This resolution came as a real shock to the traders.

Moreover, Special Order of the State Customs Committee of the Russian Federation, No. 645, of October 18, 1996, offered further guidelines for dealing with small-scale trading.[54] It stipulated that falsification of information on the use of goods and claiming goods to be for personal consumption but later retailing them was to result in confiscation of all goods and a fine of between 100 and 200 percent of the value of all items. All items had to be declared as for sale immediately, and no one crossing the border could arbitrarily change their mind without securing permission from customs officials and then paying all required customs fees (Article 2.2). Specific guidelines were established for officials as well. They were required to track the frequency of trips (repeated trips suggested peddling) and the length of absence from the country (longer trips were treated more favorably than short trips). Officials were also required to treat all items of similar use, type, fashion, and/or color as being for commercial purposes. For example, three swimsuits of different styles in the luggage of someone traveling from Turkey in July were seen as being for personal use, but five identical swimsuits in luggage arriving from Urumqi, China, in January were not.

If the weight of luggage exceeded the allowed 50 kilogram limit, most customs duties were to be paid in ECU according to specific guidelines set by this new set of regulations.[55] Customs duties depended on (a) the price of items when receipts were available or when there were minor variations in price (on products like tea, sugar, chocolate, or some fruits); or (b) the type of clothing—outerwear (other than fur) was subject to 30 percent tax or 10 ECU per kilogram; trousers and shorts, at 7 ECU per kilogram; blouses and shirts, 5 ECU; shoes, 20 percent of value plus 2 ECU per pair. Also important were size (children's clothing was taxed at a lesser rate) and the country of origin (items from Kazakhstan, Kirgizia, and a number of other "preferential" countries were taxed at a lower rate). Similarly detailed provisions were outlined in all fifty sections of the resolution, including a list of specific items that were subject to customs duty on a per-item basis (jewelry, fur coats, cigarettes, and so on).

This regulation took account of the accumulated data about the nature and scope of the shuttle trade as it simultaneously affected the shuttle-trading patterns and altered them. It aimed to make borders harder to cross, push the legitimization of the shuttle trade, and increase state's revenues from the highly profitable consumer market. By setting more rigid guidelines for the inspection of luggage, it also placed a high value on curtailing corruption and minimizing the arbitrary use of power. But its main provisions were restrictive, not for officials, but for traders. Traders could falsify many things, like the value of goods, their destination, and purposes, and were even able to produce fake receipts. But they could not alter the weight of their merchandise. The regulation effectively put an end to large-scale *un-taxed* trading in bulky items. It pushed traders who "specialized" in heavy-weight items (TVs, furniture, and similar goods) to either seek more legitimate avenues to conduct their business or to leave the business altogether, though small-scale trading in clothing, cosmetics, and similar items continued.

Ironically, the most massive blow to the trade, which undermined it and arguably ended it, came not from this government resolution of 1996 but two years later with the economic crisis of 1998.[56] As we will see later, most traders never recovered after the ruble collapse of August 1998. In relation to governmental actions, after 1998 most of these acknowledged the importance of making changes beyond the border-crossing points. To begin with, because the traders were repeatedly accused of corrupting officials, significant resources were invested in increasing the wages of such officials as well as attacking the cases of corruption more vigorously. Secondly, some changes were implemented by neighboring countries due to the expansion of the European Union. Poland is the most significant example of these changes as it now required a visa for Russian citizens crossing the border. And finally, though much effort had been made to convert this grey sector of the economy into the legitimate economy, the increase in domestic wages and the stabilization of the job market were of the greatest consequence in curbing the trade. With alternative means of employment readily available, many former traders were no longer willing to risk their well-being in pursuit of the elusive profits of the shuttle trade.[57]

The Geography of the Trade

Even after looking at the economic data, it is impossible to appreciate the scale and complexity of this trade network that bonded millions of women in a transition economy without acknowledging the broad geography of the

Figure 2.1: Shuttle traders' plaid bags dominated all train stations in the 1990s.

trade. Spanning from socialist Poland in the late 1980s to China and Turkey and to lesser extent to India and the United Arab Emirates by the mid-1990s, the shuttle trade became truly global and included dozens of destinations. In this multitude of places and experiences, we can identify three main patterns in the development of the shuttle trade that facilitate an understanding of the geography of the trade and the relative importance of each country involved in it. At first, during the early stages of the shuttle trade, most of its participants traveled to Central European socialist (and later post-socialist) countries like Poland (mainly), Romania, Bulgaria, and eventually Hungary. These countries, however, slowly lost their primary importance as Turkey and China assumed the center stage and remained the key destinations and suppliers for the duration of the shuttle trade. In a third group, a wide range of countries—India, Pakistan, Italy, Spain, Greece, Korea, Thailand, the United Arab Emirates, Egypt—supplemented Chinese and Turkish goods but functioned as destination choices for only a small number of traders or on a small scale in terms of volume of trade, or were destinations for only a short period of time.

After the law of 1987 allowed people to trade and pursue other individual activities, the earliest choice of the countries for the shuttle traders to visit was determined by the lack of convertible currency and the ease of border crossing. Hence, Central European countries of the so-called Soviet Bloc became a "natural" choice. By the late 1980s and early 1990s the Soviet people did not need a visa to travel to Poland, Bulgaria, or Romania (though references to Hungary and Czechoslovakia as trading destinations also abound), and they could easily acquire travel documents in any town in the Soviet Union. Moreover, because of the lack of convertible currency and domestic price regulations, the system of "trade" in the late 1980s was based on barter exchanges. Soviet people took canned food, photo cameras, watches, vodka, and other "deficit" items to the "near abroad" and exchanged them for consumer products that were desirable at home, or they occasionally sold these Soviet-produced items for US dollars and purchased goods for resale. Even though the limit on currency or foreign goods was set at $200 per person, this amount could bring $100 in profits, a fortune by Soviet standards. By the early 1990s, a large number of shop tours facilitated the trade by offering direct bus connections to Warsaw and other places.[58]

Yet the first traders nearly universally reported that they traveled abroad only on a trial basis, unsure of their success and even of their safety. They lacked any trading experience and did not know how to maximize their profits, though the first income was truly dizzying. The goals and aspirations of traders were also modest; they only wanted to make enough for a new pair of shoes or some cash for everyday needs. Eventually the traders would aspire to buy a new car or a flat with the profits that they made in the shuttle trade. Even in its early days, the business, or more precisely the cash flow that it generated, was addictive, and some even compared it to gambling. One risked a fortune in these travels, and often lost, but the winning stakes were high by the standards of the time. One trader, Tamara, remembered her travels to Poland:

> We went to Poland for about four years. We could not yet travel anywhere we wanted. But we had no money and nothing to buy at home. It was horrifying. That's why we traveled to Poland. There, in Poland, they had all sorts of goods, more than enough, and cheaply, too. Poland—that was a good thing, I tell you. We crossed the border at Brest, where the war for the "survival of the fittest" started. We mostly stayed with a family, and … the hostess made good profits on us. Poland then lived off the shuttle traders from the Soviet Union. But the racketeers were scary. There one could be killed and robbed. Anything. We were afraid to stay at the hotel. But the goods were cheap. For about $3,000 we could buy a cargo wagon full of goods. Everything was just so cheap.[59]

For Tamara and all early traders, a lack of convertible currency implied a heavy reliance on barter and the small-scale trading of Soviet goods. The assortment of goods that crossed the border was truly immense, just about everything that one could scavenge from the shelves of Soviet stores: vodka, canned food, watches, and so on. One trader remembered that he could buy peanuts in bulk from an acquaintance. Then he packed peanuts into small bags and sold five bags for $1, making enough profit for a new set of clothing. The early profits were spent on everyday goods, mostly clothing that the Soviet population craved badly. Jeans, an object of desire and envy for most Soviet people, became for the first time widely available. A trader could buy only a couple of pairs of jeans and a couple of other items because everything had to be carried personally and because these traders never generated enough income for more than a few coveted items.[60] But even such profits were enough to stimulate the public of the Soviet Union that was starving for deficit items.

Poland and other socialist states returned the favor manifold. Most opened bazaars and markets catered specifically for the shuttle traders, and the volume of trade in each was indeed impressive. It was estimated that in the early 1990s the Warsaw Stadium, one of the biggest bazaars of this kind, generated 60,000 jobs (ranging from manufacturing to services) and "a turnover which made it equivalent to one of the largest industries in Poland."[61] The traders appreciated such resources and according to a survey of border crossers from the (former) Soviet Union into Poland, the traders went to Poland on an average thirteen times, while one group admitted that they were making their 120th trip.[62] While the bazaars and markets were sizeable, there was little structure to regulate them. The tolerance for irregular trading was high, and there were no standards, rules, regulations, or taxation in place. All these factors allowed historian Dariusz Stola to conclude that traders were initially lured to Poland and other (former) socialist states not only because of the type of goods that these places offered but also because Central European nations offered traders "a combination of widespread tolerance towards informal markets ... and a certain basic security and stability in the operation of those markets."[63]

However, Turkey and China soon displaced former socialist countries as the main providers of goods and destination points for the traders. After the first charter flight to Turkey (Istanbul) in 1992, the trade with Turkey grew exponentially. As it turned out, it was a Turkish initiative to open up the trade with Russian shuttle traders, as Turkey had considerable experience dealing with Yugoslavian, Polish, Hungarian, and other traders in the mid-1980s. Turkey attracted traders because of its geographic accessibility (one could easily fly to Turkey or even travel by bus) and because the high-quality goods came with a low price tag. Though Turkey offered a wide assortment of goods to begin with, it also made adjustments along the way to accommodate the demands in Russia, based on the tastes and seasons there. As a result, in 1996 alone, over 800,000 "tourists" traveled to Turkey, at least 80 percent of whom were shuttle traders[64] (see Table 2.2 for more data).

Turkey attracted traders from all over the post-Soviet space. Tatiana, the keeper of a small shop in the southern Russian city of Krasnodar, was disappointed with her shopping experiences in Moscow and chose to travel to Turkey instead.

> After Turkey, I do not want to go to Moscow again. The choice of goods is more limited in Moscow, and shopkeepers there charge 100 percent more than what the goods cost in Turkey. And then in Turkey ... how can you even compare? There you can see everything nicely displayed and you can even try everything on! Even if it means 25 pairs of pants! But in Moscow you grab a bag and that is it. ... Of course, in Turkey everyone is polite, with a smile when greeting and with a smile at the end of the transaction. The shopkeepers there have respect for you. Needless to say, some people are not so honest there but they are mostly nice. I do not know the language at all but most shopkeepers there speak enough Russian.[65]

After positive reviews and experiences like that, the trade with Turkey continued to grow, and it maintained its position as the "suitcase capital of the world" for Russian shuttle traders in the 1990s. In the first two years of the decade, Istanbul became a shopping Mecca, with several routes leading to it. The most popular was a bus route through Romania, but by the middle of the decade, air traffic took over as the preferred mode of transportation. At its peak, Turkish airlines had over 55 passenger flights a week between Turkey and Russia, and Russian and Ukrainian airlines each had 10 flights a week originating in Moscow, St. Petersburg, and Kiev. Though other airlines offered charter and regular flights as well, the three above-mentioned companies alone transported approximately 7,000 people a week to Istanbul and back in the mid-1990s.[66] With over 800,000 shuttle traders from Russia coming to Turkey annually, it is not surprising that the volume of trade between Russia and Turkey reached $8–12 billion in 1996.[67]

The trade was immensely profitable for Turkish shopkeepers as well. According to research conducted by the State Higher School of Economics in Russia, 81.5 percent of all trading done by shopkeepers in Turkey was with foreign markets, of which 91 percent went to traders from Russia. A wide range of other countries were present as well—Romania, Bulgaria, Ukraine,

Azerbaijan, Serbia, Croatia, and others—but each ranked significantly lower than Russia in terms of sale transactions in Turkey. The shuttle trade also generated substantial income opportunities for new travel agencies specializing in shop tours, cargo carriers, new hotels, and the entire service sector.[68]

But Graph 2.1, depicting Turkey's shuttle exports, also demonstrates a deep crisis of the trade in 1998 and its failure to recover to pre-1998 levels. This crisis was not the first for suitcase trading in Turkey, but the two previous recessions had left no permanent scars on the trade. The first crisis took place in the late 1980s, when suitcase traders from the former Soviet Bloc left Turkey's marketplace. But traders from Poland, Hungary, and Yugoslavia were soon replaced by the residents of the former Soviet Union, and in no time these newcomers came to outnumber their predecessors. Turkey suffered from the second crisis when China and then the United Arab Emirates became its competitors. But it was the South Asian crisis of 1998 that was imported into Russia, among other countries, and delivered a devastating blow to suitcase trading in Turkey.

Suitcase trade in Turkey can also serve as a paradigm of shuttle trading and its actors elsewhere. In nearly every place the infrastructure of trading followed the pattern outlined in Graph 2.2. The Laleli market in Istanbul demonstrated that there were a great number of actors involved in—and benefiting from—the trading. Graph 2.2 does not directly represent various supralegal and Mafia-like organizations. These groups were also active players in the market, though more so on the Russian side. Respondents nearly

Graph 2.1: Turkey's shuttle trade exports

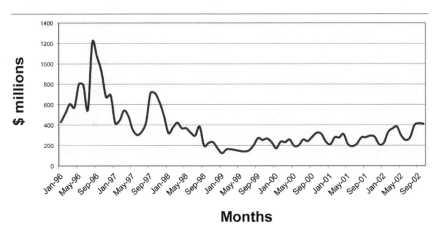

Source: Turkish Central Bank, http://www.tcmb.gov.tr/

Graph 2.2: Various actors in the shuttle trade

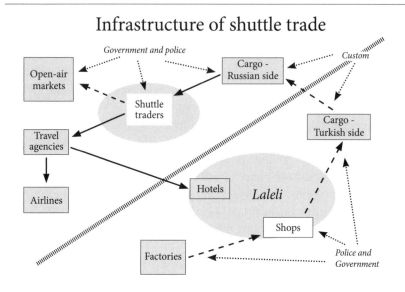

Infrastructure of shuttle trade

Source: "Redefining contagion: Political economy of suitcase trade between Turkey and Russia." IREX Research Project, 2001–2002.

universally reported that, even though petty crime and cheating existed everywhere, extortion, threats, and violence were more typical of open-air markets back in Russia than abroad. Most common were demands for "protection money," which ranged from a few hundred rubles to $2,000 USD, depending on the location, type of merchandise, and timing of trading.

The most serious competition to Turkey came from China. By late 1991 the *Moskva-Pekin* (Moscow–Beijing) train had become a true "market on wheels." Nearly every passenger on the train traveled to China to acquire goods there, though most never went farther than Urumchi. The list of items sold in China was endless and the prices were unmatched. Even the fact that Chinese manufacturers sold many damaged goods of appalling quality did not deter traders; these items looked decent enough for resale and brought the most substantial profits because of their original miniscule cost (profits of 200% were common). Of course, China also produced goods that could successfully compete on the international market and were in demand in Western Europe and elsewhere. These items were often designed and created in official state-regulated (or even state-owned) factories. But such items were priced higher and had less appealing tags than those manufactured in semilegal factories. Thousands of clandestine or semilegal (those that claimed to produce one type of product but manufactured tens of them) factories conducted business with shuttle traders from the post-Soviet space.

For a while, South Korea attempted to compete with China as the destination of choice for traders. The first shuttle traders came to South Korea in late 1992, but even at its peak in mid-1994, only about 150 traders traveled to South Korea weekly. Traders from Khabarovsk, for example, were drawn to South Korea because "it was close to Khabarovsk, the goods were of solid quality, the service was excellent, yet the prices were reasonable for the quality of goods."[69] Nevertheless, though the number of traders remained small, they differed from many other traders in various locations because of the scale of the trade. While most transactions elsewhere were in the range of $500–$600 per trader (rarely reaching $10,000), it was common in Seoul and Pusan to see individual businessmen (or more often, businesswomen) carrying suitcases of money with them and investing $50,000–$100,000 in a single trip. Even transactions of a quarter-million USD were not unheard of. Hence, the overall cash value of trade was significant in the broader scheme of the shuttle trade, or at least it was sufficient to make some traders speak of the "substantial support" they provided for the Korean economy. So the shuttle trade in Korea became significant as an indicator of shuttle traders' willingness to explore new opportunities and to travel the world, if needed, in search of the cheapest and most profitable goods, and it mattered because it became a marker by which success stories in the business were measured.[70] Yet the trade with South Korea (centered on Seoul and Pusan) remained marginal in the overall geography and volume of trade even at its best times, and it was quickly overshadowed and then completely undermined by trade done with China. "China closed the door for those who worked in Korea," remembered Elena, who used to sell fur coats from South Korea in a market in Khabarovsk in the early 1990s. Even the quality of goods was not a perfect measure of success, as "in Korea the goods were of much better quality, even though a bit pricier, whereas cheap Chinese goods cannot boast the same quality. But the buyer prefers to buy a cute outfit with a brand name label for less money. China choked many a trader."[71]

This is not to say that Chinese manufacturers were not capable of producing quality goods. The well-developed manufacturing infrastructure of China could offer all sorts of goods of all qualities and prices to customers. Yet the certified items with the required "Made in China" marking were manufactured in several dozen licensed factories in the south and southeast of the People's Republic, from where they traveled primarily to Western

European countries and the United States. These goods flooded the Western markets, where customers came to rely on inexpensive and reasonably reliable products of Chinese origin.

These factories sold to domestic stores as well and occupied a solid niche in the local economy. Yet their produce never reached the wholesale markets frequented by the suitcase traders. Hundreds of small semilegal factories catered to the designer tastes of Russian-speaking traders and offered a reasonable price–quality ratio. There also existed thousands upon thousands of private tailors' shops and illegal operations that used unsafe, half-rusted, and old-fashioned equipment to manufacture short-lived cheap clothing. Consumers joked that such pants, blouses, and other outfits lasted only to the first wash or a first trip to the ironing board, after which they simply disintegrated or became deformed beyond recognition. And still, these were the goods that made up the bulk of traders' cargo and sales.

Shuttle traders appreciated how quickly the local Chinese market adjusted to their coming. Virtually overnight "Russian zones" sprang up all over the border towns of China, and many locals learned rudimentary Russian and adopted Russian names to make communication easier for a non-Chinese speaker. By 1993, traders routinely worked with the Chinese "Sasha" and "Mitia" and were accompanied by Chinese "Katya" and "Nadya." Petty theft was commonplace, but unlike racketeering and armed assaults, it was easily prevented by round-the-clock monitoring of one's precious cargo. Shop tours and specialty tourist operators did not lag behind their counterparts in other countries. Nadezhda, formerly a border-control officer, was lured into business by its profits. "We started our business in 1992," she recalled.

> Then there was no visa support but people needed visas for China. My girlfriends suggested that I start a tourist agency that specializes in trips to Harbin. I had already tried my hand at trading and had some partners in China. So I asked them for a formal invitation, arranged for a visa, and started to take groups to China. At first, I worked in the following places: Harbin, Tongjiang, Jiamusi, Suifenhe, and Shenyang. Subsequently, it took off from there. Now I have nine people working for me full time.

Small provincial Chinese towns benefited from the trade just as much as shuttle traders. For example, the small village of Tongjiang on the Sino-Russian border, with its easy access to Birobidzhan and Khabarovsk, grew into a thriving town of 180,000 permanent residents. In the mid-1990s, local Chinese entrepreneurs even paid the travel expenses of shuttle traders from the other side of the border, reaffirmed Nadezhda. To the present day good-quality restaurants called "Moscow," "St. Petersburg," "Birobidzhan," and others serve national Russian meals to hungry shopping tourists for a low fee of $5–$7 for a three-course meal.

Shopping-tour organizers not only arranged for transportation and lodging but also used every opportunity that came their way to maximize their profits. Thus, Aleksander Shabaev, a founder and owner of a tour operator that specialized in shopping tours to China and elsewhere, wrote the first extensive manual for shuttle traders. Shabaev started his manual by acknowledging that in 1994 shuttle traders carried on their backs at least 25 percent of all the imports to the Russian Federation, though precise numbers are impossible to calculate. But the labor of former scientists, engineers, army officers, teachers, medical professionals, and people of other occupations who now invested their time in shuttling was so physically demanding and unpredictable that very few managed to stay in it for long. "Don't worry about the competition in the shuttle business," wrote Shabaev. "The work is so intense and tough that more than 50 percent of shuttle traders leave the business within the first year."[72] The manual came with a list of goods to buy for those who aspired to make fortunes in this business. The manual did not guarantee financial success to its readers, but it definitely brought success to Shabaev, who got his main dividends not by selling the book (which did well on the market) but by bringing new clients to his shopping-tour company. The clients believed that the author of such an insightful manual could offer them something special that would guarantee their success.

Shabaev's company operated not only in China but elsewhere, as some traders were not lured by the low prices offered by Chinese merchants. While the Far East region was interested in trading with China and other Asian countries, many other regions of the Russian Federation found these destinations too remote. The travel expenses of a trader going from Moscow to Pusan were hardly justified by profits made in the trade. A wide range of other countries attracted those who wanted to minimize their travel expenses or to maximize their profits by bringing high-quality (and thus high-price) designer clothing to the Russian consumer. By the mid-1990s, Greece was a popular destination as it had become one (if not the one) of the main providers of fur products (leather products were also common). Traditionally, fur coats were in high demand among residents of Russia, and it was easy to make a profit on them. Greece won the hearts of some traders with the solid quality of its fur, most of which was produced and turned into finished products around Thessaloniki. Though some attempts to cheat traders into buying sub-par products were reported, traders in general acknowledged that most Greek items made of mink fur, blue fox fur, and other furs were durable, and customers liked the quality and standard of Greek fur coats.[73]

The United Arab Emirates offered a similar advantage of high-quality goods combined with excellent service and reasonable prices. The cost of a hotel stay there was cheaper than in European countries, and the prices of various consumer goods were only 30–40 percent of those in Europe, yet the appeal (design) and durability were of comparable standards. The most common commodities were household electronics[74] and gold,[75] but the UAE retailers also offered a selection of goods from all over the world (including most Asian manufacturers and even Latin American and US goods), thus allowing traders to have access to a good assortment of products without the expense of traveling to various destinations in Europe, Asia, and the Americas. Also important was the fact that the reports of cheating (*kidok*) were almost nonexistent, and the drunken crime (street fights, debauchery, robbery, etc.) that plagued many cheap locations where traders stayed in other countries was minimal (if it occurred at all) in the UAE. The resort-type weather in the wintertime (around 80° F, or 23–27° C) and the warm waters of the Persian Gulf were an added bonus that attracted overworked and overburdened traders.

India and Pakistan were also repeatedly mentioned as places where select traders chose to go. India undoubtedly became a place of choice for jewelry with semiprecious stones and cotton items, though the trade was limited because of the high expenses associated with traveling to India. Though Pakistan was mentioned repeatedly by traders and in secondary sources, I have found no direct evidence (for example, someone who actually traveled to Pakistan as a trader) that the traders ever favored Pakistan as a country (rather than Pakistani goods) for their business. Moreover, the process of visa issuance was so burdensome in the 1990s that it casts significant doubt on the validity of claims of a direct shuttle trade with Pakistan. Thus, the minimum processing time for a visa was 21 days, the visa application required proof of pertinent immunization, and until recently, tourism was not a valid category for visa issuance (in contrast to visas for journalists or diplomatic visas).[76] Hence, the discussion of the shuttle trade in Pakistan requires more data and research before it can even be affirmed that such a trade existed.[77]

Last but not least, Spain and Italy became the choice destinations for "*exclusif*," or high-end designer clothing for those who could afford it back home. Affordability was the reason why the shuttle trade to Western Europe (except Greece) continued only on a small scale; not too many ordinary people back in Russia could buy Armani, Gucci, or Versace.[78] But traders who dared to enter this market made astronomical profits (usually about 300%) by offering consumers last year's designs, which they bought at end-of-the-season sales while claiming to sell this year's fashions.[79] In addition to haute couture clothing, traders also bought high-end fashionable clothing without big-name price tags from various factories in Milan, Rimini, Bologna, Naples, and Bari. Though these items did not have designer names, they attracted consumers with the in-demand label "Made in Italy."[80] Nonetheless, only a few managed to find their niche in buying and reselling goods from places like Italy. As one woman trader, Tamara, commented, "Italy is an expensive and fashionable country; we need something more commonplace. I did not like Italy," she added. "I am not up to these goods, and there were constant problems with my visas."[81] Even if some traders hoped to travel widely or trade in high-end clothing, the final choice of the supplier country was determined by the investment–profit ratio and the financial interests of each person involved.

A Remark on the Economic Impact of the Traders and Their Merchandise

By far the most complex and disputable question is the economic impact of the shuttle trade on the Russian economy and its share of all imports of the Russian Federation. No definitive data exists for the researcher, so we can only either repeat estimates calculated elsewhere or consider indirect evidence and information provided by such institutions as the *Roskomstat* (Federal State Statistics Service). The same goes for the type of merchandise that the traders brought in from abroad. The simple answer to the question of what they sold would be *everything,* or all types of consumer goods. Any traveler to Russia in the 1990s could not fail to notice that one could buy anything from toothpicks and clothing to weapons and allegedly even nuclear-weapon launchers in open-air markets in Russian cities.[82]

The factor that complicates the calculation of more precise estimates further is the massive inflation that was typical of the immediate post-Soviet era. Thus, the cost of consumer goods from 1992 to 1997 increased 2,400 times,[83] and in 1992 and 1993 it was more comprehensible for people to calculate inflation on a daily basis rather than as an annual number. The hyperinflation of the first few years (which was called the Great Russian Depression) was curbed somewhat in 1994, though it remained high by standards of stable economies (see Table 2.3).

Overall, the best estimate of the share of consumer goods that the shuttle

Table 2.3: Economic situation in Russia, 1994–97

	1994	1995	1996	1997
All official imports, in billions of USD	38.7	46.7	46.0	52.9
Consumer goods as percent of total	—	1.5	1.6	—
USD rate of exchange, rubles per 1 USD	3,550	4,640	5,560	5,960
Inflation, % of increase from previous year	408.0	297.0	147.8	114.7

Source: *Goskomstat*, GTK, TsB RF; Tatiana Mel'nichenko, Alberto Bolonini, "Rossiiskii chelnochnyi bizness. Obshchaia kharakteristika i vzaimosviaz's ital'ianskim rynkom," *Economisti Associati* (1997).

trade provided to the markets of the Russian Federation is generated by comparing the official data on imports into the Russian Federation and the assumed turnover of the shuttle trade. As for the latter, the most reliable information comes from three sources: the Higher School of Economics, the Federal State Statistics Service (Russia), and the Central Bank of Turkey. The IMF even advised the Turkish government to include the shuttle trade in its current account calculations.

Most sources have estimated that the trade reached its highest point in 1994–96, with sales of $10–$15 billion USD annually.[84] However, a report by the Higher School of Economics stated that the trade turnover was as high as $4.5–$5 billion USD per quarter ($18–20 billion USD annually) up to the financial crisis of August 1998, and it subsequently dropped to $2–$2.5 billion USD per quarter.[85] At a time when the government imported $1.5 billion USD worth of essential consumer goods into the Russian Federation annually, any estimate of the scale of the shuttle trade appears impressive, as it accounted for 70–95 percent of all imports of consumer goods in the mid-1990s.

A publication by the Russian Democratic Party *Yabloko* on the social consequences of the economic reforms in 1992–95 claimed that in the first half of 1995, 54 percent of all essential consumer goods and food was imported. At the same time, 25–35 percent of all trading in the country evaded any sort of control, accountability, and legitimization. The publication concluded that the share of the grey market was so substantial in the mid-1990s that it essentially stabilized the economic conditions in

Russia and allowed the country to survive this difficult period.[86]

Additional insight is provided by the Federal State Statistics Service's data on the incomes of the Russian population in the years from 1992 to 1995. In 1992 only 16.1 percent of all people of working age earned their incomes from individual activities and other sources; however, the share of such (barely accountable) income rose to 24.4 percent in 1993, 38 percent in 1994, and 38.75 percent in 1995, which roughly equaled the number of all waged and salaried workers in the state (39.4%, with the rest made up of various categories of unemployed and disabled people who received social benefits).[87] Thus, though there are variations in the data of different reports, they all point to the fact that in the 1990s the shuttle trade was of paramount importance to Russia in its social and economic spheres.

3
Women Traders
Success in Numbers

We are simply overseas trackers;

We should not be mistaken for slackers;

We have every type of a bale;

We are neither female nor male.

      —Iakov Kofman, *Chelnoki*[1]

Though it might be impossible to pinpoint the precise explanation for a female preponderance in the trade, it nonetheless is a tangible task to identify and present a social profile of the so-called typical trader. Both men and women formed the core of the trade, even if at times the trade was female by some 80 percent.[2] These women and men, if we look at the entire span of the shuttle trade across the former Soviet Union, were a diverse group of people, of various ethnic and socioeconomic backgrounds. Yet, if one is to look for a predominant prototype, then the typical trader was still a woman. Even though these women were of various ethnic origins, came from places far away from where they traded, and had different kinship networks and prior employment experiences, women traders nonetheless shared a common socioeconomic background.

The impulse to describe the shuttle trade as a significant economic phenomenon is not without precedent. Small-scale, regional research projects were especially common, and so were the thematic studies that addressed various aspects of the trade, such as its volume or its role in globalizing consumer trade. Gender-specific issues, however, received only minimal attention. Research methodology itself is partially to blame for this omission, and thus it warrants a discussion of the methodology and its limitations. Not only is it challenging to convince women to reveal all the details of their lives during interviews, but reconstructing biography in oral history through the prism of gender has proved equally problematic.

From a practical point, the process of collecting interviews was complicated by several obstacles. Common to all oral history projects are problems of extracting particular information from an interviewee without superimposing one's agenda onto the answers. It was constantly tempting to ask former shuttle traders their opinion on whether women were the driving force of the shuttle trade and what role they played in facilitating Russia's transition to a market economy. Yet the question itself might have prompted women to construct their answers in ways that they might not have otherwise considered. Thus, when toward the end of the interview some women were asked about the gendered aspects of the trade, they nearly universally produced the same answer regardless of their prior comments: "The topic of women's role in the shuttle trade is very important … and must be studied, or our women would continue suffering for the sake of their families and their children."[3] These women became instantly convinced of their unique role in the shuttle trade by the mere fact that a researcher worded the question in such a way.

Predictably, there were also some contradictions and discrepancies in various individual accounts. These variations are common to all recollections and could be explained by memory lapses, normal reversals of the exact chronology, and some confusion and repression inherent in all life-altering experiences. This fact, of course, did not render the accounts less valuable, even if it made some details impossible to reconstruct (for example, though most respondents recalled that they only had "a few hundred bucks" when they got into the shuttle trade, very few remembered exact amounts or the profits made in each transaction). Overall, though, normal reversals and poor chronology were easy to remedy and reconstruct with some additional research.

A far greater challenge was posed by the fact that all former traders were extremely reluctant to share financial aspects of their business and even more reluctant to have the interviews recorded. Informal economy was not fully legal (though neither was it illegal), and as such some hesitation persists about sharing too much. Some shuttle traders understood clearly their legal rights and had no fears, but many others asked for anonymity as if they were accomplices in some grave crime. Moreover, many people bought into the idea that researchers would somehow make marvelous profits out of these people's life stories, but these profits would be lost to the main participants in the interviews. Several women explicitly stated that they would "talk openly" with a researcher but refused to be taped because, as one of them put it, "What if you turn this into a TV program and make a fortune, would I get anything then?" The derogatory attitude toward shuttle traders of the early 1990s made still others reluctant to admit that they participated in the trade. One person at first willingly shared details of her retail trading career in the 1990s, but once she heard the word "peddling" (*chelnochestvo*), cried out, "What's that? I have never heard of such a thing!" and shunned all further questions.

As a result, all but four women asked for full anonymity, and all agreed to a longer interview only after a prior personal conversation. It is important to point out that the respondents repeatedly commented on the fact that they could talk about these matters only to "one of us," meaning a native speaker, a cultural insider, and a woman. Nonetheless, if identifying people who did shuttle trading in the 1990s was as easy as it gets, getting them to talk was much more difficult. In the first round of fieldwork, 37 people were identified as suitable for an interview. They were chosen because it was established, usually through friends and acquaintances or personal conversations, that they indeed had partaken in the trade in the 1990s and were intimately familiar with its functions and operations. Of this number, nine people politely declined the offer to participate in the study, five were outraged by the offer and became downright hostile, and six more initially agreed but later failed to participate, citing reasons such as lack of time or other commitments. Seventeen women, however, answered most questions, with a typical interview lasting one hour or longer.[4] In other words, more than half of all the women refused to participate in the study, even though they were asked by friends or by someone with whom they had shared many pleasant conversations. Other fieldwork experiences were identical to the first one.

When supplemented with published life stories, these interviews became a rich source of gender analysis. Various studies, conducted specifically in the context of post-Soviet Russia, demonstrate the specificity of the male versus female self-narrative. When resolving the dilemma of how to combine employment and family obligations, Russian women depart drastically from men by prioritizing marriage, motherhood, and family relations over professional interests, training, and employment.[5] This is reflected in the fact that in female self-narratives women pay significantly more attention (compared to men) to marriage(s), childbirth, raising children, building relations with their mothers-in-law, improving living conditions, dealing with a housing shortage, and taking care of household chores. Men, in contrast, limit their personal stories to brief, questionnaire-like answers ("married, have children") and prefer to emphasize their professional training and employment in their self-narratives. On the same page, male narratives tend to be based on a model of "I, independent," whereas female self-narratives can be described as "I, in relation to others."[6]

When explaining their work-related choices, women most commonly cited external and circumstantial reasons for their employment choices rather than a personal active choice of their own. Listed in the order of descent (from the most to the least common), explanations of work-related choices demonstrate that women typically expressed their biographical narratives as someone who responded to external pressures.[7] The model was adopted from Meshcherkina's study of women's biographical models, and it worked perfectly well when supplemented with statements from traders' interviews:

* Marriage and childbirth as the main factor of employment choices, e.g., "I had to leave my job and find something else because I had to care for my family";
* Women have no personal choice, e.g., "That's life, it had to be that way";
* External circumstances, e.g., "I had to find another job because the Soviet Union collapsed";
* A failed marriage or a poor choice of husband, e.g., "My husband was a drunkard so I had to do something to earn a living";
* The death of a relative, e.g., "My father died and I had to go to work";
* Divorce and being a single mother, e.g., "Someone had to provide for the kids";
* Parental poverty, e.g., "My parents could not afford to give me anything";
* Hard to say, e.g., "I don't know why I ended up doing what I do";
* No personal qualities needed for success, e.g., "I didn't have the will-power or self-esteem to do anything better";
* No personal interest in career;
* Inability to marry;
* Rampant unemployment.

Overall, sociological studies like the one by Meshcherkina demonstrate that women in Russia in the 1990s were twice as likely to cite their private lives than any other factor in explaining their employment patterns. Specifically, 66.1 percent of women identified their personal lives as the driving force behind their job-related decisions, whereas only 33.9 percent identi-fied other factors, such as personal character traits, education, and inde-pendent professional choices, as important. Moreover, only about a third of all women who participated in Meshcherkina's and similar studies used the active voice in describing their lives (e.g., "I chose," "I decided," "I man-aged"). The majority, however, relied extensively on using passive verbs when explaining their life circumstances ("I was called," "I was convinced," "I was drawn into this," "I ended up getting involved," etc.).[8] Of all women, 46.1 percent also believed that they had never planned and should never plan anything in their lives; their lives are so much controlled by external factors and other people that planning is pointless and hopeless.[9] On the other hand, men were twice more likely than women to say that they were responsible for their own successes or failures, and twice as likely to use the affirmative verbs (active, even aggressive verbs) than women.[10]

These patterns were true of the female shuttle traders as well. Women traders largely affirmed that, to them, attitudes of society and family needs were formative in their own choices, and societal norms and socially ac-ceptable behavior were more instrumental than institutional support or a lack thereof. As subsequent examples demonstrate, women prioritized family values and social attitudes in explaining their roles in public and domestic spheres, often downplaying personal ambitions or the financial aspects of their trading activities. In an unstructured part of the interview, few spoke of the monetary value of their transactions; instead, women opted to highlight how much they contributed to the family's financial and emotional well-being and how much of what they did was a matter of self-sacrifice for the family. Even the traders' evaluation of their financial suc-cesses, which were often positively assessed, were measured by their ability to provide greater opportunities for their children rather than by self-gain or capital accumulation.

So who were these women? Though none of the survey methods are per-fect or immune to criticism, most studies, including empirical evidence col-lected during fieldwork for this project, demonstrate that the majority of women had post-secondary education (90% by some estimates), most were in their late twenties and thirties, and nearly half claimed to be of ethnically Russian origins. When it came to their place of residence and where they traded, over half of such women were originally from and conducted their business in central and Far Eastern Russia.[11] Other studies confirm this gen-eral pattern, estimating that shuttle traders were mostly women between the ages of 30 and 40 (though traders between the ages of 20 and 30 years old came a close second), mostly married and/or with children, predominantly with professional training or higher education and work-related experience (see Table 3.1).[12]

While precise numbers vary from one location to another, the data presented in Table 3.1 demonstrate that the traders were well educated, with a majority having post-secondary and professional training. One trader in the sample had the equivalent of a PhD; several had training as medical professionals and engineers. The age distribution, presented in Table 3.2, also suggests that most traders had at least a few years of working experience when they entered the trade.

At the high point of the shuttle trade, most traders also abandoned all hopes of finding employment elsewhere or of combining their regular jobs with trading activities. If in prior years traders could bring an item or two from near abroad and then go back to their full-time jobs, by the mid-1990s, as Table 3.3 demonstrates, only a small share of all traders could combine their jobs with international peddling.

This data is comparable to what the researchers found in various former Soviet republics.[13] For example, case studies of Lithuanian and Ukrainian markets (both former republics of the Soviet Union) demonstrate that the largest group of women traders during the time of study were between the

Table 3.1: Educational levels of traders (averages, with minimum and maximum of all samples shown in parentheses)

Type of education	Percentage
High school diploma*	24% (8%–39%)
Professional technical education / training	38% (38%–39%)
Post-secondary (minimum of four-year college)	38% (22.6%–54%)

Note: The overall size of the sample is 311 traders.
*Traders without a high-school diploma did not represent a statistically significant percentage.

Sources: Correlated with data from V. I. Il'in and M. A. Il'ina, "Torgovtsy gorodskogo rynka: shtrikhi k sotsial'nomu portretu." *EKO*, no. 5 (1998).

Table 3.2: Age distribution among traders, as of 1996

Age group	Percentage
18–30	39.5%
31–40	42%
41–55	11.5%
Over 55*	7%

Note: Age 55 was chosen as a marker because the official retirement age for women in Russia was and still is 55 years old. Most women can claim retirement benefits after this age. Though, as chapter 4 reveals, access to retirement benefits became limited in the 2000s for former traders, in 1996 most women could receive pension payments after age 55. The overall size of the sample is 311 traders.

Source: Includes data from V. I. Il'in and M. A. Il'ina, "Torgovtsy gorodskogo rynka: shtrikhi k sotsial'nomu portretu," *EKO*, no. 5 (1998).

Table 3.3: Trading as a share of overall employment, as of 1996

	Percentage
Trading on a full-time basis (no other employment)	83%
Retired but trading on a full-time basis	7%
Combining trading and other job/ employment	9%
Students, trading only in spare time	1%

Sources: Once again, this is based on the same sample group as figures 3.1 and 3.2, and it includes data from V. I. Il'in and M. A. Il'ina, "Torgovtsy gorodskogo rynka: shtrikhi k sotsial'nomu portretu," *EKO*, no. 5 (1998).

ages of 40 and 49 (41%, although 34% were 30–39 years old), thus indicating that these women were in the age group of 30–39 when they entered the business. Moreover, in the case of Ukraine, which experienced tougher economic acclimatization to new market conditions in the 1990s compared to Lithuania, women under 30 were more likely to enter the business than in Lithuania. In other words, most men and women were mid-career, when social and family pressures were high (e.g., a need to provide for children) but employment opportunities were low. This conclusion is also supported by data on educational levels among traders in both countries, though exact numbers diverge. In Ukraine 57 percent of women and 87 percent of men had a university education, and the number was 73 and 83 percent respectively for Lithuania.[14] Repeatedly, high educational levels were cited as a common feature of self-employment in transition economies.[15]

Similar data emerged out of the former socialist countries of Central and Eastern Europe. Although there was some chronological discrepancy (trading and female entrepreneurship appeared there earlier than in the USSR), the typical social profile roughly corresponded to what was witnessed in the Newly Independent States. An example from Hungary demonstrated that in the mid- to late 1980s the average age of women in business or self-employed was 38.5 years old. Most of these women came from well-educated families (54% had parents in professional and professional technical fields), 80 percent had a college-level education of their own, of which 34 percent had graduate (post-baccalaureate) degrees. An equally high percentage (78%) of women had children, and married women had husbands who had training on a par with their own education (78% of spouses had college-level training).[16]

The economic forces that pushed shuttle traders in post-Soviet Russia into trading were not inconsequential and led to a substantial debate about whether these women were necessity entrepreneurs. Social studies conducted in the 1990s about employment patterns demonstrated that, among unemployed women, trading was the most common way to supplement the family income or to survive in the shattered economy.[17] Moreover, the study of the Syktyvkar market, undertaken in the mid-1990s, demonstrated that only 10 percent of all traders were involved in it to realize their entrepreneurial ambitions, while the rest argued that they were forced into this business by external circumstances.[18] Undeniably, women who had no professional opportunities and could not be employed according to their professional training and skills were attracted to the shuttle trade. The terms "necessity" or "crisis" entrepreneurship were at least partially suitable for describing their motivation.[19] But at the same time, of the range of options available to the traders-to-be, they picked the one that promised the greatest financial success. People chose to forsake poorly paid alternatives for the promise of financial success, and many believed that they won by making this choice (Graphs 3.1 [a and b], 3.2, and 3.3 demonstrate this popular perception). More than anything else the factor of geographic proximity of foreign countries and foreign goods assured the irresistible attraction of the trade. This was true of all border regions.

Moreover, there were always other options of "survival": one could work on a private gardening plot, care for the elderly or children, get new professional training, or find a second job elsewhere. All these options were widely used, applied, and realized by people of the former Soviet Union. But surprisingly none of the respondents (i.e., the shuttle traders) even attempted to find a new job or supplement their income by other means. All chose, to use their own words, to change their lives radically for the better. It was impossible to earn decent wages working for the government or even for private individuals, and very few could expect incomes higher than those earned by traders. By the mid-1990s, traders were not the object of pity but, rather, of envy among the general population. Women who became housecleaners or those who sold their meager possessions were more miserable and in greater financial need than the international peddlers. The traders would not have chosen this path under alternative and more normal circumstances if they had had steady employment and decent wages. Indeed, they were "pushed" into making tough decisions and taking risks. But theirs were not the most

Graph 3.1a and b. In your opinion, are [were] shuttle traders richer, poorer, or as well-off as most people in Russia? (public opinion)

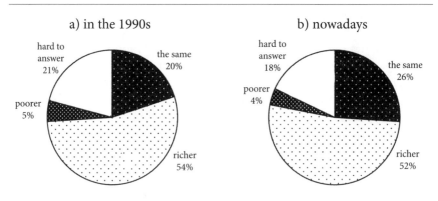

a) in the 1990s   b) nowadays

Source: "Shuttle Traders: Lifestyle, Revenues, Character," The Public Opinion Foundation, June 30, 2005.

Graph 3.2: Have shuttle traders become rich?

(as answered by traders and their relatives)

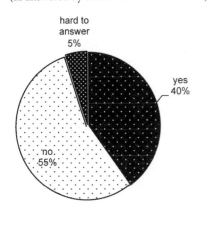

Graph 3.3: Do traders do their jobs willingly?

(no = forced by circumstances)

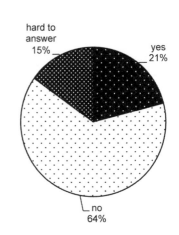

Source: "Shuttle Traders: Lifestyle, Revenues, Character," The Public Opinion Foundation, June 30, 2005.

unfortunate circumstances of all, and they should not by any means be mistakenly imagined as being on a par with impoverished women who are forced to sell tinware to feed their children. As a matter of fact, various studies concluded that by 1998 shuttle traders constituted the rough equivalent of the middle class in Russia, which was 20 percent of Russian society, coming below the top 20 percent but above the 60 percent mark of those who were relatively poor or poor. They were clustered together with the staff of the few commercial firms that existed at the time, junior government officials, and racketeers, all of whom combined made up the amorphous but financially comfortable fledgling middle class of Russia.[20]

Only a few recent studies began exploring the notion that even though the push factor and necessity are important in analyzing the motivation of the traders and entrepreneurs in transition economies, the predominant reliance on such factors simplifies the reality in an undue manner. Thus, traders in Ukraine and Lithuania cited that the most frequent motivator to partake in retail and wholesale trade was not need ("necessity") but the craving for independence, though the need for extra income was also repeatedly reported. As the authors of the study conclude, "Although female entrepreneurs may be 'necessity-driven' when starting their businesses, this does not necessarily determine their subsequent development path, which may involve a recognition of entrepreneurial opportunity as external circumstances change, and [these women] themselves grow in confidence, competences and ambition."[21]

Graduates of technical colleges and vocational schools, as well as those with degrees in business studies and economics, were believed to be especially well suited to the task. They did not necessarily have any prior experience in retail, yet their education had exposed them to the basics of trading. Elena, a former shuttle trader in Khabarovsk, who currently has her own business in interior design, spoke highly of the role of her professional training in assuring her commercial success:

> People need to do what they are best suited for. What if I start healing people now? That would be nonsense. It's the same with trading. There are specialized programs and colleges that prepare for a career in retail. Many think that it's easy to do it [international peddling]. They are mistaken. I am a graduate of a technical college that prepared professionals in light industry. I worked according to my qualifications after graduation, and thus I had real experience in retail trading. I was not a novice in the market … and that's why I did not have "to discover the Americas" over again when I started trading on my own. At college, I learned how to check the quality of each and every product.

At the same time, as most interviews demonstrated, the higher the training and educational level that the traders received, the less likely they were to admit to having it at all. These professionally trained women had imagined—predictably—professional careers when they earned their advanced degrees. They did not want to come across as losers or, worse yet, to be pitied for what they did to earn a living, and they carefully concealed their diplomas. "By the way, if we talk about training, well, I finished a vocational school," says 56-year-old Tatiana from Khabarovsk:

> And then I got a diploma from the Higher School of the Moscow Financial and Economic Institute [one of the best schools in finance]. But I am ashamed to admit it. I only mention vocational training, or else people question why I do this nonsense [trading] when I have a degree. I am ashamed of it. It is better if [no one knows]; let them think that I am uneducated. I did not think of trading as a student—who did? … I respected Grandfather Lenin and obeyed my parents. The borders were closed, the speculators were prosecuted. And then I got into this.

While some were ashamed of their unrealized potential, other women boasted with pride that they knew how to make financial calculations and estimate costs correctly. If trading a pair of jeans to supplement one's regular wage was a rather straightforward matter, then estimating the potential profitability of various destinations was more complex. One respondent from Khabarovsk, an economist by training, reported with a great deal of pride that careful calculations and market assessment allowed her to conclude that trips to Moscow were more profitable than trips to China, even though the latter seems to be much closer to her hometown. At first, it appeared that nothing could beat China. Made-in-China clothing was so cheap that it allowed the trader to mark it up five times. But once converted to real ruble value, the profits were not so astounding; buyers were willing to pay only so much for clothing that was a priori known to shrink, fade, or even fall apart after a wash or two. At the same time, trips to Moscow seemed rather expensive. The airfare was 30,000 rubles (about $1,000 USD), lodging, transportation, and meals ended up costing another 10,000 rubles. This was not an insignificant overhead cost for a trader. Yet with capital of 200,000 rubles, it was realistic to buy about 250 pieces of clothing. Add rent and other miscellaneous expenses to this equation, and Tamara ended up selling a 1,200-ruble dress for 2,000 rubles on her stall. This was not a stunning 500 percent markup, but it was a much higher price in real terms, and it represented the price that many people were willing to pay for quality items. Once all the math was done, it turned out that Moscow paid handsomely. "It's pure math," said another respondent with professional training. "You've got to realize," she added, "that a 20-percent profit can mean a lot of money in some cases."

The difference in profits in real terms implied that there was a difference in the capital that these women possessed. All traders had to invest something to start off, and even $100 USD was not an insignificant amount of money in the context of the Great Post-Soviet Depression. Access to capital, be that borrowed from friends or owned, was what distinguished these traders from the rest of the population who struggled to survive at the time. To the present day, traders are often ambivalent about the origins of their capital and limit their discussions to only vague statements like "I had the money to start off" or "you could say I got it from nowhere, little by little, you know how things are." Only a few are open enough to admit that they borrowed money from friends or started by selling their personal items. One trader, for example, related that in the late 1980s, when the system of social distribution was still in place and when people still could not purchase goods at will, her father finally got a permit to buy a car (a Soviet model). Such a permit allowed its owner to make a desirable purchase (in this case, a vehicle), and this was the only way to obtain certain goods. Instead of buying it himself, the father exchanged the permit for a box of stockings, a VHS player, and a few jars of instant coffee. The profit made on the sale of these goods was so fantastic (double the combined monthly wage of all family members including grown-up children) that it inspired the entire family to get involved in trading.

Informal kinship and friendship networks were highly valued and indispensable in a system that lacked any formal institutional provisions for acquiring start-up capital. Thus, the banking system remained underdeveloped for the duration of the trade (from 1988 to the mid-1990s), and there were few if any opportunities for formal sources of financing. Loans and microloans were only available for target purchases (to buy a car, for example), and there were no formal institutions that could have offered traders microloans for international peddling. Persistent socialist-era attitudes also played a role; though women complained of the need to self-finance their initiatives and the difficulties of accumulating such capital or borrowing it from equally hard-pressed relatives and friends, few ever considered obtaining a bank loan and none had actually tried to get one. All of this aligns with the growing body of scholarship that emphasizes the role of social capital in financing strategies as well as the importance of formal institutions in creating and regulating the market economy.[22]

Informal institutions (traditional attitudes toward women, employment, and family values) were no less significant, and on occasion it was socially acceptable for younger women to pursue a different path into the business compared to their married counterparts.[23] Some college-aged women started in the trade as a sideline to their main jobs abroad. In the 1990s it became common in the eastern (Asian) parts of Russia to seek employment in Japan and South Korea. Young women, specifically those between the ages of 18 and 25, were hired to work in bars, restaurants, and cafes as hostesses, dancers, waitresses, and kitchen help. The job of a hostess in Japan was highly desirable, and Oksana was fortunate to get the job in 1995 when she turned eighteen. She recalled:

> It was dangerous to work in Europe for young girls. I have children now, and I am a normal person. I was not interested in prostitution. But it was tough there in Europe. There the dividing line [between formal economy and the sex industry] was so thin. But this problem was not even on my radar in Japan. When we went there for the first time, we were the third group to arrive from the Russian Far East. The first thing we were told was that we could not go anywhere alone,

we could not date locals, and we absolutely could not become prostitutes—or we faced immediate deportation. Nothing happened there! I've heard that in Korea they have, you know, "those" clubs but I've never heard of anything like that in Japan. No one could force us, and I can guarantee that 100 percent in the case of Japan. The guys from Greece told us that there, the girls said "no" at first but eventually everyone got into the [sex] business of their own free will, for the sake of money.[24]

There was much truth to that story. Although personal relations of an intimate nature among traders were less than satisfactory to many women (as will be discussed in the subsequent chapter), here was something different altogether: the risk of getting involved in sex "trading" was a pervasive threat that many traders contemplated and feared. Even though many traders believed that girls who ended up as prostitutes abroad "knew what they were getting into," nonetheless rumors were plentiful that some young female traders were threatened, blackmailed, or even kidnapped into sex slavery. Indeed, international prostitution was thriving at the time. Some young women were lured by advertisements that promised well-compensated jobs in "modeling agencies" for girls with good looks and certain bodily criteria (the phrase "90–60–90" referred to the fact that young women were paid the best if the circumference of their breasts-waist-hips matched 90–60–90 centimeters respectively). Various European countries as well as Turkey, Egypt, and China were the leaders in attracting "ladies of the night," and lax visa regulations and levels of corruption among officials were the most suitable of circumstances for this thriving export trade.[25]

The shuttle traders, however, consistently denied having been involved in any aspect of the sex industry and systematically preferred to emphasize that theirs was "a clean" start, even if this early phase of their trading was shrewdly made vague or even disappeared from their self-narrative completely and got lost in the aura of complete mystique or silence. Several other women related the same story of working overseas and bringing goods from there for resale. "When I worked in Japan, I did not bring cash but goods for resale from over there," added another former trader. "The working conditions there were great, and here [in Russia], the wages were a hundred bucks while there, in Japan, the wage was $500 USD plus bonuses and tips and we really had the means to bring goods from there."[26]

The accumulation of the early capital also changed over time. It shifted from schemes that used—and abused—the remnants of the socialist distribution system to a reliance on private moneylenders to finance first trips. Tamara remembered that she started trading in the early 1990s when a friend of hers was appointed a director (manager) of a store that sold personal-care consumer goods. Instead of retailing them at the store, Tamara and her friend sold goods of a particular type (for example, all toothpaste or all deodorant) at a local market with a slight markup and then deposited money for goods at the store-appointed prices. The difference was theirs to keep. This was an illegal speculation on store-owned goods, and Tamara admits that "it's embarrassing to remember what we did. We could have ended up in jail then for what we did."[27]

Trip after trip brought new acquaintances in the business, familiarity with its internal workings, and new ideas of goods to buy and ways to sell them. All of these necessitated more capital, which some traders accumulated by themselves and others borrowed from relatives. Relatives and friends were routinely nagged to lend money, but they were a less than perfectly reliable source of support. Some simply did not have anything to lend, others recalled their loans sooner than anticipated for family and personal reasons. New lives and new needs created new people, and that need for short-term loans created a niche that was quickly filled with new private lenders, or *rostovshchiki*. Their minimum interest rate was 10 percent weekly, and quick profits made in the trade and high rates of return justified paying the interest on small short-term "loans" from private lenders. Private lenders were often part of the criminal underworld; they cared little for the personal needs of their borrowers, and tragic stories circulated in abundance. Unpaid loans and the consequences that people faced are the fodder of many urban legends, though precise evidence is hard to come by.

The attitudes of women traders to the early days of their trading diverged in at least one significant way from the life stories of women who attempted to legalize their business and become well established in "proper" entrepreneurial niches. Businesswomen of the 1990s reported that they "associated risk-taking with masculinity" and that men were "the forerunners" of all business activities.[28] Women traders, on the other hand, perceived *themselves* as being at the forefront of this new emerging opportunity to earn extra income. Neither did they recognize problems of legalizing the business in the same way as businesswomen did. Traders feared the scorn of their neighbors and dealing with racketeers and the criminal underworld while businesswomen reported that their main problem was "the attitude that women should remain in their role as homemakers instead of pursuing entrepreneurship" and the refusal of various (male) officials to sign proper documentation on the grounds that women "should stay at home with the dishes and children."[29]

Women traders systematically reported that being a "shuttle trader" was a physically and emotionally demanding task and only women were capable of such a workload and risk-taking. Women's perception of their activities was far more complex than the official view of the trade. For example, the shuttle trade is typically defined as individual activity in which traders make regular trips and personally buy (legal) goods abroad and bring those goods back for resale in local markets. Women traders see the problem as being more complicated: "It is an interesting question whether I am a *chelnok* [shuttle trader]. Of course, [I am] a *chelnok*. What else? I am neither a butterfly nor a migrating bird that brings light loads from place A to place B. Of course, I am a *chelnok*. To define ... *chelnok* equals hard labor. And that's it. 'Hard labor' really captures it all."[30] This sentiment about hard labor that only women can handle was shared by all respondents with no exceptions, and Tatiana also made the point even stronger by adding, "*Chelnoki* are women who scramble for goods; we forage for goods for resale. Yes, we don't just buy goods but forage for them."[31]

This general sentiment about the hard labor and the need to forage for goods was indeed universally shared. It almost seemed as if the women could not brag outright about their achievements even in the case of success; instead, they had to adopt and relate to the listener this common narrative of suffering and pain. Although by all means there was much truth to it, it might also mask the financial rewards that the traders earned in their endeavors, and the rewards were quite substantial in relation to the low living standards for the majority of the population. The traders were typically hesitant to share the specifics of their financial success, and thus at times it could only be wrested indirectly from their self-narratives. Tatiana, for example, complained that even though she has many girlfriends and they all have special talents, "none of them wanted to get into this business ... because this business is a ton of work, and you have to treat it as such, and not everyone can take it. You need to work, so to speak, till you drop, without a minute to spare for yourself." Yet these hardships did not prevent Tatiana from reinvesting the profits made in the shuttle trade and eventually opening four different retail clothing stores, all of which are staffed by waged employees and offer a wide assortment of clothing from Italy, Holland, Sweden, Germany, and Japan.

By far the most common comment that hinted at financial success was related to a belief that traders, especially in the mid-1990s, had to combine their business with travel to exotic destinations for vacationing. One woman, in her late thirties and early forties in the 1990s (and currently unemployed) commented with a clear sense of nostalgia:

Working at a research institute [before the collapse of the Soviet Union], I could have never dreamed of seeing the countries that I did. I wanted to travel so badly, and shuttle trading gave me that opportunity. I explored not just the Black Sea but also the Mediterranean! I could not have wandered around St. Peter's Basilica and seen the statues by Michelangelo any other way.[32]

Several traders reported that personal contacts abroad were crucial to success because acquaintances provided information on two most valuable topics—what to buy and where to *vacation*. Other traders complained that they could not spend much time on sightseeing "like normal people" and instead had to rush through sites. Still others added that "we were so sorry to miss the shopping tour to China because, you see, we want to see some sights and travel, in addition to buying goods there." Some traders were more openly cheerful about their vacation opportunities abroad. One trader fondly remembered her trips to Turkey: "In the winter time, I used to go to my destination [Turkey] for just a couple of days, but in the summer for at least four or five days. I took my husband with me, and every time, after two days of buying goods, we used to spend two more [days] on the beach, and then we had all sorts of sightseeing excursions."[33]

Vacationing was only one of several aspects that women appreciated. Tatiana from Krasnodar was more open about her own financial success and that of her peers. "We had to get into that business," commented Tatiana, "but at the end many women earned enough in that business to buy new housing, new cars, to dress themselves and their families, and some even to open their own permanent small businesses." Galina from the same city added to the statement with a bitter emotion that "indeed, we had money all right, but only at the cost of our health. And that's the truth of it."[34] This narrative of suffering and joy was intimately intertwined to reproduce a reality that was equally complex and hard to define.

Life "on the go," on trains and buses, required some serious stamina, and yet women found joy in this lifestyle. "A woman in this business could not be depressed," related one of the traders. "Russian women suffer, but what for? Because it is written in books? Nonsense. We need to enjoy our lives and we did what we liked. We have only one life, after all, so why would you do something that makes you suffer?" Another trader admitted that she had no time to spend with her son when she was in the business. "Time was a luxury," she commented, "but not because I was forced to work like that but because business sucks you in, you get addicted to it. When success came, I got new ideas, new contacts, I met new people, and I saw an income potential everywhere. My son had every material possession that he could dream of, though possibly he did not get the time and care that I should have given him as a mother."[35]

Speaking of children, women repeatedly commented that even though the trading was physically strenuous and that they would never have wanted their children to enter the trading business full-time, nonetheless trading offered these women an opportunity to finance their children's education. While the Soviet system provided access to free college-level education (once students passed a rigorous examination in core subjects) and even paid them a stipend, post-Soviet Russia saw a near-collapse of government-subsidized education and a massive proliferation of newly emerging private schools at all levels. The problem at the level of post-secondary education was exacerbated by the fact that college-level educators, facing a situation when their salaries were chronically in arrears and too meager even to cover the cost of the public transportation to get them to their jobs, privatized public education de facto if not de jure. Bribery became so pervasive that there emerged "official rates" of bribes for getting into the school of one's choice, though such bribery was often masked as exaggerated tuition rates for private lessons that prepared a student for entry exams into a specific school. Anecdotally, a single private lesson in preparation for a high-ranking university could set the family budget back by $100–$150 USD.

Though not all traders had college-aged children at the time (and younger children will be discussed separately), nonetheless women repeatedly reported that they "gave a good education" to their daughters and sons. "I invested so much money into my sons' education," reported one trader. "They both got superb technical education and that's why I do not want them to ever do trading. They do something else altogether for a living." Elena from Khabarovsk also noted that her son could never do a business like hers because he did not have the stamina that the business required and because "now, of course, he is professionally employed with an excellent education [that I paid for]. I raised him to be a different person."[36]

The comments were not gender-specific in the sense that women traders reported on the success and educational levels of their daughters with the same sense of pride and investment as their sons. "I earned enough to give some real estate to my daughter and to pay for her education, and I want her to have a meaningful job," reported Tamara. She added that she would only allow her daughter to get into a retail business if the profits were significant and there was a chance to buy a better property. Nadezhda, a former trader from a southern part of Russia, commented that her daughter was "smarter than I am, not least because I paid for her education and she now has a nice job." Though most of these comments were systematically framed to reflect that these women needed to get involved in trading, such commentaries nonetheless reveal a sense of pride in being able to meet at least some of the women's financial goals. Once again, most women reported their successes and failures through the prism of their relations with others, not only or not at all in terms of their own well-being. "It was all for my children" was a prevailing comment among women traders. One trader ably summarized this common notion when she said, "We did not have much and we were not rich but we earned enough for a decent living ... enough to buy an apartment, to afford a family vacation, and to finance our children's education."[37]

In comparative perspective, men echoed women's assessment on financial success but added that the business was important to their self-esteem. The themes of improving the housing situation and a need to provide for the family were comparable for both. "I worked as a shuttle trader for two years and, in general, I got what I wanted, I bought an apartment," shared a woman trader, while another recalled, "Thanks to this business I had an opportunity to pay for my children's education and have enough money for everything we needed." Two male respondents, in their mid-thirties at the time of the business, also emphasized family values: "Thanks to the trading I could provide for my family at a good level. I say 'good' because we could afford to vacation abroad—in some years even two or three times a year. And then I built a family estate."[38] Another male trader added that he "did it all for children, who most definitely won't face the problems we had. Meaning that they won't have housing problems, they won't struggle with financial problems; they've already started from a different financial platform."[39]

Most men, however, repeatedly reasserted that the trading was important for their self-esteem, for gaining experience, starting new social connections, and for their personal social status and the self-realization that came with financial security. "I take any experience, including this trading experience, to be invaluable in establishing contacts with other people and for perfecting yourself," noted one man (age 40–44 at the time of trading). "I wanted to test myself, to expand my boundaries," commented another, "and I enjoyed [trading] at the end of the day because it allowed me to do something unusual." Yet another male respondent added, "I gained so much in trading because I became more self-assured, confident, relaxed. [I say] 'relaxed' in the sense of being able to communicate with different people easily and with confidence. I know that this is a result of our shuttle trading trips to Turkey." For many men, the confidence was indeed identified as the main gain of the entire experience, not least because the trading pushed them into contact with people of different backgrounds and nationalities. "The mentality of Turks, Hungarians, Americans is different from Russians, and to understand other peoples and their mind-set—this is huge, this is the main benefit of it all. All of that plus an opportunity to see the world—this is what trading was for me," and indeed, for many other men who chose to emphasize "self" in their assessment of trading experiences, unlike women who always explained what they did in relation to others.[40]

This might help to explain why the two books (one of which is auto-biographical) about the shuttle traders were also written by men. Genrikh Paloian, in *Chelnoki v Vengrii,* states directly that the reasons that men got involved in the trade were to buy a car or a *dacha* (a country house) but primarily to earn the respect of others and to improve their social status because of their financial success. Status and self-esteem are the dominating motives of male traders in Paloian's book, and though they lost more than they gained on their first trip to Hungary, none of these men despaired. After all, their pride was at stake and they continued to aspire to financial success that would build their confidence.[41] Vitalii Vladimirov in *Chelnok* uses Lyudmila, a female trader turned entrepreneur, as his main protagonist. Her path into trading seems typical at best; with a postgraduate degree in economics, Lyudmila is forced into trading to make ends meet. Unlike most, however, Lyudmila is highly successful in the end; she opens a boutique-style clothing shop where her employees do most of the work while she enjoys the spoils. Yet, through her life Lyudmila is portrayed by the author as needing constant reaffirmation of her self-worth that she can find only in endless sexual affairs. For men, trading is a way to build their *self*-worth; for Lyudmila, trading is the way to appeal to men, to attract them with her looks and money, to find her self-worth *in relation* to male companions. After all, to Lyudmila and the people around her, the independent *self* is the domain of men.[42]

Interviews and self-narratives also demonstrated that men and women alike who participated in the shuttle trade in the 1990s reflect back on their experiences in relation to their present-day occupation, family situation, and income. When traders managed to thrive financially as a result of the trade and to maintain or reestablish their personal relations, they argue that, for them, the shuttle trade became an opportunity not to be missed and that they provided for their families at a time when much of the country was in the midst of the Great Depression. Their experiences were not always easy, and at times they learned their lessons the hard way. Yet, in the end they emerged victorious from their trading experiences, not so much because of what they do now but more because of what they could afford at that opportune moment in their lives. Many others, however, argue that their engagement in trading led to their financial demise long-term and that ten to fifteen years later they feel financially deprived and find themselves in a worse situation than they would have been without trading. Moreover, they lost spouses, companions, and partners because of the constraints imposed by trading, and they continue to lack emotional and sexual intimacy in their lives. The perception of the trade among some members of this group might even appear irrational, as they tend to blame others—the Soviet Union, Gorbachev, and Yeltsin, even America and George Bush, to name a few—for their hardships. They identify the trade as a temporary solution to their financial insecurity in a tough transition era but a solution with far-reaching family consequences.

The price of their success was indeed high, as the subsequent chapter will reveal. The entire impact of trading on the social and familial fabric of life did not become apparent until the 2000s. Before then, the traders served both as the backbone of consumer trading in the nation and as unconscious shapers and promoters of globalization, and the latter function was especially important for reshaping the popular consumer culture of the post-Soviet Russia of the last two decades.

Globalization in the Making

When the borders of the Soviet Union, and later Russia, opened and the traders rushed to the markets, Russia quickly became a land of new consumption opportunities for its residents, consumption that was indeed unprecedented in the context of prior Soviet experiences. Thanks to the shuttle traders, for the first time in a decade, if not ever, Russian citizens saw their markets flooded with goods that differed in styles, place of origin, and affordability. By flooding the markets with all sorts of goods, traders in many ways promoted globalization and the westernization of the former Soviet people's desires and demands in the post-Soviet space; even more, the traders brought not only new goods but new lifestyles to their customers. At the same time, they influenced the image-making process in supplier countries (such as Turkey and China) that sought to market their goods to post-Soviet consumers as "Western." Many supplier factories abroad embraced styles and goods that could be marketed as "Made in Italy" in the Newly Independent States, where customers craved symbols of westernization. Thus in the 1990s, the mobility of traders across borders facilitated the flow of signs and images.

Yet another force was at work in this process of globalization. As goods proliferated, Western images and fashions were remolded and acquired new meanings in the process of circulation. An obsession with specific brands (and the quality and style associated with those brands) to the point of craving fakes eventually devalued brand names and dissociated specific labels from their places of origin. Everyone involved in the process—fashion-label companies, local producers who falsified labels, and consumers—were fully aware of the fact that the product was not authentic. Yet, as one historian put it, in the 1990s the "mere devotion to Western attire was so great" that it made customers either oblivious or indifferent to the original place of production of goods with labels stating "Made in Italy." This obsession with valuable fakes drastically revolutionized and globalized the consumer culture of Russia, yet it simultaneously undermined the value of such consumption long-term. Twenty years later it became clear that, progressively, Russian citizens "engage with products for cultural consumption with relatively little concern for their origins or intrinsic meanings."[43] Diversification and glocalization (a blend of globalization and localization) shape the current patterns of consumption more than westernization, yet both were born by access to those valuable fakes.

The primary role in this process was assumed by the shuttle traders and the foreign factories that rose to the demand. Yet much of the consumption pattern was rooted in the Soviet experiences of the Russian people. The complex Russian history of the last century severely challenged the prevailing notions of the West as the producer of images and ideas that had to be emulated. Traditionally, dating back to the days of Peter the Great in the early eighteenth century, Russia aspired to westernization, often by adopting the dress codes and outward signs of that westernization as the first and the most crucial step in the process. Even though the admiration of the West was limited to those few who could afford it, Russian elites progressively embraced Western culture and consumption to the point of nearly abandoning any attributes of what they perceived as Russian backwardness. The Soviet regime cut the cord that used to tie Russian ambitions to Western Europe (though never completing isolating itself). Some of that severing was ideological, as the Soviet Union aimed to position itself and to indoctrinate its citizens with the notion that it had moral and cultural superiority compared to the West. *Veshchism*, a Russian word for consumerism, was identified as a symbol of the worst moral and ethical decline, and though hippies and other movements trickled into the Soviet Union despite its strictest prohibitions, it was only the very few with "connections" who could get access to Western goods on the black market. They even dared to wear those attributes of westernization with a risk to their social position and even physical well-being.

At the same time, in a paradoxical relationship of sorts, the Soviet experience worked as a catalyst to the Soviet people's desire to consume Western goods. Part of that desire was prompted by the reality of chronic shortages of basic consumer goods. The ability to buy at will, the consumerism itself, seemed like an unattainable mirage in the desert of empty store shelves. Yet, to a great extent, the proverbial sweetness of the forbidden fruit also played a significant role in stimulating the fascination with foreign brands and foreign products. Denied access to even information about the consumer culture of the West, Soviet people imagined levels of consumption in the West that were greatly exaggerated compared to reality. All these factors combined to assure that the consumption of foreign-made goods—any goods that were labeled as made in places other than the USSR—became deeply sacramental in the 1960s and even more progressively so into the 1970s and 1980s. People did not go through the pain of buying Wrangler jeans on the black market simply because they aspired to wear a comfortable and durable pair of jeans (this would have rendered consumption non-sacramental). They were willing to pay as much as a month's wage for a pair because it represented more than clothing: it was "sacramental" in symbolically representing the West and its values of consumerism and freedom of expression.

There emerged a strict hierarchy in the value invested in the place of origin and brands of each item. The closer ideologically was the country of origin to the Soviet Union, the less value its products had, and vice versa. Thus, goods with labels "Made in Poland" were ranked higher than those made in the Soviet Union yet significantly lower than goods produced in West Germany. Those notions also assured that products made in Hungary ranked higher than those from Bulgaria, while Czechoslovakia ranked in between. Products with labels and logos of major American brands had an almost mythical aura to them as the ultimate carriers of that message of rebelliousness and freedom. When clothing was out of reach, the niche was filled with music, postcards, pictures, calendars, and anything else that was discernibly foreign.

The Soviet experience profoundly altered the people's behavior in yet another way. In a state of self-proclaimed equality for all, there was little room for expressing one's social status. Social classes did not cease to exist, unlike what the Soviet people had been assured, and the gap between the haves and the have-nots reached down to all layers of society by the 1970s and 1980s. The party elite always enjoyed special access to goods and facilities that distinguished them from the rest of the population. But for the population at large, which was becoming increasingly stratified, there were few avenues to express their social position and distinguish themselves from their peers.

Housing was distributed by the state, and property was not privately owned, and thus the housing situation could not be improved or changed even with greater financial resources. In short, it could not function as a sign of one's social status. Cars, refrigerators, TV sets, and other valuables were "sold" according to a distribution system, and they were not purchased at will. And thus the only true outlet for visibly asserting one's social position was clothing, which was priced on the black market out of all proportion to incomes precisely because it represented more than a way to cover one's body. Not store goods but "made in" labels were cherished and invested in, and the ownership of foreign-made goods (clothing specifically) was a crucial marker of identity. At a time when an average engineer earned 120 rubles a month, a shirt with a "Made in Germany" label went for 50 rubles or more on the black market; a comparable dress for 100 rubles; and a coat for 300 to 500 rubles. Purchasing large pieces of outerwear was celebrated as a special occasion, and one could literally determine a person's status by looking at what was on his or her back.

By the time that shuttle trading began assuming endemic proportions in the early 1990s, traders were discovering that the post-Soviet consumers, much in a reflection of their prior desires, demanded not just any type of goods but specific brands. This trend was at first obscured by the mere hunger for consumer goods; people were ready to wear any pair of jeans or swimsuit. Yet once the first craving was satisfied and the first gap was filled, the Soviet preference for specific places of origin and brands returned with a new force. The obsession with brands was so intense that even late Soviet factories started faking goods for local consumers (by pirating commercial logos such as Marlboro and Levi-Strauss). By the mid-1990s, everyone wanted to wear Nike and Reebok when they went jogging and appear with Chanel N° 5 sprinkled over a dress at a cocktail party.

Predictably, the traders involved in the trade quickly realized that they could not reconcile the gap between the purchasing power of their customers and their consumer demands. While people wanted to buy "Made in Italy" brands or craved Gucci, Versace, and the like, they could at most afford to pay for cheap goods made in Turkey and China. It was in this context that both traders and manufacturers in China (and later elsewhere) rose to the challenge by creating "valuable fakes." The Chinese producers assured that the traders were attracted to Chinese markets by the low prices of clothing and domestic goods but also by *designer names*. Almost universally, outfits were labeled as "Made in Italy" or "Made in Germany" and had Nike, Adidas, Reebok, and other logos on them. Ironically, it was also common to see, for example, jackets with logos of Nike on the front, Puma on the sides, and Adidas on the back all at the same time.[44] This contradiction reflected the same feeling among consumers as well. Some traders laughed at designer labels and commented that "if someone wants to buy real Reebok or Adidas shoes, he won't go to [an open-air] market. People who buy Reebok shoes [there] know that they are not Reebok, and for them it doesn't matter whether it says Reebok or Raabok or Ruubok." But other traders and consumers disagreed, often citing the fact that many brand-name products were produced in China, Korea, and elsewhere anyway. This fact did not make brand names less authentic or labels less valuable. After all, one trader argued, if "Adidas shoes are produced in Korea and sold in America, are they original or not?"[45] For others, however, the craving for Western brand names was so great that they chose to ignore the place of origin of goods labeled "Made in Italy."

One of the criticisms of this chase for the brand or a "made in ..." label was that it drove choices and markets too much. Instead of buying fashionable clothing and this season's styles, traders systematically preferred to go "for a sure thing." They purchased whatever had sold best the last time around, and they opted for cheap-with-logos goods ("fakes") over any other options. Those consumers who aspired for better quality and authenticity but could not afford it came to rely on a chain of secondhand stores. At first, these stores used "humanitarian aid" packages from the West and resold clothing at a low price; the business was so profitable that some store owners started buying secondhand in Western Europe and the United States on their own. Yet the movement remained marginal to the overall culture of consumption that was still driven by whatever shuttle traders brought to their local markets.[46]

Ironically, the near universality of foreign-name products with recognizable labels dislodged the meaning and value of those labels. Valuable fakes made brand names and logos commonplace and even mundane, and this was true even considering that these were not authentic items. One could get instant access to Gucci or Armani regardless of income, location, and social status. Obtaining those valuable items was a matter of a short walk to a local open market, and everyone had a "Made in Italy" tag sewn on the back of their clothing. Fakes dominated the consumer markets to such a degree that very few knew what the "real thing" looked like or could distinguish a fake from an authentic item. And even fewer wanted to do so. The instant availability of goods was comforting, even if their abysmal quality was shocking. Consumers knew that nearly all cheap goods were manufactured in places other than Western Europe (mostly China and Turkey), yet they systematically preferred to rank those higher than clothing without brands at all or with clear markings of "Made in China."

Hence, the massive influx of foreign clothing that the traders brought into the post-Soviet space, especially when it came to "valuable fakes," was neither a giant scheme in which consumers were simply cheated out of their money (after all, all were fully aware of buying fakes). Nor was it a linear process of westernization, in which people became sacramental consumers at all costs. The process was more complex: one that involved consumption in the context of the social past that linked clothing to status; of perceived quality of goods depending on their origins; and, at times, one of peer pressure and a sense of "fashion." The main role of the traders was that they changed the patterns of westernization and consumption for Russia; the consumption of the late 1990s and progressively into the 2000s became non-sacramental. Traders flooded the markets with "valuable fakes," and as a result consumers stopped seeing them as signs of rebelliousness, freedom, or even westernization. Instead, consumption became deeply rooted in notions of "coolness" (and social class) that could be displayed only through looks (clothing). The shuttle traders in many ways promoted globalization and the westernization of the former Soviet people's desires and demands in the post-Soviet space; after all, they brought those valuable fakes to the Russian population. Yet they also assured that globalization was not a top-down process with its origins in large corporate headquarters. In a more complex way, "the mobility of 'ordinary' people across borders facilitated the flow of signs and images [but] Western images and fashions got remolded and acquired new meanings in the process of circulation."[47] As mentioned earlier, glocalization and diversity dominate the current consumption pattern, and in the new century the intrinsic meaning of goods has very little to do with the "made in" tag that they carry. This was only one of the unintended consequences of the shuttle trading, but it was no less important than the impact that the trade had on regulating the border-control regime and the one on the social and familial space of the new Russia.

4

The Price of Success

My life started to get in order. From being unemployed, I became the
breadwinner of my family and a work horse of [the post-Soviet con-
sumer] trade. No one cared, and I can not tell anyone, what it took—
legally and illegally—to carve out this prosperity in life. During my
trading years, I saw things that one cannot describe; I have seen about
just everything in life. I have been both on the main deck and in the
hold of the ship.

—Anna S., 47 years old, a former employee of the Ministry of Trade of
the USSR, now an entrepreneur and the owner of a middle-size business

Every scholarly work that deals with the shuttle trade includes at least a
marginal reference to the hard life of the shuttle traders, but these works
do not tell us what such "hard labor" exactly entailed. To be sure, being a
successful shuttle trader required long work hours and a lack of adequate
sleep. But what about the psychological aspects of the trade that are mentioned vaguely and only in passing? What emotional and psychological
factors shaped the experiences of the shuttle traders and soon became an
integral part of the business? Even the lack of sleep and the weight of their
bulging suitcases meant little compared to the psychological stresses of this
business that produced a whole range of health problems. The fear of being
robbed at the airport or in the market, the uncertainty inherent in dealing
with customs officials and racketeers, and the constant dread of being recognized by acquaintances and former coworkers who initially looked down
upon the shuttle traders were more persistent and emotionally draining
than the heavy physical burdens of the shuttle trade. The main goal of most
women traders was to provide financially for their loved ones, but often-

times the price that the shuttle traders had to pay for the material comforts of their "shuttle families" was indeed high.

Different risks and problems constantly weighed on the shoulders of female shuttle traders, some of which were objective and some only perceived. They risked losing their husbands because of their own prolonged absence from home. These women also risked losing their children, although in a different sense of the word. Accustomed to their mother's care and attention, many children of shuttle traders were left unsupervised and often found themselves in problematic situations when they developed substance-abuse problems or became part of street gangs. Female traders also risked becoming just a mere statistic of the human trafficking and sex-trade flow, which proliferated alongside the shuttle trade. When added to fears of bribing officials and paying racketeers, all these aspects of the trade created a severe psychological trauma for many women. The emotional aspect of the shuttle trade dominated female traders' lives and actions. As a side effect medical problems stemming from the physical and emotional hardships of female shuttle traders proliferated and contributed to ruining the health of many of them, adding to the already impressive list of emotional costs that these women endured to secure their financial well-being and that of their families.

The stresses of the shuttle business started for many traders with the fear of being recognized, at least during the early years of the business. "I had a specific goal, that is to earn enough for a flat," says Elena Semienova, a business woman from Barnaul and a former professional philologist, who further recalls, "But at first, when my acquaintances passed by, I had to hide from them. We were raised to believe that trading [*torgovat'*] was immoral, that it does not befit a well-bred person. But then I was told: you and your business are not the same. Of course, I adapted, but it was difficult nonetheless."[1] Another trader remembered: "I never told anyone about it [trade] ... I used to wear a baseball cap that I pulled down over my eyes. ... I feared to meet my teacher most of all."[2] Even those who managed to earn significant profits and could afford material comforts that were out of reach for many people around them shared similar sentiments. One shuttle trader, who earned enough in the early 1990s to send her children to an elite private school with a high tuition, feared being recognized and kept her occupation a secret even from her relatives. She explained that she "feared that [her] children would be bullied by others. ... Even [her] parents did not know what [she] did for a living because they also believed [the shuttle trade] to be nonsense, something that was 'below' [the] family."[3] For economists, teachers, and other college graduates, who were raised and educated in the Soviet Union and had held high-prestige positions most of their working lives, the change of occupation from professional to trade implied more than a change of jobs. It was a real transformation of their social milieux and status, accompanied by the loss of friends and familiar interests. "We were just degraded, even in our own eyes," summed up one woman trader.[4]

The sense of discomfort and embarrassment at being involved in trade accompanied traders not only in their hometowns but also when they were abroad. When medical professionals, lawyers, teachers, musicians, and economists changed professions and entered the shuttle business, they were received with surprise by their businesses "partners" in more stable economies. After the first shuttle flight to Korea in 1992, many traders were traumatized to see that

> most Koreans are simply shocked when they learn, for example, that this Russian or Ukrainian trader is a doctor and that one is a lawyer or an engineer. Doctors and lawyers and engineers in Korea are well-paid professionals and their incomes are incompatibly higher than the profits of even most successful shopkeepers; and in general Koreans look down upon trade, especially retail trade, as being not such an honorable occupation. That's why the sight of a surgeon dragging cargo bags containing leather coats utterly shocked them.[5]

Indeed, even though many people in the Soviet Union and post-Soviet Russia relied on the services and goods offered by the shuttle traders, initially old Soviet clichés about "speculators" prevailed, and people generally did not favor traders, insisting that such people did not produce anything as they only speculated on the difference in prices in various locations and nations. Even shuttle traders shared these sentiments. R. Volgina, the founder of the Moscow-based company "Novyi Disk," which sells household appliances, bluntly stated, "I started my own business as an ordinary speculator; I was involved in the shuttle business."[6] Indeed, public opinion polls demonstrated that despite their role in providing for the consumer market, many traders were believed to be rude, insolent, and greedy, while a third of respondents thought that the shuttle traders damaged the Russian economy because of the influx of poor quality goods and capital flight.[7]

Women who were involved in the trade in the 1990s also emphasize the physical demands of their business. In the shuttle trade, the weight of the trader's bag was directly proportionate to the profit of the trader. That is why all the bags were loaded to the limit allowed by customs regulations and the bag's size and beyond. The weight of each bag often exceeded the norms that medical professionals consider appropriate for women without harming their reproductive health and injuring their backs. During the Soviet era managers in state factories and industries observed state laws that limited the amount of weight that women had to carry. While these laws were rarely enforced in labor-intensive occupations, they existed at least on paper. No such laws applied to the shuttle trade, and traders maximized their profits by carrying ever-heavier bags on their backs. The easier it became to bribe customs officials, the heavier the bags became. Many women paid with their health by carrying bags that usually weighted 40 to 100 kilos each (88 to 220 pounds), and shuttle workers commonly "accumulated" sprains, strains, hernias, lower-back pains, and prolapsed wombs along with their profits. Though the various health problems of female shuttle workers merit a lengthier discussion at a later point, the sentiment, stated by a former teacher turned trader was shared by all women involved in the shuttle trade: "It was inhumanly difficult and heavy when there was a need to lug a hundred kilos of merchandise. We got used to it after several years of work, [one] gets used to anything."[8] Another trader argued that the weight of her bags was almost beyond the limits of human capabilities:

> Indeed, it takes such sweat and blood to do this [trading]. I remember those years with horror! Constantly traveling, carrying unthinkable loads, trying to pass through all these borders, all these control [posts]. You take a flight but carry a bag of 40 kilos with you when only TU [Tupolev, older Soviet planes with small passenger seats] were used. This meant that you sat on top of that bag with no room for your arms and legs for four hours.[9]

In Soviet days many men offered a helping hand to women with heavy bags in trains and airplanes as a common courtesy and a part of a shared culture, but such courtesies were rarely offered to women shuttle traders in the post-Soviet space. Traders could not count on help from men, unless men were directly involved in their trade and shared in their profits. The sheer volume of trade and the number of traders made such courtesy gestures rare. Even passersby noticed this change:

> I admire the dexterity and the ant-like strength of the women shuttle traders: tiny and seemingly so frail, they carry and shuffle on the third shelf [of railroad bunk beds] bags larger than they are. The sign of our times is that men do not offer their help to these "ladies," arranging their luggage on trains, and men even refuse to help when asked to do so. They say: "Hire a loader, I am not about to sap all of my strength for your profits."[10]

Figure 4.1: Clothing on display. Hangers and enclosed stalls were a marked improvement compared to the early years of the shuttle trade. Photo taken by the author, Moscow, 2004.

Larisa Dorofeeva is no longer a shuttle trader but a successful entrepreneur in Barnaul. But she shudders with horror when recollecting her first trips that took place in 1993:

> After arriving in China, we went to the market the first thing in the morning. Of course, no one knew the language; in dealing with Chinese, we did not understand each other. We communicated only with the help of a calculator and just punched in the price we were willing to pay on the display. Then we traveled to the hotel with our acquired merchandise. The conditions there were horrifying; there was no hot water, and cold water was supplied with interruptions. As for furniture, there were only three beds, but we did not sleep. We packed the merchandise into boxes all night. There were no storage spaces; we kept everything in our room; barricades of stacked up boxes reached the ceiling. ... When we approached the Kazakistani border, we unloaded our merchandise and ... dragged the bags of many kilos by ourselves. There was no difference if you were a man or a woman. Everyone worked equally hard.[11]

The shuttle trade was practiced in all the towns and cities of the former Soviet Union, where any merchandise acquired abroad had to be carried personally to major railroad hubs or airports and only then home. This pattern of travel also implied that shuttle traders had to spend a night or two on each shopping trip somewhere away from home, preferably paying as little as possible for their overnight accommodations. For example, many traders preferred to sell their goods in markets in major cities, where prices were higher than at home, like the Cherkizov market in Moscow, which was the closest to the three main railway stations. Some women, who were willing to pay a fee, used train wagons set aside for traders with only minimal accommodations (one restroom for forty people and no showers). But others could not afford even such luxuries and preferred to sleep on their bags on the railway station floor rather than reduce their profits by paying for housing. When it got especially cold outside during harsh Russian winters, traders who made high profits occasionally managed to get into women's hostels, established in Soviet times for women traveling with small children (usually under the age of eight). For a minimal fee, the lucky trader could get a warm bed at such a place. But getting into such a hostel was not easy. The director of one of these hostels at the Yaroslavl train station in Moscow explains:

> The women traders cause the most problems. They want to bring their bags into the rooms. But we have newborn children here while [the traders'] bags bring all the dirt of Moscow on their wheels; it's a railway station after all. ... [The director explains that she knows everyone who comes to her hostel, for example, a woman named Tamara.] Tamara takes a train to Vladivostok tomorrow; she is a certified day care teacher; she has a child with cerebral palsy waiting for her at home and a mother [who is] a pensioner. They live for several months only on what Tamara makes by reselling her goods in Moscow. This time it is not much, she says. If you subtract the cost of transportation, only 20,000 [rubles] are left [app. $800 USD]. When the money runs out, Tamara again goes to Moscow and again, to this Yaroslavskii train station.[12]

If a profit of 20,000 rubles can last a trader's family for several months, it is easy to understand why none of the traders stayed in a nearby hotel, like The Leningradskaia, with room rates that started at 1,800 rubles a night.

In addition to the physical challenges, the fears and emotional stresses that accompanied border crossings, especially when traders traveled by train or bus, also added extra pressure on shuttle traders. Bribery and abuses of power by border-control officials were commonplace, and it was crucial when crossing the border to hide one's cash well enough so that it could not be discovered by officials and would be transported to its final destination rather than left at the border in the hands of officials. The prospect of having one's money confiscated at the border meant more than a financial disaster; it was a constant stress that was not easily forgotten by traders, though most looked at it as a given and an inescapable fact of life. It was common for traders to say that "the fear you endure makes you shiver in horror; but who is free from fears among us these days?"[13]

Bus drivers and train conductors also played a significant role in transporting cash and merchandise across the border. These people could side with either the traders or the state, and their choice often depended on personal connections and the size of a bribe. The most seriously affected by such practices were traders who commuted short distances across the border and sold their goods immediately in the nearest border towns. Unlike traders who went far away to Turkey, China, and various other remote destinations ten times a year and sold their merchandise in large urban markets, traders in small towns that bordered Poland and other Eastern European countries went to buy goods every two or three days. These women usually bought and sold cigarettes and chewing gum in small quantities for small profits. But they crossed the border up to twenty times a month, and they directly depended on their ability to hide goods, bribe officials, and at times just beg for mercy. Women who were involved in this type of shuttle trade had to have strong nerves, but they also had to overstep the boundaries of fear, humiliation, and shame.

For these "transborder" shuttle traders, the crucial task was to bring in more than the one bottle of vodka and two packs of cigarettes allowed by a law that had been put in place back in Soviet days and remained "the law" officially for the first decade of post-Soviet Russian existence. Shuttle traders had to get enough goods through customs to resell in order to make even marginal profits, and the only way to make such profits was to break the law. Even though such smuggling was illegal (or at least more so compared to the sale of clothing and some types of food), it often attracted people en masse. For example, in the town of Bagrationovsk in Kaliningrad *oblast*, in some years half of all residents, and at times the overwhelming majority, were involved in such trade. Indeed, in most border towns, the proportion of residents involved in the shuttle trade was significant; in places like Sovetsk, Neman, and Krasnoznamensk, 15 percent of all people regarded the shuttle trade as their main occupation. They thought that decent income was about $200 USD a trip (after the payment of a bribe of approximately $30). But the risk and the stress were all-encompassing and inescapable. The allotted norm of one bottle of hard liquor and two packs of cigarettes taken over the border per month could yield a profit of only $6.00 a month.[14] This implied that the rest of the merchandise—thirty times over the allowed norm—had to travel as illegal contraband, which women, fearing the worst, hid every place they could think of. Occasionally, women traders asked other passengers to transport a share of their merchandise as a part of their allowed quantity of duty-free goods. But it was nearly impossible to distribute all the bottles of vodka or cigarette packs this way. The remaining items had to be hidden on the bus, and this required the traders to pay a share of profits to the driver or to hide the goods on their own bodies. Even when the merchandise traveled safely, the stress associated with such risk taking was high.

Worse yet, many women fell victim to criminal bands, who robbed traders at all points of their travel. "The fear was always there," reported one woman trader. "Everyone knew, and especially the criminal elements—they knew all too well—that [traders] go to Poland with money and from Poland [they return] with goods. It was easy money [for criminals], and there were many cases [of robbery]."[15] Train conductors recommended that travelers stay in their compartments at all times. When night came, traders used all means at hand to block the doors of their compartments; they used a special blocking device distributed by the conductor and further fixed the door knob by tying it to the bed frame with a towel. Even train conductors who escorted trains on popular trading routes feared violence and refused to leave their rooms during the night. Traders remember that ingenuity was a mark of the criminals, who managed to rob the traders while trains were en route and when they stopped, even when all possible precautions had been taken.

At the same time, racketeering became widespread in all major cities, especially in Moscow. From the early days, traders complained:

> Bandits were already in our way. ... You know, bandits from Russia, Ukraine, Belorussia. Boys who saw that you had sold [your goods and] travel with money; they can even take your merchandise along with your money. ... Once [they] took $200 from me; this money was earned by my hard labor, my penal servitude-like labor. ... They came and met you in the morning at the Belorussian train stations, when the train arrived. This is dangerous! No one can protect you, of course.[16]

The fear of being robbed by criminals or being approached by racketeers was prevalent not only in Russia but also abroad, where many racketeer groups traveled in order to make more "profits." Oftentimes problems started at the marketplace abroad, as one woman recalled:

There are special buses that go to Poland. These buses go straight to the market. When you arrive [on these buses], racketeers come right away—our
Russian guys! [They] collect a payment from all bus passengers. Then [you]
arrive at your hotel, and the Russian racketeers come again, though a different bunch. Then when you cross the border with Belorussia, the Belorussian
racketeers arrive. Then we reenter Russia; traffic patrol officers stop us: they
tell us that they need to check the bus and [we] need to unload all our things.
Of course, no one wants to unload everything. Then we pay them $50 dol-
lars per bus so there won't be a problem. And so it happens along the entire
route. And if you travel alone, that is even scarier, for [racketeers] can take
away your merchandise, your money, and can even beat you up, if [they] do
not kill you.[17]

The same was true of many other destinations. Turkey, for example, did not
lag behind Poland:

In 1995–96 *our* racketeers came to Turkey; they robbed in small alleys by cut-
ting off money pouches. All sorts of fraud existed. [These criminals] presumably
drove a trader to a factory on the city outskirts [to buy] leather, offered what they
passed off as a cup of tea, then the traders fell asleep and woke up without their
money [and] their passports. … [These criminals] usually picked on women or
elderly men, anyone who looked like they could not stand up to them.[18]

Many women also tried to save on accommodations and stayed in private
lodging or cheap and shady dorms and hostels in questionable neighbor-
hoods. Women usually shared a room, five to six women in one, both as
a safety precaution and to save money. Yet despite all efforts, women were
especially prone to become victims of criminals and false law-enforcement
officials in such places. Such hostels attracted many gangs:

In one such hotel women were awakened by masked intruders—eight unknown
men with metal rods and clubs and armed with guns (though [the guns] were
fake). They beat up one of the women, probably just for the sake of scaring the
others, and broke her head. They did not touch the others, who were already willing to part with anything valuable they possessed. The crooks were not squea-
mish about anything: they took merchandise intended for resale, cell phones,
and even costume jewelry. Some women traders did not even have money for
their return journey after such visits. In this incident, the bandits left with six
thousand dollars plus golden [jewelry] and merchandise.[19]

This particular gang was captured and prosecuted shortly thereafter. But cases like this abounded, and everyone seemed to know a trader who had to part with their hard-earned money. Crucially, even if most traveled safely, the traders were nonetheless under the constant stress and fear of being robbed, abused, or even killed.

Many traders in large marketplaces in major cities were content to pay a fixed sum or a share of profits to racketeers who offered protection from other racketeers and criminal groups. In smaller towns, racketeers were not as prominent as in major cities, thus alleviating some pressure on traders but also increasing the risk of being approached unexpectedly. According to various opinion polls conducted in marketplaces in Naberezhnye Chelny, racketeers rarely took regular payments from traders. Traders, again primarily women, explained this lack of interest by the fact that they "have no big items" and no significant profit (46.3%); that they "have no one to fear" (15.2%); that "everyone knows them" (12.7%); or that they are protected by "the guys they know" (13.9%), their husbands (6.3%), or their family (5.1%). But all respondents more or less agreed that the small scale of trade, even compared to shuttle traders elsewhere, is what safeguarded small-town women traders from being approached by racketeers.[20] One woman reported: "I am a single mother. This market is the only means for me to feed my child and not to die myself. You barely have enough profit for food, and even then you have to save hard. Racketeers do not even approach [people] like me; they know that we have nothing that can be taken away."[21] With time women learned to recruit "guards" to help them along the way. Most commonly policemen and military personnel joined the ranks of security guards to supplement their meager official incomes by escorting women traders en route. But even such "escort" was not a guarantee of complete safety.[22]

Even though women learned to hide money in places where criminals did not check (like underwear and feminine sanitary napkins), criminals in turn learned to recruit fellow traders to spy on women, who were keen on hiding their money in not-so-obvious places. In a widespread scheme, the recruited female traders started a disorderly catfight, ripping other women's clothing apart. In most cases, money hidden "on the body" (taped to the body, in undergarments, etc.) disappeared after such brawls. Even accepting a hand from fellow traders could have severe consequences. Traders who did not know each other usually did not trust others to supervise luggage or help in any way. But after several trips abroad and after spending days working their way through the markets of Turkey, China, or Europe, some traders came to trust each other. Criminals learned to use even these shaky relationships. Albina N. often saw a man after her trips who passed himself off as an airport worker, and they chatted on several occasions and seemed to befriend each other. After one especially tiring trip, the man offered Albina a ride home and help in getting her luggage to his car. This man subsequently disappeared, after he had been entrusted to carry Albina's luggage, and Albina lost all her money, which had been invested in the merchandise in her stolen bags. She had to quit the shuttle trade and survived only because her sister, a manicure professional, took her in.[23] In other words, from the moment women traders left their homes until the moment they sold their goods, they risked their incomes and even their lives. Anxiety and fear accompanied these women on their trips, and even if the theft was mostly petty, the anxiety was not.

The post-Soviet era was marked, above all, by a rapid increase in the number of divorces and separations, a sharp rise in common cohabitation without marriage registration, and a growing number of children born out of wedlock. Abortions and contagious diseases were on the rise, including diseases like tuberculosis, that had been curbed or eliminated in the Soviet Union. Sexually transmitted diseases spread like wildfire, and female alcoholism consumed a large number of women who had previously lived healthy lives. The media started to talk about a resurgence of the well-forgotten practice of infanticide. The word "foundling," which had left everyday vocabulary in the 1940s, resurfaced to describe the increasingly common phenomenon of child abandonment. Orphanages and state boarding schools for the disabled could not accommodate the excessive and ever-growing number of parentless and abandoned children. The government was forced under these conditions to allow the adoption of children from Russia by foreign citizens, partial adoption for weekend visits, or even the boarding of children in families without official adoption at all. Because of their sheer numbers and the type of work that they performed, a good share of these problems belonged to women of the shuttle trade.

From the early days of the Soviet Union, state propaganda had emphasized a stable family as the core of good moral values. Moreover, in practice and in some cases by law, Soviet people continued to rely on the normative gender roles that had been established in predominantly rural communities. These roles emphasized strong patriarchal control and placed children at the center of the household. Public opinion and official regulations condemned "vicious" relations that bonded unmarried men and women sexually. The country continued to be predominantly agrarian until well into the 1960s;

the values of patriarchy, female virginity, and childbirth nine months after the marriage that people brought from the countryside persisted well into the last years of the Soviet Union's existence, and the official propaganda masked any deviations from these norms.[24]

These values underwent significant transformation under the new cultural and material pressures of post-Soviet realities. Though most couples continued to prefer marriage as an end result of their relationships, most young and middle-aged people started to practice common cohabitation without registering marriage as a way "to get to know each other better." The number of divorces increased steadily in the 1990s,[25] but divorces only partially indicated the changes taking place, as many couple never registered their relationships and many became separated without filing for a divorce.

Beyond doubt, the lifestyle of a female shuttle trader added significantly to these statistics. Men of the Soviet era accepted female employment only insofar as women remained solely responsible for the upkeep of the house and all chores associated with child care. Women accepted this role, but they could perform duties associated with this double burden of domestic work and public employment only if they were physically present at home at least some time during the day, meaning that they worked in the same town or city where they resided. When women started to earn their incomes in the shuttle trade, it became impossible to maintain the same level of involvement in mundane operations of the household. These women were away from their homes for days and weeks out of each month, and they clearly recognized the challenges of their prolonged absence from home. But they explained it away by their lack of choice:

> I became a shuttle trader because of desperation after my husband was not paid for seven months, my daughter at that time gave birth, but her husband worked as a gym teacher in school and was paid meager wages or not paid at all. There was no money in the family at all. I stood in the market for four years. … Of course, I only got involved in the shadow economy because I had to work where the pay was better. [One] wants to eat more than to work for an honest local enterprise.[26]

Few men partook in the shuttle-trade business. Some husbands got involved in the trade only as household "bosses," who took control of profits. Many others did not work but were not satisfied with trading as an occupation and started to drink abusively. Women repeatedly asserted in their interviews that men took advantage of their wife's profits and relied on the shuttle-trade income to provide for all their needs, yet they also complained about the lack of female care and attention. Such men failed to participate in domestic duties and started to quarrel or even beat up their wives, especially when the wives "failed to do any laundry for days on end."[27] Most women remember that they wanted to preserve the family and tried to cheer up their husbands during this difficult transition era by offering them moral support paired with material comforts. But, overwhelmed by the many stresses of the trade and the complaints of their unemployed, often drunken husbands, these women preferred to divorce and to raise their children on their own rather than continue to live in an abusive domestic environment.[28]

United by a common business, men and women engaged in the shuttle trade often joined not only forces but also their lives. The family dynamic and family relations changed under the pressure of a new occupation, when one family member entered the shuttle trade. If it was the wife who became a trader, then her financial independence rose along with her self-esteem. The trade demanded a carpe diem attitude from its participants, and more than once a wife's character was transformed by this demand from that of an all-accepting caretaker to a physically and emotionally sturdy and increasingly communicative new woman who had to deal with all sorts of people from all social backgrounds. This new woman found more understanding in someone who shared the burdens and responsibilities of the trade than in her own husband:

> In 1993, my husband suggested we go to China to purchase some merchandise [for resale]. The first trip brought profits. I started to travel two–three times a month. I sold all merchandise by myself at a flea market. After a year, my husband decided to divide the capital, and he split off because he thought I was not frugal enough and used too much money for the trips. This offer of his was a psychological shock for me: how was it possible if we are one family? I continued to travel, counting only on my money. I met Victor during a trip. We became companions. I was the brain [of the business] and he supervised everything.[29]

Nina, the woman who told this story, later married Victor. Though Nina is an architect by training, she now boasts of her ten-year experience in the shuttle trade.

In some cases husbands joined their wives in the business precisely out of fear of losing their spouses. Yet the process of forging new alliances and establishing new relations and new families based on a common participation in the business was also widespread. This process did not imply that women shuttle traders never tried to preserve their existing families; many preferred to support their husbands, both emotionally and financially, under any circumstances. It was common for women to make trips and for unemployed or underemployed husbands to stay home and occasionally take care of children and do household chores. In such families women became the "de facto heads of the household." Galina, a 45-year-old former accountant with two children, explained that "my husband after perestroika could not find his niche; [he] broke down and started to drink. Hence I had to feed the family. My husband then started to steal money that was put aside for business and drink it away."[30]

Women often attempted to boost men's self-confidence and preferred to compromise when it came to women's feelings in order to preserve their marriage and assure that their children would grew up with their father present. At times, such attempts even became grotesque or tragic. Marina E. wanted to keep "the love of her life," a former cabdriver turned unemployed and constantly drunk father of two, in the family at all costs. She quit her job at a factory after she failed to receive her pay for six months. At first Marina sold ice cream, watermelons, and then fish to feed her family. But she had a dream of working for herself, and after she saved up enough money, Marina entered the shuttle trade and traveled to Turkey, the United Arab Emirates, and Poland to buy goods. Marina's financial success outraged her husband, who became physically abusive. But Marina did not yield to her relatives' persuasion to part with her husband; she justified her actions by saying that "he cannot live without us. He will just die somewhere under a fence." His physical abuse escalated: once, trying to stand up to his drunken violence, she stabbed her husband with a kitchen knife and accidentally killed him. Marina was sentenced to three years in prison but was pardoned under a general amnesty shortly thereafter. She continued to justify her late husband's rage and abuse and her persistent desire to stay by citing his good grace when he married her pregnant from another man, his "unjust" unemployment, and her strong beliefs that "it is very tough [for a woman] to be alone" and "you do not throw men around."[31]

But even women who avoided such unfortunate family dramas realized and feared that their frequent absence from home was a possible cause of a future divorce. Tricks and lies that women used in order to safeguard "their men" were countless. One woman remembered that she recruited a bunch of relatives to spy on her husband: "I am not an idiot; I asked my mother to 'look after mine' [to spy on my husband]. My mother has a girlfriend who lives in a house adjacent to ours so she is on watch from dawn to dusk to spy on what [my husband] does without me. My mother says that no, he does not cheat."[32]

This, of course, does not mean that all men reacted to their wives' involvement in the business in the same manner. Some, though identifiably the smallest group, enjoyed the benefits of having a working wife who took full financial responsibility for the entire family. These men were typically unemployed and performed "honor" tasks like driving their wives to markets in the morning or home from train stations after the trip. Women in these cases agreed that their husbands were victims of the transition economy; yet, it was not a man's job to get involved in retail trade. More than once women echoed a sentiment expressed in one trader's comment: "My [husband] says that trade is not a man's business. I agree. And in the market only women sell; what if he likes someone? Why would I want to lose my husband?"[33]

Realistically, other women in the markets were a minor nuisance compared to the real health risks that the traders faced in the marketplaces. Selling retail in the marketplace was not only a way to earn an income but also a job with severe repercussions. In the 1990s most marketplaces were not covered, so women traders there were exposed to all the weather conditions. They had to come in early and leave late during all seasons regardless of whether it rained or snowed, whether it was bitterly cold or suffocatingly hot. Women traders also had to disregard their health problems. The only excuse to miss a day of sales was a life-threatening sickness and a stay in the hospital. Colds, flu, ear infections, arthritis, back problems, and other "minor" aches and pains were disregarded, even when the outdoor temperature dropped well below freezing. Even then, women had to stand outside in such weather for hours. In addition, markets were often unsanitary, lacked basic facilities, and had nothing to offer in the way of hot food. It is not surprising that under such circumstances, health problems among women traders started to increase dramatically. Emma, who traded in one of these open markets, recalled that she shivered from the cold all day long in her kiosk in the midst of her merchandise because no matter how warmly she dressed, she could not stay warm in freezing weather for long. When her children came to pick her up at the end of each day and took her home, she could not undress herself; her fingers could not bend from overexposure to the cold. This story repeated itself day after day. After several months her arthritis pain became unbearable; Emma had to sell her merchandise at a minimum price in order to sell it fast and then she switched to housecleaning as a source of income.[34]

Marketplaces that were covered and presumably protected traders from frostbite and a wide range of other problems were not much better when it came to health risks. In the 1990s a visit to just one covered market, Cherkizov in Moscow, at a time when the city had up to 30 such markets, could reveal a host of problems. Dirt was everywhere and sanitary norms were never met or enforced; it was suffocating to breathe as there was no ventilation system of any sort. The lack of ventilation provided a safe haven for illness and a breeding ground for respiratory problems and contagious diseases. Noise there exceeded tolerable levels and was unbearable after several hours. Yet the Cherkizov Market continued to attract women traders, who hoped to profit from retail sales even at the cost of their health.

Faced with these harsh working conditions, many traders warmed up by drinking hard liquor, skipped on meals, and ignored all health problems even though most women traders were of childbearing age. The problem was exacerbated by the fact that these women commonly lacked the local registration that would have allowed them to get health insurance and use the local medical facilities for free. When they had to go to a local emergency room or other medical center, the fees that these facilities charged were often beyond anything the traders could or were willing to pay.

These difficult conditions and the constant demands of the trade had grave consequences for the institution of motherhood among traders. Most female traders did not intend to have children in the near future because they could not relinquish their business responsibilities even temporarily. In the 1990s, the birth rate declined to 1.17 children per woman of childbearing age in Russia. This decline was indeed significant if we compare it to the reproduction rates of 2.63 children per woman in 1959, 2.0 in 1970, and 2.41 in 1985.[35] Most traders believed that they had no right to have more children when they could barely feed their existing children, or they argued that children could wait until life became more stable. Abundant research demonstrates that the decision to postpone childbirth was one of the main contributing factors to the demographic crisis in Russia after 1991.

When women chose to keep their babies rather than have abortions, they often lacked the means for proper prenatal care. Medical records in the 1990s show a sharp increase in the number of pathologies in newborns that resulted from a lack of adequate nutrition on the part of mothers. Many disabled children were abandoned by their mothers, and those who remained in their families required special services and support from the government. In the 1990s the number of disabled children who received state pensions increased fourfold over the course of the decade, reaching the astronomical number of 675,000 disabled children receiving the state aid. In this business and beyond, a mother's ruined health became a child's ruined life.[36]

Moreover, children born out of wedlock amounted to no more than 10 percent of all children in the Soviet Union. Since the end of the 1960s, fathers in these cases were recognized as legal guardians who shared responsibility with the children's mothers in providing for them.[37] But the number of children born out of wedlock rose dramatically in the 1990s; at least one-third of all children, and as much as 40 percent in some regions in the Far East, were born as a result of cohabitation or after a brief liaison.

The choices were not much easier for women who already had children. To begin with, many women realized that they spent most of their time traveling or in the market and failed to have quality time with their children. They felt guilty that the work they chose to perform took them away from home and their children for weeks at a time and left them with no choice about whether to stay home with a sick child or stay at the market with their merchandise. When women felt that they neglected their own children, they tried to compensate for this by showering their children with gifts and various material possessions. Inevitably, such a response fostered a new sense of consumerism. A VHS player became a coveted item and the dream of many, fully replacing the more social movie-going habits of Soviet youth. Money that could go into securing a better future for "shuttle" families went to buying tapes with soft-core pornography and action movies that had been censored in the Soviet Union. For many traders and their families it was a Catch-22: the more the women worked in the shuttle trade, the more they wanted to justify their prolonged absence by acquiring new coveted items for themselves and their children. But the more they acquired in terms of material possessions, the more they had to work, performing the same strenuous and nearly inhuman labor. Simultaneously, these women also eroded the very values that they tried to compensate for by immersing themselves and their children in consumerism.

Many women placed their hopes in round-the-clock day care (where parents could leave their children for five days and take them home on weekends) and in after-school programs, which they thought could compensate for the virtual absence of parents in their children's lives. However, the Soviet institutions that were created to free mothers for public employment had disintegrated along with the Soviet Union itself, and whatever was created in their place could not satisfy the demands of millions of shuttle traders. Soviet day-care facilities were transformed into private specialized learning centers with high tuition fees that emphasized arts, language training, or other academic fields. But the overall number of day-care centers dropped to 50,000, half of what had existed in the Soviet Union. Though tuition was high by Russian standards at the time, these facilities could not satisfy popular demand; 4.3 million children were placed in these centers while 303,000 more were placed on waiting lists.[38] Some day-care centers claimed that they could not enroll enough preschoolers to stay open, and they closed down, mostly in order to use their buildings for other, more profitable purposes (like renting them out as storage spaces, for example). Well-off women traders resorted to hiring nannies to watch their children in the comfort of their homes, but the number of women who could afford such luxuries remained minimal.

The problem of child care and supervision was especially pronounced in the summertime, when school-aged children were left unattended. During the Soviet era, most organizations and factories had access to the so-called pioneer camps, that is, summer camps located on a lake or seacoast, where children were sent for 21 or 24 days at a time. These resorts for children included not only facilities in nearby villages but also extensive permanent camps in prime resort locations in the Crimea and the Caucasus. Even if the key goal of these programs was indoctrination, they nonetheless provided free meals, supervised activities, and entertainment for all children. Access to these summer camps was limited to employees of the sponsoring organization, but nearly every employed parent—and unemployment officially did not exist in the Soviet Union—could get a free or nearly free place for a child in one of these resorts. A pass to such camps was guaranteed on an annual basis to all children in large families and with single mothers. By the late 1980s there were 90,000 Pioneer camps that offered their services to over 16 million Soviet children annually.[39]

When these camps lost state financing in the early 1990s after the demise of the Soviet Union, they were almost universally closed down, and the buildings in them were subleased as dorms for temporary workers or in some locations used as refugee camps for the victims of internal wars or ethnic discrimination. Hence, one of the crucial dilemmas of the shuttle traders was the supervision of their children during the summer vacations when schools closed down and the camps and other institutions that cared for children collapsed. Parents, especially mothers, could not afford to stay home and instead spent weeks away from their homes in the shuttle trade importing foreign goods and the rest of the time selling their merchandise in the marketplace. More affluent shuttle traders earned enough money to finance their children's vacations in Bulgaria or Romania; the less fortunate ones had no choice but to let their children spend summers on their own, without any adult control or supervision of the children's activities and actions.

Though the problem of school-aged children was less severe during the school year, the lack of extended care centers also assured that children roamed around unattended after school instead of doing their homework or playing sports. Various after-school programs that offered instruction in music, arts, sports, or tutoring in school subjects serviced nearly 15 million children on a daily basis in the Soviet Union in the 1980s.[40] Yet, like other child-care facilities they ceased to exist once the Soviet Union disintegrated, as the state lost control over local institutions and lost its ability to finance these establishments. Of course, private lessons and private arrangements could be made for children who wanted to take music or art lessons or were interested in academic tutoring. But too many women traders had neither the money to pay for costly lessons nor the time to take their children around to different places. Almost overnight, millions of children were left without adult supervision, and this was especially true of children whose mothers spent the day conducting business and were not present at home even after regular work hours. All the consequences that one might expect of such a situation followed suit. Substance abuse among teens and teen pregnancies and abortions reached endemic proportions; mandatory secondary education became mandatory only on paper, when thousands of children without adult supervision dropped out of school; and material goods, like popular brands of jeans or portable audiotape players, became items of obsession.

All too often a drink of vodka or any other hard liquor seemed the only solution to the emotional and moral dilemmas that the women traders faced. It is not a coincidence that the rapid jump in alcoholism occurred in the 1990s, when former Soviet peoples faced severe financial and psychological challenges and uncertainty. Alcoholism among women grew at a much more rapid pace than among men. Medical professionals noted that most women who turned to hospitals for treatment or ended up in the hands of doctors were traders. Too often such women related a story like this: "You spend all day at your stand, watch crowds of people, and listen to the same pop song over and over again—the boredom [and depression] is horrifying! Many could not handle it. Former scientists, teachers, doctors broke down after several years 'behind the stand' and fell head over heels [to become] the scum of the earth."[41]

Elena tells the story of how she was left alone with her daughter after her divorce. Her pay as an engineer was not high, but at least she was paid regularly. Combined with the child-support payments that she received from her husband, she had a sufficient income. Then came a bolt from the blue—the factory went bankrupt. It was not easy to find another job, when all factories were already fully staffed or shut down and private firms did not want to hire "elderly women" like Elena, who was 38 years old at that time. Unfortunately, Elena's husband lost his job as well and could no longer send her child-support payments. The only place where Elena could earn any income was the market stall, and by the end of each day, she had a migraine from tiredness and stress. Her girlfriend advised her to get a drink to relax, and when Elena had her drinks, she "started to feel like the problem was solved."[42] At first Elena was ashamed of her actions and only drank by herself. Then she found drinking companions at the market and on various trips. After several months she realized that she needed to drink every day, and after six months or so she could not function without taking a drink in the morning, throughout the day, and into the wee hours of the morning. This situation continued until Elena's relatives could no longer take it and forced her to see a doctor.

Many doctors who specialize in substance abuse treated this story as typical. They explained that at least half of all female patients in the 1990s were shuttle traders, though no official statistics exist.[43] Women traders argue that they were forced into becoming alcoholics because of the conditions of their trade. Trips undertaken with constant risk and stress, health problems, the physical demands of transporting overly heavy merchandise, long absences from home, domestic problems with their spouses and children, poor trade turnover, and even sudden luck in selling goods—all these factors contributed to women's decisions to take a drink or two, and many more thereafter. In addition, traders were often forced to deal with the personal emotions and reactions of their customers. Some customers left home in a bad mood and lashed out against the traders; others complained about the price or quality of goods; still others threatened to call upon the internal revenue services and fine the seller for whatever reason. In short, these women traders were the buffer zone in their customers' relations and the new post-Soviet consumer economy as they had to absorb all the shocks and challenges of the trade. They became a risk group for substance abuse, according to various studies. Clinical psychologist Ol'ga Kunitskaia, currently employed in the psychiatric ward of a substance-abuse clinic, explained that trade was not necessarily a stressful or problematic occupation, especially for those who possessed appropriate communication skills and were genuinely interested in it. The real problem was that "recently many teachers, economists, engineers and even artists poured into the marketplace [who are] not fit for it. … At this stage, alcohol seems to facilitate the process of adapting to new conditions." Dr. Kunitskaia further explained that to these women alcohol seemed to have almost miraculous properties: it helped them warm up when it was cold; it helped them relax after a tough day; it helped them calm down after brawling with a particularly picky customer. Nearly universally, such cases are complicated by women's denial of their problems: "These women do not consider themselves alcoholics. Even when they drink regularly they are convinced: I cannot become an alcohol addict! I am just cheering myself up!"[44] Women, according to Kunitskaia, crave the sense of security and comfort that comes with a drink. They want to experience it so much that some of them admit that "the desire to drink can be so intense at times that if you put a glass of *samogon* [homemade vodka] in front of me [and] put a gun next to it and say that I'll be killed if I drink but spared if I abstain, I would still drink."[45]

Women alcoholics hurt their children even more than themselves, as these children had no choice or voice in situations like this. Children in families where mothers became alcoholics experienced a real emotional crisis. They wanted to believe their mother was the best because she worked hard for the family and because of the strength of the biological mother-child bond. Children of female traders with a drinking problem loved their mothers, but they also learned to hate them. These children hated the shame of having a drunken mother show up at home; they hated the responsibility of taking care of the household and younger siblings; they hated that they could not invite their friends over because there was always a risk that their mother would show up drunk. More than once children of shuttle traders who succumbed to this addiction echoed the words of 14-year-old Nastia:

I fear above all in this world that my friends will find out that my mom drinks. I constantly think in school and at home: what is to be done now? Should I hide a bottle or call relatives? Sometimes I want to run away from home but then I pity my mom. She wasn't always like this. I remember her cheerful, happy, [and] beautiful. It all ended the day she left to become a trader.[46]

Similarly, 42-year-old Natalia was in the business for eight years. She started off by traveling to Turkey, Greece, and later Poland. She had to spend most of her time en route. She slept on the floor of train stations, waited in lines, and suffered from chilly weather and constant colds. She always had a bottle of vodka with her; after all, it was the best solution to deal with a particularly annoying customs official or a border-crossing inspector. Some traders shared a drink or two to warm up and chat while waiting for their trains or airplanes. With time, her dependency became so severe that Natalia could no longer travel. She was hired to sell items retail in a local market and immediately found a nice group of women "with similar interests." Soon, after a particularly prolonged spur of hard drinking, she ended up in the emergency room in a crisis condition and was subsequently admitted to a rehabilitation hospital. "There is a need to admit," says Valerii Usenkov, a psychologist in a rehabilitation clinic, that "there are many women with advanced education among these [patients], former economists, teachers, accountants, even doctors." Typically, all of them followed the same path: a job loss, possibly divorce, financial difficulties, and eventually the choice of the shuttle trade as a suitable occupation. However, added Usenkov, "once women found themselves in the unusual conditions of the shuttle trade, many started to drink to ease up the tension. At first many women drink by themselves, hoping that no one finds out [and that] a small dose will bring relief. But it is a trap: drinking becomes addictive fast."[47]

Indeed, female alcoholism is particularly dangerous because alcoholism in females progresses (turns from occasional drinking to addiction) much faster than male alcoholism.[48] An "addictive interest" develops after just a few months of habitual drinking, and full-scale alcohol addiction develops over the course of two years. A woman's body is less able to break down and digest alcohol than a man's, so the level of alcohol in the blood and intoxication is higher in women than men even when the same amount of liquor is consumed. Emotional dependency also develops faster among women than men. But the main paradox and challenge of treating alcoholism among women traders was that, after undergoing treatment in a rehab facility, women went home to their problems and their need to earn money. And once again, the only place to turn to was the shuttle trade. With few or no rehabilitation facilities, poor understanding of the condition, limited knowledge about the role of nutrition and lifestyle in treating it, and little emotional support, these women found alcohol addiction extremely difficult to overcome. Persistent stress, lack of adequate sleep or insomnia, paranoiac fears, and other factors contributed even further to these traders' mental problems.

Short-term liaisons seemed to alleviate these problems for a while. Women who entered the shuttle trade were in their late thirties and forties and were forced into the trade after divorce or prompted by the need to feed their children. Residing in a small town with children to support, these women had very few chances of meeting "Prince Charming" back home. Hence, a romantic encounter with a foreigner was like a dream come true for women who went abroad to purchase items for resale. Several women reported, for example, that men in Turkey, regardless of their incomes and social status, attracted overworked women by courting them and displaying affection in chivalrous ways. Once home, these woman boasted that they had "unusual success among men" and could even attract a foreigner (not only a local man) with their beauty and looks.[49]

Some affairs matured into long-term relations and even marriages. One former trader tells her story of how she met the owner of a jewelry stall in a market in Turkey and married him. Now she works as a guide for Russian-speaking tourists in Anatolia and tells everyone about her unbeatable luck and surreal happiness. Her only regret is that her husband forced her to sign a marriage contract under which she can be left without a cent after divorce if her husband ever sees her wearing a miniskirt.[50]

However, such relations brought with them negative consequences and connotations as well. Soon after the massive influx of female traders from the former Soviet Union, salesmen in various countries (Turkey and Egypt being the most prominent examples) started to fly banners with signs like "One Natasha, one sex, one dress" (or one coat, one jacket, or anything else the trader had in the stall). Needless to say, since the offers to have "one sex" with "one Natasha" for the price of "one dress" proliferated, this was a sign that some women traders actually responded to these offers. Once again, scholarship on this topic is scant, to say the least, yet even a casual observer could not miss such signs. The common Russian name Natasha soon became slang for prostitutes, a development that flattered few Russian women and was a sad reflection of an even sadder reality.

For various reasons (all of which are beyond the scope of this study), there existed a significant regional variation in the type and number of relationships forged by women traders. Anecdotally, if Eastern European or Middle Eastern men commonly became traders' partners, the same was not necessarily true for places like Korea and China, and very few women traders found their emotional needs satisfied by local men in Far Eastern countries. Several women even argued that in Korea and China only women who intentionally wanted to expand their incomes from trade by offering intimate services engaged local men. In fact, the main center of Russian prostitution in Korea was Harbin, located in the northeastern part of the country. From there, women in this ancient profession traveled to Beijing, Shanghai, Hong Kong, and Macao. Their services were the cheapest in Harbin itself, where "Russian students" charged at most $50 USD per hour. Though the demand was high in Harbin, so was the supply. "Students" arrived in groups of 25 to 50 at a time. Once these women earned some money by selling their bodies, they then purchased goods at local markets—jeans, sweaters, cosmetics—and sold these in their hometowns. Most of these women were divorced and were relatively young, 25–30 years old, though some were much older or worked with their husband's explicit or implied approval. Nastia, who traveled from a small village near Komsomolsk-on-Amur, commented that her husband was fully aware of how she made money, but he never complained.[51] According to Eric Wittman, the press secretary of the International Organization against Female Slavery, in 2003 alone over 6,000 Russian female citizens and over 12,000 Ukrainian women were engaged in prostitution. They earned an average of $5,000 USD a month by offering sex services, an astronomical sum by their standards.[52] Though it is not the purpose here to tell the story of Russian prostitution abroad, it is nonetheless important to acknowledge that traders routinely encountered such stories, and the fear of falling victim to human trafficking and the sex industry was one more stress factor of their jobs.

Romantic or not, multiple sexual relations with untested partners was the reason that many women traders brought back with them not only their merchandise but also STDs. The resurgence of STDs was especially noticeable in the case of syphilis and gonorrhea. Syphilis had been almost nonexistent in the Soviet Union (3,800 women and 4,100 men contracted syphilis in 1990), but this disease grew in the 1990s. In 1995 there were 130,000 women infected with syphilis; in 1996 197,000 women were diagnosed, and by 1997 there were 208,000. Even these numbers are incomplete because many patients preferred to use private clinics that offered anonymous services.[53] While women traders repeatedly acknowledged in their interviews that short-term affairs resulted in nothing but STDs, nonetheless at the time the lure of a romantic encounter with Prince Charming outweighed any concerns.[54]

Women traders also realized that they could have affairs but not children from these affairs. The most common solution to the lack of adequate birth control was abortion. Mini-abortions were most common, though the exact occurrence rate can only be speculated upon since there is only indirect evidence. Thus, all Russian newspapers in the 1990s advertised services by "medical professionals," who performed mini-abortions inexpensively and privately. The number of such ads commonly exceeded the number of ads for apartment rentals, housecleaning services, and hairstyling. Bleeding and other complications were also common, and some medical professionals have attempted to compile data on abortions by counting the number of complications treated in major hospitals and giving a ballpark figure for the number of "private" abortions. But even the official statistics that have been compiled based on data available from large clinics that were formerly state-subsidized show that in the 1990s the number of abortions was twice the number of births.[55] Especially worrisome was the fact that nearly 5 percent of abortions made women inadvertently sterile, and the number is higher for women who had an STD at the time of abortion.[56]

Equally problematic for researchers is the growth of infanticide and child abandonment. Though there might never be precise and verifiable data on such acts, especially in relation to one social group like traders, press organs commonly reported in the 1990s that infants were found, both dead and alive, in trash dumpsters, city sewer systems, on the streets, in parks, and oftentimes on the steps of residential buildings or near children's hospitals and day-care facilities. Though parents of such children were rarely, if ever, discovered, the large number of women who participated in the shuttle trade in proportion to the overall female population of Russia indicates a high probability that some of these foundlings were the children of traders.

However, this dramatic and radical method of getting rid of unwanted children attracted only a few. It became more commonplace to leave newborns in a delivery room to have them put in orphanages later by hospital administrators. Even though in the 1990s there were twice as many orphanages in the Russian Federation as there were a decade earlier, reaching 1,265 in 2001, these orphanages could accommodate only an insignificant number of children in hospitals who awaited their place in an orphanage. The orphanages housed 74,000 children, 1.5 times more than their allotted norm, in the 1990s, and thousands of children were left in children's hospitals for a year or longer before being placed in an adequate child-care facility.[57] Some children with living parents could not even count on being placed in any child-care facilities. In 1990 about 50,000 children were orphans or de facto orphans (with parents who were either alcoholics, in rehab facilities or hospitals, or away from home for more than 80% of the time). This number reached 130,000 by 2001, which in real numbers translates into a fourfold increase in rates because of the difference in population from Soviet to post-Soviet times (the population of the Soviet Union was close to 320 million, whereas the Russian Federation that emerged after the Soviet collapse had about 150 million).[58]

Despite the bleak picture of life among those female traders who failed to achieve even a moderate level of financial success, more affluent women traders commonly believed that this business was a means by which they regained their self-esteem and realized their potential. Such women were no longer ashamed to meet acquaintances or former coworkers because they felt like "keepers" in this life. They no longer feel displaced and alienated; their sense of belongingness to a community of traders gives them also a sense of being included in "their own" society. These women have a sincere interest in maintaining their position of "small owners of big market forces." Some of these women add that they lacked education and social status prior to their involvement in the trade, but now they feel superior to "all those intellectuals" who struggle financially. "If you cannot turn around," they argue, "then live on those crumbs that the government throws you with a huge delay."[59] Women who started their own businesses (as we will see in the next chapter) pride themselves on their accomplishments and see the changes in their financial lives that took place since the early days of the businesses. They lament, like Galina from Irkutsk, that "I am offended when someone calls me *chelnochka* [female singular for a shuttle trader]. I am not *chelnochka*, I am an entrepreneur, a businesswoman."[60] These women share a sense of achievement in their lives and pride themselves on living according to the harsh rules of the marketplace.

But the rules of the game have proven to be unacceptable or too tough for others. Nearly half of all women left the shuttle trade in their first year, and many others wanted to leave the trade but remained in it only for financial consideration. A survey of Syktyvkar Market conducted in 1996 demonstrated that over 70 percent of traders wanted to leave this business, and many of them agreed that they were "all fellow victims [of our lives]. Do not believe anyone if they say that this trade is their dream come true." Nearly all professionally trained traders wanted to return to their former occupations under ideal circumstances, which included getting paid at least what they earned in the shuttle trade. Sentiments like "I would go back to school [to teach] any minute … but how would I earn money to raise my son?" and "if they paid a decent wage at the tailor shop, I could make enough clothing for the entire town" are commonplace among traders. Still others say they would agree to perform any job other than sell retail. One woman noted, "I want to leave this place desperately and to feel like a normal human being again, but then I need money for that."[61] Even the most successful traders who earned the most believe that they paid too high a price for their success, and they hope that their children will do anything it takes to avoid the trade. Larisa Dorofeeva, now a successful entrepreneur, says, "I do not want my child to do the same. This is a cruel path."[62]

5

Where Did All the Women Go?

You can still meet an old-fashioned shuttle trader on the border of
China every once in a while. But they are more like a dying breed,
dinosaurs of sorts—virtually extinct.

—From an interview, 2007

The default of the ruble in 1998 assured that the shuttle trading of the
1990s almost disappeared by the turn of the century. What emerged
instead was a new kind of trade that had only a marginal relationship to
prior forms of trading, one that swept across Russia in the decade after the
collapse of the Soviet Union. The devaluation of the ruble and the decline
of profit in the economic collapse of 1998 played a massive role, but so
did the eventual improvement in the Russian economy in the new century. If in the first few years after default most traders could not afford to
reenter the trade, then by the mid-2000s (2004–2005), the thirty- to forty-
year-olds who used to dominate the trade had found new and oftentimes
more reliable and desirable ways to earn a living. Thus directly linked to
economic development and growth, there emerged a significant regional
variation in the patterns and scale of trade. This is not to say that there
were no differences between Moscow-based and Far Eastern traders from
the outset. Yet the gap that separated the ever more expensive Moscow region and the less affluent peripheral regions continued to widen at a rapid
speed in the last decade. The high cost of imports pushed some traders to
consider retailing domestic goods, which had been practically absent in
the 1990s. New occupations appeared as well; a few sellers emerged successful enough only to sign contracts for wholesale deliveries of goods by
cargo careers while the market stalls were staffed by low-paid employees.

The 2000s was a decade of the new age of international peddling that had only superficial links to its predecessor.

The financial crisis of August 1998 was in the making for a long time, and the signs of impending doom were everywhere. Still, the Russian default came as a shock to many observers, investors, and ordinary people both domestically and internationally. Only three days before August 17, 1998, Boris Yeltsin had declared during a press conference that "there will be no default of any sorts."[1] The declaration was prompted in the first place by Russia's shaky economic situation. In the three prior years the government had resorted to issuing short-term Russian Government Treasury Bills (GKO) to compensate for the massive state budget deficits.[2] Though the revenue made on the sale of bills was reasonable in the first few years, it quickly turned into a Ponzi-like scheme. The government could only meet its obligations on the previously sold bills by making more sales. As the revenues declined, the government had to borrow money to pay the interest on its bills and the payments became more and more burdensome. Buyers could be fooled into purchasing more bills only through promises of ever-increasing interest rates, which had to be financed by more sales and further borrowing.

Two external factors contributing to the collapse were the Asian financial crisis of 1997 and the declining price of petroleum products and nonferrous metals. Commodity exports were Russia's main source of income, and as was the case in 1985 the government's ability to meet its own financial obligations rested on revenues from the sale of natural resources. But when the price of petroleum fell from $26 USD a barrel to $15, it dealt a devastating blow to the Russian economy.[3] In combination, massive foreign debt, low commodity prices, and the unsustainable pyramid of the State Treasury Bills pushed the government to announce its default on GKO payments and to withdraw its support of the ruble on August 17, 1998. The consequences were felt almost immediately: the exchange rate of the ruble against the US dollar collapsed by a factor of three, inflation hit hard, and living standards declined even further compared to pre-1998 standards (see Graph 5.1 on the US dollar exchange rate to Russian ruble for specific details).

The Black Monday of 1998, as observers labeled the crisis, was unprecedented in its structure and scale, and it dealt an equally unprecedented blow to the shuttle traders of the 1990s. The trade never recovered in the form and shape that existed prior to the financial crisis. Traders' profits depended directly on the currency exchange, and massive fluctuations led to substantial

Graph 5.1: The exchange rate of the US dollar to the Russian ruble, 1998

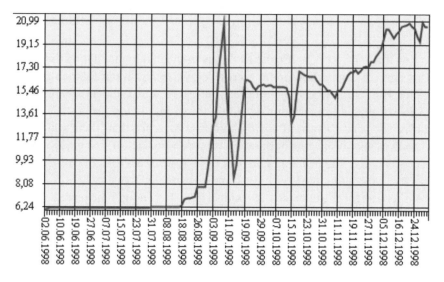

Source: Central Bank of the Russian Federation, cbr.ru.

losses. When the trade bounced back, it reemerged in a new form that was shaped by the new economic and social realities of the 2000s. Research conducted by the Sociological Institute of the Russian Academy of Sciences demonstrated that at least 40 percent of all traders left the business immediately following the default of 1998. The percentage might be even greater if we compare the popular participation in trade in the mid-1990s. The "human capital" of the trade was estimated to be at least 15 million people in the 1990s (pre-1998), with the highest points occurring at mid-decade with 30 million people earning a livelihood from activities associated with international peddling. By 2006 the highest estimate was about 6.5 million people, though, once again, precise numbers are hard to come by.[4] Other sources indicate that no more than 10 percent of the former traders sustained their business into the first year of the new century.[5]

The monetary volume of trade, however, increased over the years, suggesting that the per capita capital and the scale of transactions increased as well. The volume of trade experienced a steep decline in the months following the default of 1998, but it bounced back in the early 2000s. The Russian Trade Committee and the State Committee for Statistics demonstrated that in February 1999 the monthly volume of the shuttle trade fell to $0.8 billion USD (estimated $5.6 billion annually), which was a 55.2 percent decline compared to the same month of the previous year.[6] However, by 2004 the annual volume of trade, according to the study done by the Highest School of Economics, was estimated at $22 billion USD though the State Committee for Statistics quoted a lower figure of about $12 billion USD.[7]

If the initial departure from the market was a result of Russia's default in 1998, then the subsequent remodeling of the new trade had to do with broader macro- and microeconomic changes in the nation. The growth of the Russian economy in the 2000s and the stabilization of the job market offered traders new opportunities for employment. The economic growth (demonstrated by Graph 5.2) also meant better incomes for consumers who could finally afford better-quality goods. For some regions, especially Moscow, this implied that the traders needed more capital to invest when entering the trade, thus creating a new obstacle for newcomers.[8] Lower profits, greater capital investments, and rising employment opportunities elsewhere became a potent force drawing many traders away from international peddling.

Unemployment data can offer insight into popular participation in the trade, even if the evidence is only suggestive or indirect. The official unemployment reached its all-time high at 13 percent of the working-age

Graph 5.2. Russian GDP

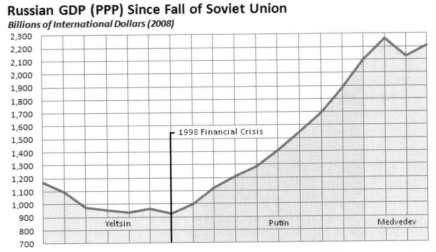

Russian GDP (PPP) Since Fall of Soviet Union
Billions of International Dollars (2008)

Source: International Monetary Fund, http://www.imf.org

population in the second half of 1998 and in 1999, but it started to scale down thereafter and by 2002 was at 8 percent, the level of 1994.[9] By 2005 official unemployment dropped to 5.2 percent nationwide, though regional variations were significant. Thus, Moscow, St. Petersburg, and a number of other central regions had unemployment rates well below 5 percent, while the Chechen and Ingush regions topped the list with 15–18 percent unemployment rates.[10] These numbers might suggest that more people opted to register their small businesses or seek gainful employment in spheres other than illicit trading. In combination with the data on Russian economic growth presented above, it also implies that the financial circumstances of more and more people were improving into the 2000s, and this is confirmed both anecdotally and in interviews. Economic growth and changes in other sectors of the economy also influenced the outflow of people from peddling, even if at times indirectly so (by creating jobs). For example, two women who were interviewed for this project now work as real-estate agents. They reported that this occupation practically did not exist in the 1990s and what did exist was too corrupt to be even considered as an option by "normal" people. The situation changed in the last ten years. Though the housing prices skyrocketed, people for the first time had access to mortgages (all real estate was sold for cash in the 1990s). Not every family can afford the high interest rates and the high prices of housing, but the availability of mortgages made real-estate transactions appear more mundane and legitimate. Middle-class families could now aspire to hire middle-class real-estate agents and buy middle-class housing. The better economic situation in the country and the lower unemployment rates played a substantial role in the transformation of the shuttle trade, even if this cannot be measured in precise numbers.

Beyond any doubt, the structure of the trade changed dramatically when it reemerged after the default. While a small minority of traders continue to perform all tasks involved in the process, like traveling abroad to buy merchandise and then selling it retail, much of the retail trade after 1998 has been done by waged employees. Typically, the sellers are paid a guaranteed wage, usually the equivalent of 1,500–2,000 rubles ($50–$80 USD) a month, plus 5–10 percent of the profits made on the sale of goods. On average, this implies an income of about $150–$200 USD a month, though the type of merchandise can significantly affect the incomes of retail sellers.

In various short interviews done among current retailers in multiple markets in Moscow and several cities across Russia during and after 2007, sellers nearly universally confirmed that they started trading in 1999 or later and were hired to work at stalls. As a general rule, they never travel abroad and earn a margin of the profit. Only one woman in the Mar'ino Market in Moscow admitted that she attempted to get into trading back in 1992. She invested all of her borrowed money into both the trip and buying a few pieces of clothing, but she could not retail them afterward and suffered severe financial losses. She could not explain exactly what went wrong; "a poor choice of styles or bad luck probably explain it all." The experience was traumatizing enough to dissuade her from ever trying to get into trade again, until she was offered a seller position in one of the stalls in 1999. Like most traders, she resented the long hours and the lack of social benefits; there are no sick days or vacation days whatsoever, and the market is open from 8 am to 9 pm. But some counted their blessings to have a job like that; a woman from Armenia, now employed by the owner of a retail booth, admitted that she had no "paperwork" (immigration papers) and could not find any work when she came to Moscow seven years earlier. Selling retail did in fact imply low wages and long work hours, but as she recalled, at least no one asked her at first if she had legal residence or any work permit. She had legalized her status by the time of the interview but chose to stay in the market. "What else is there for me to do?" she questioned and then added that the job became more emotionally acceptable as her children got older and no longer needed her constant supervision.

The shuttle traders themselves, if we may call them such, are no longer the same breed of traders either. They do not sell retail themselves (the only exception are those "start-ups" with less than $2,000–$3,000 USD in capital), and they also no longer travel abroad on all occasions. Some hire "camels," while others prefer to buy in wholesale markets in various locations across Russia and make profits by retailing those goods. Regional variations play a significant role in this pattern as well. Graph 5.3 explains where the goods come from and clearly demonstrates that in southern parts of Russia, the sellers acquire the bulk of their goods from other regions in Russia (mostly wholesale markets in and around Moscow)—though this has no relation to the origin of an item. At the same time, in the Far Eastern border regions, traders still travel to other countries (mostly China) to buy their goods for resale. The "traditional" shuttle trade remained important only in those border regions, as most sellers prefer to use wholesale depots as their supply bases. Curiously, the number of traders who use a combination approach (i.e., those who travel abroad and to wholesale markets) is not very high either; the logistics of combining the two are too complicated, just as traveling to various locations is simply too expensive.

The place of origin of the goods circulated by traders has also been changing. If in the 1990s goods were almost exclusively imported and brand names mattered a great deal, then in the first decade of the 2000s, domestic goods

Graph 5.3: Patterns in acquisition of goods

■ the trader buys from a domestic / wholesale market ■ the trader personally buys from abroad ■ combination

Source: Adapted from A. A. Iakovlev, V. V. Golikova, and N. L. Kapralova, "Rossiiskie chelnoki," *Mir Rossii,* no. 2 (2007): 84–106.

came to form as much as 40 percent of the goods sold in the open-air markets. Domestic textiles, shoes, and all sorts of clothing became progressively more popular because they became affordable and were made of cotton, linen, wool, and other natural products. Some of that popularity was a reaction to various concerns that low-cost and poorly manufactured imported goods posed potential health hazards for the consumers. High-profile television channels such as *Pervyi Kanal* and *NTV* aired programs that showed children poisoned by dyes used in the production of clothing in China, as well as adults who had severe allergic reactions to these dyes. The poor quality of imported goods was also a matter of constant concern; some better-off consumers were beginning to seek out locally manufactured goods that were more durable, while less affluent customers preferred healthy options, like cotton underwear, over pricey nylon imported equivalents. Though the following sample is not a complete overview of all goods, it is representative of the share of the market that domestic goods occupied by July 2004.

The same increasing reliance on domestic producers is evident in the general overview of the place of origin for goods that the sellers offered in their stalls. Once again, though regional variations are important, the number of sellers who rely exclusively on imported goods (purchased either at wholesale depots or elsewhere) had declined to slightly over 20 percent in the first decade of the twenty-first century. The rest, in roughly equal shares, offer either only domestically produced goods or an assortment of items of both domestic and foreign origin.

The sellers who continue to buy abroad now use new avenues for their acquisitions and hire others to act as carriers when needed. In the Far Eastern part of Russia, young people make some quick cash working as "camels" (*verbliudy*). Though similar schemes (on a small scale) could be found in various border regions across Russia, this has become a "Chinese phenomenon" since most trips are made to China. In this scheme the "boss" hires a group of people, typically thirty to forty-five people at a time (roughly equivalent to a full bus) to cross the border into China for a quick day trip. "Camels" report to a bus or docking station at about 8 am, find their "boss," and have their name checked off the list. Then all "camels" get specific instructions about what they need to buy, where to do so, and how much they can buy for themselves. Logistics are also taken into consideration; "camels" get information on departure meeting places and times, and they also get tips on where to eat cheaply and what to look out for. Families are especially welcome on these trips as they appear less suspicious to the border-control officials and can carry more goods of different styles and sizes. "Camels" are furthermore advised to wear their worst clothing possible, as most are expected to trash it and pile up new outfits onto themselves. Outfits on their backs do not count toward the maximum weight allowance, and most "camels" look like cabbage on their return journey, with layers and layers of clothing on them. Tricks of this kind are especially worthy of the risk for fur coats. Many are known to leave Russia in a worthless piece of clothing that can only nominally be classified as a "fur coat" and come back in a fur coat that later sells for $3,000–$5,000 USD. Needless to say, none of those goods are for personal consumption.

Graph 5.4: Share of domestic goods on the markets

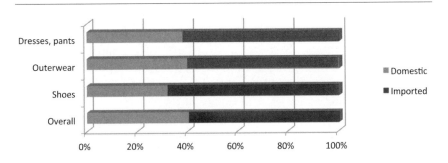

Source: Adapted from A. A. Iakovlev, V. V. Golikova, and N. L. Kapralova, "Rossiiskie chelnoki," *Mir Rossii*, no. 2 (2007): 84–106.

The "boss" in this setup pays only for the "camels'" transportation; even when helpers stay abroad overnight, they cover their own expenses. Some "camels" are also asked to pay for their visas, and they all must have valid passports. Initially "camels" received no cash payment (at least no one was willing to admit it), but the trip was lucrative anyway because helpers could buy discounted clothing and household goods for themselves or for resale. In the last five to seven years, professional "camels" started to charge for their services—with a fee anywhere from 100 rubles to 5,000 rubles per trip (the rough equivalent of $3.50–$160 USD). Various press organs estimate that up to one million "camels" crossed the border with China annually in the mid-2000s.[11]

The vocabulary of this trade also became region specific. For most locales, though the term "helpers" (*pomogaiki*) was widely used in the 2000s, they were not to be mistaken for helpers abroad. In many locations, especially in China, it became commonplace to hire bag carriers for shopping trips. These locals pay a licensing fee to "carry *bauly*" (bulging bags) for foreigners like Russians and are reliable as far as safety and service go. But in some places, for example in Blagoveshchenk, the term "camel" was not used at all. Instead, the "brick" (*kirpich*) hired about thirty "flashlights" (*fonar'*) to cross the border with goods for "personal use." These people "flashed" their passports to demonstrate that the goods were for personal consumption and thus were not taxable. Whatever the specific term that was used to describe the people involved in these dealings, the scheme itself was nearly identical for the border regions.

Border regions, in fact, assumed a new role in the trade. Domestic retailing and legitimate high-end trade dominates much of the central and western parts of Russia, but the Far East sees a far greater rate of international peddling compared to other territories. The structure of the trade has changed significantly, and both the microeconomic growth and proximity to China played an important role in this transformation. Scholars of the far-eastern gray market have diverged in their interpretation of the new trade. Some argue that the cases of informal international trade, as it came to exist in the 2000s, are highly comparable to various examples across the world and demonstrate a great flexibility of the border population to use resources available to them "on the frontier" to earn their livelihood. The temporary engagement in trade is one of the innovative personal uses of the advantages that come with living so close to the different cultural and economic spaces of a foreign country.[12] While this "matter-of-fact" observation carries no positive or negative connotations, other scholars see it as a part of "the other side of globalization."[13] Though much of the international peddling is in consumer goods, it might be considered as one of the links in the illegal trade in biological resources or even human trafficking. Wild ginseng, sea cucumbers, and more rarely, Siberian tiger body parts cross the border from Russia to China and fuel Chinese interest in stimulating this illegal trade. The fear of illegal Chinese migration (scornfully called "the yellow danger") is routinely discussed by locals and at times even scholars, though much of this "danger" is greatly exaggerated.[14]

At any rate, the nationwide popular participation in international peddling had scaled down significantly in the twenty-first century. Most respondents cite the default of 1998 as a turning point. The trade never bounced back because of the subsequent low profitability of the post-default years, tighter border regulations, tariffs, and quality controls, and because there progressively emerged new opportunities to earn income elsewhere. The cargo business slowly absorbed the lion's share of the low-key trading done by individual peddlers. Most companies have large-scale operations and can afford to work off a relatively small margin of profit because of the sizeable capital and low overhead costs of goods per kilo. Large cargo operations also have access to bank loans that either still are unavailable to private individuals or carry interest rates that individual peddlers cannot afford to pay. At the same time, regulations for legalizing a small enterprise were dramatically simplified by 2005–2008, thus prompting peddlers to find their local niche and file the proper paperwork. According to the Union of Business Women, the service sector (hairstyling salons, spa services, tourist operations, as well as notary public and consulting services) became particularly attractive to women who used to be involved in the shuttle trade. The Khabarovsk branch of the Union, for example, created a "one window" service: aspiring women could file all proper paperwork for founding their own small company in one place. The benefits of legalization were significant. By the late 2000s the income tax was fixed at 13 percent, and all other legal costs were brought to a minimum. Legalization also brought access to special subsidized loans (no matter how imperfectly functional the system was), some degree of legal protection from demands for "protection" money, security vis-à-vis the police, and a chance to claim social security benefits upon retirement (which remained unchanged since the late Soviet days for both men and women, set at sixty and fifty-five years, respectively).

It is also worth noting that the popular attitude toward traders did not become as positive as we might assume, considering how many people were actually involved in the process. The All-Russian Center for Public Opinion administered a survey in 2005 in order to study the popular attitude to shuttle traders. Though some respondents found it hard to evaluate the role of trading for Russia, 38 percent believed that the shuttle trade was bad for the country and 37 percent assessed it as good.

However, written comments submitted in response to an open question about the role of trading were more revealing in terms of popular attitudes. While some respondents spoke of traders as persistent, entrepreneurial, and energetic, just as many respondents labeled the traders "mean swindlers," who share such personality traits as boorishness, rudeness, impudence, intrusiveness, and greediness. Some even called traders swindlers, cheaters, thieves, and speculators, revealing an attitude that harked back to the Soviet days.[15] The generalized scornful attitude to shuttle trade was also evident during interviews. Even in 2009–2010 most sellers refrained from using the term *chelnok* or were offended when the term was used to describe them. Anecdotally, some traders also wanted to leave the business in the last ten years because they were tired of feeling ashamed of what they did for a living and opted for more steady jobs. The attitude was not universally shared by traders or the general population by any means, but it cannot be discarded in trying to explain the evolution of the trade in the years following 1998.

Another significant feature of this transformation was the change in the quality of imported goods or, to be more precise, the share of quality goods that reached Russia in the 2000s compared to the 1990s. As one respondent commented: "The overall quality of goods that Russian shuttle traders buy has not changed at all because they still bring both quite expensive quality goods that are aimed at affluent customers and cheap, poor-quality items. But what has changed is the percentage of each; the share of quality items

Graph 5.5: Assessment of the shuttle trade by the population of the Russian Federation

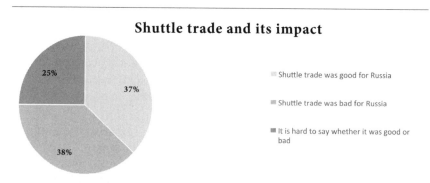

Shuttle trade and its impact

25%

37%

38%

■ Shuttle trade was good for Russia

■ Shuttle trade was bad for Russia

■ It is hard to say whether it was good or bad

Source: Adopted from Public Opinion Foundation, "Shuttle Trade," June 30, 2005.

was 15–20 percent at most in the 1990s and now it is more like fifty-fifty." This concerns mostly clothing and household goods (nonperishables), as the trade in processed and raw foods has practically disappeared. To begin with, the Russian State Committee for the Safety and Quality Control of Consumer Goods (*Rospotrebnadzor*) began to strictly enforce regulations that perishable items can only be sold with the export-import certification of quality and in places that have undergone a sanitary and epidemiological inspection and clearance, and the traders surely had none of the above. Moreover, consumers also expressed considerable concern over foods sold in unsafe conditions. For example, a popular demonstration broke out in August 2011 in Smolensk when it was discovered that several traders attempted to sell raw meat and dairy products in 90°F heat off newspapers spread over a paved but dirty street.[16] The registered and certified import of Chinese products into Russia is not a guarantee of quality either; take, for example, a well-known case in which a number of children were accidentally poisoned with melamine, a substance commonly used in the production of dinnerware, which was added to Chinese-made baby formula.[17] Yet beginning in the 2000s and moving progressively into the present, most consumers prefer to limit their purchases from the shuttle traders to nonperishables. Most consumers are fully aware that toys, clothing, and other items that are available in brand-name stores are also manufactured in China. They hope, however, that the higher price of these goods can be associated with higher quality. As the general per capita income increased, so did the number of consumers who were willing to pay a higher price for the hope of getting a better-quality item.[18]

The same consumers' hopes of securing quality goods drove a new and rapidly expanding retail trade in secondhand clothing. If the sacramental consumption of brand items along with popular attitudes toward social status and prestige made such trade almost unthinkable in the 1990s, the slow but steady devaluation of general consumption and its more mundane nature made secondhand clothing appealing to some buyers in the 2000s. The popular attitude to the secondhand stores changed dramatically, and so did the stores themselves. If during the 1990s a few places existed that sold humanitarian-based aid packages of clothing in abysmal condition (hardly a piece of clothing without damage), now the secondhand stores buy selectively; the owners rent well-equipped store spaces, and most advertise that they even spot *real* Prada, Levis, and other brand-name clothing. Fashion magazines played a role in this transformation as well, as many (*Prelest'*, *Zhenskii jurnal*, *NJournal*, and others) published the "revelations" of major European and international pop stars that they, too, frequent secondhand shops, thus making such shopping more desirable and less degrading. As one respondent commented, "It is not just the fashion for the poor anymore!"

Another curious feature of the new trade of the 2000s was its relationship with informal (Mafia-type) structures. In the 1990s much of the racketeering was done face-to-face, when "protection money" was demanded directly from the traders and could vary significantly. But as the trade transformed, so too did its "protection." The criminal underworld started to work with the more important subsidiaries in the trade, leaving the meager and the mundane to the official administrators of the market spaces.[19] Some criminal gangs morphed into security services with registration, licenses, and all paperwork needing to be legitimate in appearance. They fulfilled the prophecy of Vadim Volkov, who called them "the violent entrepreneurs."[20] Others disappeared, being pushed out by "ethnic Mafias" that came to control most open-air retail markets. These are called "ethnic" because they typically bring together people from the same ethnic background—like "the Armenians of Gera Obeziana" (or "Gera the Monkey")—or assume the ethnic title based on the background of their leader.[21] But these ethnic Mafias evolved as well, now working for the control of entire market zones and not getting bogged down with individual peddlers. Though an in-depth discussion of the criminal underworld is beyond the scope of this study, most traders acknowledged that in the 2000s the relationship with those structures became both more predictable and indirect. All traders were asked to pay official rent to the administrator of the market space in addition to the unofficial but fixed fee to the same person (the fee was customarily set at ten times the official rent). The administrators later took it upon themselves to handle all negotiations and payments with criminal structures, and the traders knew little of the specifics of that arrangement. The new law, passed in 2011 and effective as of January 1, 2012, required a total liquidation of all ad-hoc, open-air, and/ or temporary markets. These were to be replaced with permanent shopping-mall-style buildings with better regulated and fixed rents for each space. Though the implications of this change are unclear at the time of this publication, the expectation is that this law will curb corruption and minimize the role of the criminal underworld in this sector of the economy.[22]

As the structure of the trade changed, so did the lives of its former participants. In general, all of the former traders could be classified into three groups according to their biographical trajectories after the default of 1998. Some traders, though a clear minority of them, have established their own businesses of varying sizes; they assess their involvement in the shuttle trade as the starting point of a successful career and a way to accumulate sufficient capital. The second group consists of traders who remained in the shuttle trade in one capacity or another but failed to legalize their endeavors or who became wage earners, oftentimes working for the first group. Finally, the last group consists of the overwhelming majority of traders who "reversed" their biographies after 1998; they left the business for good and oftentimes went back to their prior occupations and professions. These people typically assess their shuttle-trading experience as a transitional phase in their lives—as a short-term occupation that filled in the gap between two points on the vector of one's life.

The discussion of the first group prompts the question of whether they shared some traits that could have indicated their future success; that is, some "key to success" or at least some "key to private enterprise" that allowed them to move on to the next phase of their careers. What distinguished them from the rest of the group? The question seemed most pressing in trying to understand their experiences, but an analysis of their life stories did not produce a clear-cut answer. Most traders, both men and women, who emerged as successful had professional training before they entered the trade. But as we discussed in previous chapters, traders by and large were somewhat well-educated, and the type of education among the successful group was not qualitatively different from that of the other traders. Gender also seemed to matter little. Thus, professional education and gender played little role as determinate factors in traders' success. At the very least, neither of the two factors guaranteed success. Men failed in the shuttle trade just as often as women (in proportion to their overall numbers), and professionals across the board fared equally in their endeavors as a group. Nor was there any other common denominator that could predict, or at least retrospectively indicate, future failure or financial crisis in one's business. Finger-pointing was common but without much basis for such judgments. Age was also a variable that was difficult to assess, although most traders who turned into entrepreneurs in the 2000s were relatively young in the 1990s, as were most other traders. If age mattered, it was only by being indirectly linked to risk taking and energy levels that might wane with time.

Nonetheless, the first group seemed to demonstrate certain behavioral patterns that distinguished it from the rest. Some of these patterns were not intentionally chosen or strategically adopted, even if some traders insisted that they were. Other things—such as, for example, intuition—are so nebulous and intangible that their study is difficult to quantify. Overall, though, members of this "success" group from the start seemed to diversify their individual initiatives on multiple levels. They combined shuttle trading with other profit-generating activities, and when trading, they never relied on a single type of merchandise, unlike most other traders. As a result they were less fearful of financial disasters and bankruptcy and more likely to take financial risks. Their failures in one area were less consequential compared to other traders; it was definitely not as significant as a total loss of investment, which pushed many traders relying on one type of merchandise to leave the market. One woman reported that she started to tailor clothing for her closest friends as a parallel business to shuttle trading. Trading exposed her to an assortment of designs and fashion trends and thus helped her as a tailor while her skill as a designer improved her assessment of the quality of goods that she purchased abroad. Crucially, when one business failed, the other sustained her during reported "dry spells" in her careers—when designing clothing did not generate any income or when shuttle trips did not return her investment. In tandem, the two businesses worked marvelously. This trader currently owns several designer boutiques that sell brand-name clothing and her own designed and tailored clothing as well. In a similar way a male respondent reported that he never stopped working as a private taxi driver; such "privateers" had no registration but were in high demand among the general population. The trader continued to work in this capacity at least two nights a week for the duration of his involvement in the shuttle trade. He generated enough income driving people around that he was not concerned about losing his income from peddling. As a result he experimented with various types of merchandise to find, by trial and error, the most profitable of all.

The diversification of merchandise was no less significant and was directly linked to another behavioral pattern among more affluent traders. Unlike their peers, these traders strategically planned their business, oftentimes because they took time to analyze the market and had a keen sense of popular demand. The traders attempted to assess the market, or more specifically consumer tastes, in order to identify unique niches that were not occupied by other traders. "I walked around the market and literally questioned all people there about what they wanted to buy," one trader recalled. "Though I met people who refused to answer, enough shared their perception of what was lacking in the market and what they wanted to see there." Another trader from Khabarovsk quoted his hobby and intuition as guiding forces in this market analysis: "I loved reading but could not find at all the books that would be interesting to me. So I started buying them for myself first, and then for resale. In no time, I was the only person in town selling books and my business took off from there." A trader from Novorossiysk shared almost an identical story. Petr came across the first one-volume translation of

Ann McCaffrey's *Dragonriders of Pern* and was so taken by it that he wanted to buy other books by the author. But the only way for him to finance the purchase of the next book was to sell the first, which he did with a sizeable profit. In two months' time he started selling books regularly, and by the mid-1990s he had become the main wholesale supplier (and later store owner) for all booksellers in the town. Yet overall, the analysis of life stories strongly suggests that the most successful in the long-term were the traders who moved away from clothing and cosmetics and into the sale of electronics, household appliances, cars, furniture, and building supplies.[23]

Unlike most other former traders, businessmen and businesswomen who built up their capital from peddling assert now that they never felt ashamed of their activities and actions. They never thought that trading was a moral compromise but perceived it as an intriguing and innovative way to earn a better living. They actively sought the support and assistance of their relatives and friends and were eager to receive advice from those who had tried the business before them. "Unfortunately, I had to cheat and lie on occasion in this business," recalled a male respondent who currently owns a chain of residential building supply stores in Moscow. "But that was an unfortunate reality of life and the only way for me to 'catch the big fish,' to become successful. Any job is a good job, and it helps as well if it pays handsomely." The overall standard that seems to distinguish those successful today from the rest is their high self-esteem, a broad social network, and a willingness to take risks while carefully analyzing the market and differentiating both business activities and merchandise.

Nadezhda Kopytina is a case in point.[24] Nadezhda came to Moscow in 1988 to take exams for university admission but did not pass them. Going back and admitting her failure seemed shameful to her, so she decided to stay in Moscow and see what she could do to survive in the capital. Kopytina failed the exams again the following year and realized that the situation was becoming dire. Jobs were nowhere to be found, but Nadezhda had the chance to go to Poland with her friend. She grabbed a couple of irons and kettles with her and bartered them for a few Polish goods, mostly hair clips. For three years the trips either were complete financial disasters or brought only marginal profits. Nadezhda tried different strategies, buying toothpaste from Bulgaria, then curtains from Syria, videotapes from Singapore, and then T-shirts from China. But the goods either arrived damaged or the buyer for a particular product was nowhere to be found.[25]

Nadezhda was not satisfied with her marginal profits and, unlike most of her friends and peers, chose to borrow $20,000 USD to invest into her trading. At a time when most traders made profits of $100–$300 monthly and when apartments were sold for $5,000–$10,000 in most large cities, the amount was indeed astronomical and so was the risk. But it paid off, and Nadezhda sold all the merchandise that she acquired, profiting upward of 200 percent. Her friends and acquaintances were speechless and advised Kopytina to keep buying whatever she had bought in the first place. However, she had a better idea. Nadezhda saw that relying on a single product was extremely risky, and she recognized that particular designs could go out of fashion virtually overnight, bankrupting those who invested in them. "It was my school of marketing," comments Nadezhda now; instead of an easy profit, she chose to try out something entirely new and underrepresented on the Russian market.[26] She chose to import raw and processed fish and seafood products. Even though the first few years were challenging, to say the least, Kopytina states that she had "extreme confidence that everything would be fine at the end."[27]

In her early actions and to the present day, Nadezhda, like others in this subgroup of traders, came the closest to displaying the entrepreneurial mentality and thinking that many hoped—but most failed—to see emerge among shuttle traders of the 1990s. As a result, Kopytina acknowledges that nearly all her friends and acquaintances left the business in 1998 or shortly thereafter. She, on the other hand, became the founder and the CEO of Ledovo, a company that imports, produces, and distributes frozen and refrigerated seafood products with an operating budget of over a quarter billion US dollars. She received an "Entrepreneur of the Year" award in 2003, was named among the top ten most powerful and successful women of Russia by such leading journals as *Finansy, Kompaniia*, and *Kariera* in 2006, and owns and leads one of the largest Russian companies in the food sector. When assessing her early days, Kopytina says she can even now "pick up anything and go sell it on the street for the fun of it. Those days were great, it was so much fun."[28] She feels no resentment or shame, and she continues to diversify her business initiatives and personal activities as she has always done. In addition to expanding her company into the agricultural sector by growing mushrooms, for example, Kopytina is a successful writer, producer, educator, and even a singer.[29]

Success stories like Kopytina's are notable but exceptional. As noted earlier, approximately 90 percent of traders left the business after 1998, representing the "return" of the biographical model, or those who assumed other activities after they left the business. This group is too numerous to find any stable common denominators in their behavior or actions. They nonetheless had the strongest interest in their training and occupation prior to trading, compared to other two groups, and most treated trading as a temporary occupation. Furthermore, in a random 20-person sample of those who found professional employment after trading, all had a postgraduate (or university) education, and three had defended doctoral dissertations. Though the sample is too small and random to make any definitive judgment, it still suggests a slightly higher than average educational level. Admittedly, many were also reaching retirement age (55 for women and 60 for men) and chose to spend their time with grandchildren and on their dachas.

Lower trading profits and the changed nature of the trade had an important role to play but so did new economic possibilities—a common reference point among respondents. Elena, a university professor teaching English to linguistics students, recalled that she was attracted to trading when she realized that her teaching job paid less than the cost of public transportation to work. But after several years as a full-time trader, she picked up a few private lessons after 1998. By 2003, her regular teaching job (which she resumed in 2001) paid enough to cover basic necessities and private tutoring covered the rest. "I was glad to leave the trading and go back to what I love," she remembered. The benchmark for her stood at 30,000 rubles, or approximately $1,000 USD a month. Once she could make this amount by teaching English, she left trading without any regrets.

Other traders reported that the hardships of international peddling became unjustifiable for them, especially when other job opportunities became available. The list of those hardships should sound familiar by now (racketeering, corruption, physical exhaustion, shame, family problems, health problems, etc.), and grotesque or exaggerated stories made things even worse. If in the 1990s most fears were of the Russian Mafia, then in the first decade of the twenty-first century, traders complained that Egyptian, Turkish, and other authorities began routinely to jail traders from Russia who broke some rules unbeknownst to them; Russian embassies and consulates rarely offered any protection to those traders, and some people were rumored even to be stoned to death for a petty crime.[30] Yet overall there was no clear indicator guaranteeing a priori that particular traders were likely to leave the business and resume their old jobs or find employment elsewhere. Though the overwhelming majority of traders left the business, this group nonetheless demonstrated its successful adaptation to the socioeconomic instability that accompanied the collapse of the Soviet Union and the first decade thereafter.

Finally, the third group of shuttle traders has stayed in the business and continues with small-scale trading to the present day. But although their number is small, this group comes the closest of all three to identifying themselves as "necessity entrepreneurs" or as accidental traders. Talking to them at the present day, it becomes obvious that these traders have a rather low self-esteem; they often comment about the "rude but successful youngsters" who operate in the marketplace and about "those who made it big time," or the few of their friends who managed to use trading as a platform for their own small businesses. The traders' goal was and continues to be the immediate financial reward; they often do not see any value in analyzing the market dynamics or trying to expand or change their work patterns.

Yet their role and functions are significant. They became the only group of all shuttle traders to become and stay self-employed and demonstrated the sustainability of such an employment model with all its pros and cons. Moreover, if in the 1990s the traders were a diverse and even chaotic mix of people from all walks of life, in the first decade of the twenty-first century the traders who stayed in business formed the core of a clearly recognizable social group with its own occupational markers and vocabulary. Members of this group frequently use terminology like "the brick" or "the helper" that might have no meaning to an outsider, they recognize the limits and restrictions of their competitive environments, and they mastered the acceptable behavior and limits when dealing with the authorities (it does take a good deal of practice to know when and for what offense a bribe is expected and appropriate and the amount of the bribe that corresponds to each situation). Though complaining hard in the process, the representatives of this "stable" group learned the mechanisms and dynamics of the imperfect and ever-changing marketplace of new Russia.

Overall, the diversity of these biographical models once again demonstrates that the traders of the 1990s were not a coherent social group, and applying a common term like "entrepreneurs" to them is challenging. The lack of a common guild-like or occupational mentality might also explain why traders never aspired collectively to change anything, whether their relationship vis-à-vis the government or their resistance to racketeering. These people, of course, were linked to the same type of business, and if we look at entrepreneurship as any form of individual activity geared toward the acquisition of profit, then the traders could qualify as such. But if we look at entrepreneurship as a more complex set of values and initiatives, as most scholars have done, then the position of traders is less clear. For example, the term "entrepreneurship" could be interpreted as "a process of continuous search for patterns of change in consumers' tastes and demands for both goods and services; a process of satisfying those demands by the means of production organization and the finding of most innovative and optimal means of marketing, logistics, managements, and the delivery" of those goods and services. Finally, the term implies a "rational combination of the most optimal means of business that can be achieved through the informed, ingenuous and risky approach."[31] Most traders (except for the small success group), though often risk takers by the nature of what they did, nonetheless did not qualify for any features of that definition. Of the numerous standards and categories developed for qualifying a micro-, small, or large enterprise, traders failed to achieve even the minimum threshold as a "microbusiness."[32] Their role was significant in the 1990s and continues to be through the present, but it was not in achieving the status of small and large legal enterprises that could directly form the basis of the middle class in the new Russia.

To the same extent but on a smaller scale, we see the same patterns in the countries of the former socialist bloc and Yugoslavia. With some regional variations, the remnants of the trading survived there to the present, but such trading is not typically associated with small-business and entrepreneurial development.[33] In Romania, for example, one can encounter women peddling clothing (especially underwear) and small household goods even on the streets of Bucharest, yet residents do not fail to comment that peddlers are "just Roma, you know, gypsies." Though there is no indication that Roma as an ethnic group dominate peddling in Romania, the derogatory attitude and the choice of words used to describe peddling is indicative of popular notions of the trade. It is considered the activity of marginalized groups of people who are only slightly higher on the socioeconomic ladder than beggars. In Bulgaria retailing homegrown produce is seen as labor intensive and as a rather honorable task that continues to thrive, but shuttle trading has only a marginal existence. The same is true of much of former Yugoslavia, where only the sale of pirated video and audio materials survives to a sizeable and noticeable extent. These observations and examples are anecdotal and do not aspire to convey statistical accuracy. But they do highlight the notion that international and domestic peddling lingers at the verge of disappearance and is by no means favored as a way to earn a living. Furthermore, peddling is not seen as a gateway into private business, and aspiring entrepreneurs try to avoid it at all costs.

At the inception of this study, I aspired to demonstrate that for the former Soviet people, who from birth were indoctrinated into socialist norms of economic behaviors, international peddling became a school of capitalism, a way to learn how the free market functioned. Yet the more I researched the topic, the less evidence I saw to prove that this was actually the case. This is not to say that none of the traders emerged as successful or learned from their experiences. As the biographical models above demonstrated, some shuttle traders used their peddling activities as a platform for subsequently founding their own businesses. Yet these examples turned out to be proverbial exceptions that in turn proved the general point. The masses of people who participated in the trade during the 1990s largely treated it as an opportune moment in their lives with few long-term financial outcomes.

What role, then, did the shuttle trade play, and how do we assess its meaning and significance? To begin with, the shuttle trade confirmed that during times of massive political, economic, and social transformations, ad hoc and spontaneous forms of mass social mobilization can play a role as significant as any institutional development. Moreover, these spontaneous and widespread popular practices impacted the emerging social, legal, regulatory, free-market, and labor conditions in these societies. For example, we saw earlier that none of the participants of the trade aspired to change the border-control regulations. Yet collectively they have achieved just that—not only in Russia but in neighboring countries as well. They impacted the manufacturing and retailing sectors of both the domestic and international economies. They exposed the shortcomings of the regulations that governed the emerging small-business sector, and they demonstrated the personal risks of long absence away from home at a time when the social support system had all but collapsed. They also became the vehicle that changed, or at least challenged, old Soviet attitudes when it came to consumption and individual activity. In these ways shuttle traders became the actors who transformed the social space of the new Russia without ever aspiring to do so.

Yet they also remain the forgotten actors of the massive social transformation of the 1990s. The first post-Soviet years were ones of cheerful popular and academic optimism for a new Russia, though the scholars tended to hold on to their views for longer than ordinary people. Opinions had changed dramatically by the turn of the century, and few continue to assess the "transition" of the 1990s as the "Russian Boom" or the rise of "Russia's market economy."[34] Scholarly and popular opinions of the Russian economic performance and life experiences of the 1990s have changed, but as the two spheres have merged and morphed in traders' lives, the traders themselves remained significantly underrepresented in the scholarly perception of the tumultuous decade. The shuttle traders and their experiences challenged the separation of economic forces and its human meaning, and the traders became the salient force that transformed the social and economic space of the new Russia.

Notes

Introduction

1. The word "shuttle" (*chelnok*) is used by analogy with a shuttle used in weaving (a movable part that carries a thread back and forth).

2. Shuttle trading did not include small-scale peddling and women who sold domestic goods and food in the open markets; suitcase traders traveled abroad rather than domestically and resold merchandise that they did not produce at home. Most international peddlers were not previously involved in the Soviet shadow economy, and shuttle traders constituted a group highly distinct from street sellers and *babushka*s. Some street vendors (as opposed to shuttle traders) resold fruit (e.g., the number of banana traders was so significant in the 1990s that "Moscow must have been the only world capital in which slipping on a banana skin was an ever-present danger rather than a music-hall joke," Bridger, Kay, and Pinnick, *No More Heroines?*, 150), but the majority were engaged in selling produce from their own garden plots or selling their own meager possessions. For this form of retail trade, see ibid.

3. All of these points will be discussed in detail in the main body of the book; refer to pertinent sections for references.

4. "Chelnoki," *Delovaia gazeta*, no. 4–94, January 26, 2001.

5. E. Leontiev, "Chelnok ne professiia, a diagnoz," *Rossiiskaia Federatsiia*, no. 11 (1997): 50–51; also see explanation in note 6.

6. Gosudarstvennyi Komitet Rossiiskoi Federatsii po Statistike (hereafter, GKRFS), 162, 164. Statistics are given for 1994, though these numbers did not change substantially from year to year between 1991 and 1995. Many sources offer similar statistics, e.g., the Institute of Transition Economies estimated the unofficial shuttle trade in 1995–96 at $2.5–$3 billion USD each quarter, totaling $10–$12 billion annually (in addition to $1.5 billion USD confirmed officially). Overall, data and statistics on the volume of the shuttle trade (i.e., both its dollar value and the number of participants) are primarily derived from "Suitcase Trade Problems"; multiple publications, including Iakovlev, Golikova, and Kapralova, "Rossiiskie 'chelnoki,'" 84–106; Eder, Yakovlev, and Carkoglu, "Suitcase Trade." These estimates are also available in Humphrey, "Traders 'Disorder,'" 19–52; also E. Leontiev, "Chelnok ne professiia, a diagnoz," *Rossiiskaia Federatsiia*, no. 11 (1997): 50–51; Iakovlev, "Nepotopliaemyi chelnok"; G. Charodeev, "Nashi 'chelnoki' pokinuli bazary Stambula," *Izvestiia*, September 5, 1998.

7. E. Medvedeva, "Chelnoki pereimenovany v korobeinikov," *Izvestia,* October 28, 1998.

8. This number is based on the author's research, although a more precise number of women involved in this semilegal, often clandestine, business is impossible to calculate. Similar estimates have been made in the following works and range from 72 to 85 percent: Il'in and Il'ina, "Torgovtsy gorodskogo rynka"; Kandioti, "Pol v neformal'noi ekonomike"; Barsukova, "Zhenskoe predprinematel'stvo."

9. It is only with great hesitation that I use the term "transition" in this work. The term has been criticized for implying a transition from the centrally planned economy to Western-style free-market capitalism with all of its features almost preordained. In fact, the changes did not imply a predictable and inevitable outcome in only one form and shape. However, keeping these reservations in mind, the term "transition" helps to chronologically bracket the era of economic, political, social, and other changes in much of socialist Eurasia in 1985 (or 1988)–1998.

10. Sperling, *Organizing Women,* 155.

11. See, for example, Ball, "Lenin"; Davydov, *Nelegal'noe snabzhenie.*

12. See, for example, Hessler, *History of Soviet Trade*; Randall, "Legitimizing Soviet Trade."

13. See, for example, Ledeneva, *Russia's Economy of Favors.*

14. Humphrey, "Traders 'Disorder,'" 20.

15. See, for example, Wallace, Bedzir, and Chmouliar, "Spending, Saving"; Morawska, "Malleable Homo Sovieticus."

16. Keck-Szajbel, "Shop Around the Bloc," 374–76.

17. For further discussion of the trading patterns in the socialist bloc, see, for example, Kochanowski, *Tylnymi drzwiami*; Kochanowski, "Pioneers"; Dessewffy, "Speculators and Travelers"; Zatlin, "Scarcity and Resentment."

18. See, for example, Babb, *Field and Cooking Pot*; Clark, *Onions Are My Husband*; Salaff, *Working Daughters*; Seligmann, *Women Traders*; Wolf, *Factory Daughters.*

19. Humphrey, "Traders 'Disorder,'" 19–52; also Hohnen, *Market Out of Place?,* 4.

20. Chudinovskikh and Zhulin, *Ekonomiko-demographicheskie aspekty,* 14.

21. Though globalization is a multifaceted process with many global emitters, I use the term "westernization" here to underline the desire of people in the post-Soviet space to consume or approximate Western European and US brands, fashions, styles, everyday activities, and even lifestyles, though the diversification of consumer tastes has expanded in the 2000s.

22. Deniz Yükseker, "Shuttling Goods," 60.

23. Both quotes are from Eder, Yakovlev, and Carkoglu, "Suitcase Trade," 1.

24. Though contestable on some arguments, Klimova, "Shuttle Traders," presents a short discussion of the trade that might also be of interest to readers.

25. On the formal definition of "small businesses," private enterprise, and the deviation of shuttle trading from these forms of activities, see, for example, Ponomarev and Burtseva, "Malyi bizness."

26. For more information on the shuttle trade as an integral part of the gray market, refer to Holtom, "Shuttle Trade."

27. See, for example, Radaev, "Entrepreneurial Strategies."

28. Hass, "Trials and Tribulations." Italics are mine.

29. For further discussion, see Iakovlev, Golikova, and Kapralova, "Rossiiskie 'chel-

noki'"; Shcherbakova, "Siniia ptitsa"; Il'in and Il'ina, "Torgovtsy gorodskaogo rynka." Finally, as subsequent research has demonstrated, only a tiny proportion of these traders remained involved in peddling post-1998; most eventually returned to waged employment.

30. E.g., Marangos, "Preventive Therapy."

31. On the question of the systemic change in learning, knowledge, and motivation, see, e.g., Csaba, *Capitalism Revolution.*

32. Holtom, "Shuttle Trade."

33. Though all interviews were conducted in the 2000s, the respondents were asked to reflect on their shuttle-trading experiences back in the 1990s. Many of the respondents are no longer in the business; most left in 1998 (as discussed later in the work). These locations were chosen because of the centrality of the location (for Moscow) and to demonstrate regional variations (southern Russia for Krasnodar, the far eastern region for Khabarovsk). But many other towns and regions were evaluated as well.

34. This also explains some discrepancy in numbers throughout the book. For example, I could calculate the age of most respondents (including for short statements and interviews collected by others), but I limited a more substantive analysis to only in-depth interviews conducted for this study.

35. Ogloblin, "Gender Earnings Differential," 613.

36. Young, "Fetishizing the Soviet Collapse," 119. On the question of interdisciplinary borrowing, Young specifically refers to Cooper, *Colonialism in Question.*

37. Osborne and Rose, "Social Sciences," 367.

38. Bradshaw, Stenning, and Sutherland, "Economic Restructuring," 147.

1: Origins of the Shuttle Trade, 1987–91

1. Ryzhkov, *Desiat let*, 78–79.

2. Gorbachev, *Zhizn' i reformy*, 268.

3. "Opros naseleniia po reprezentativnoi obshcherossiiskoi vyborke ."

4. "Historical Crude Oil Prices."

5. *Strategiia reform*, 253.

6. RGANI, fond 2, opis 5, delo 45, l. 3.

7. Ibid., fond 9, opis 5, delo 33, ll. 168–170.

8. GARF, fond 5446, opis 149, delo 1439, ll. 72–94.

9. Ryzhkov, *Desiat' let*, 93.

10. GARF, fond 5446, opis 147, delo 374, l. 32.

11. Babikov, *Sorok let*, 161.

12. Ryzhkov, *Desiat' let*, 101.

13. Sinel'nikov, *Biudzhetnyi krizis.*

14. K. Z. Terekh, Minister of Trade of the USSR, "Informatiia o sostoianii torgovli otdel'nymi tovarami na 2 dekabria 1987 g," GARF, fond 5446, opis 148, delo 950, ll. 7, 8.

15. Blacker, *Hostage to Revolution*, 57.

16. V. G. Panskov, Vice-Chairman of the Ministry of Finance, and S. A. Sitarian, Vice-Chairman of the State Planning Committee, a report to the Soviet of Ministers, "O poriadke i srokakh osushchestvleniia radikal'noi perestroika finansovoi sistemy, perevoda ee na normativnuiu osnovu," April 12, 1988, GARF, fond 5446, opis 149, delo 1, l. 149.

17. *Izvestiia TsK CPSS,* no. 1 (1989): 48–50.

18. *Voprosy ekonomiki,* no. 1 (1990): 26–32.

19. RGASPI, fond 591, opis 1, delo 90, ll. 3, 11, 12.

20. Ibid., fond 591, opis 1, delo 112, l. 36; see also delo 243, l. 174.

21. Interview with Tatiana O., Moscow, 2007.

22. Koriagina, *Plantye uslugi*, 139.

23. Ibid., 142–43.

24. Ibid., 143.

25. Ibid., 149.

26. Ibid., 144.

27. Wallace, Bedzir, and Chmouliar, "Spending, Saving," 14.

28. "Russkii biznes." Comparatively, an average monthly wage was 200 rubles.

29. For example, a female respondent from Novorossiysk (aged 35 in 1988; interview conducted on June 12, 2004) reported that she made eight trips to Poland in 1988–89 with a business passport as a Komsomol activist and was never once searched or inspected at the border crossing.

30. "Russkii biznes."

31. See also Wallace, Bedzir, and Chmouliar, "Spending, Saving," 14–15.

32. State Bank of the Soviet Union, "Material k dokladu o sotsial'no-ekonomicheskom polozhenii strany. 2 ianvaria 1990 g.," RGAE, fond 2324, opis 33, delo 741, ll. 54–58.

33. *Toplivno-energeticheskii kompleks*, 108–9; *Toplivo i energetika Rossii*, 158, 408–9.

34. Gorbachev, "Ob osnovnykh napravleniiakh," 8.

35. Goldman, *What Went Wrong?*, 159, 160; also "Iz zapiski v TsK KPSS 'O predlozhenii po uregulirovaniiu zadolzhnosti razvivaiushchikhsia stran, po vystupleniiu tovarishcha M.S. Gorbacheva v OON,'" in Protocol of Politburo of the Central Committee of the Communist Part of the USSR, August 23, 1989, RGANI fond 89, opis 9, delo 23, ll. 3, 4.

36. GARF, fond 5446, opis 163, delo 1192, l. 113.

37. *Narodnoe khoziaistvo v SSSR v 1985–1990 gg.*

38. VTsIOM, Report of 1991, 85.

39. Report of March 25, 1991, "O rabote upravleniia denezhnogo obrashcheniia v 1990 godu," RGAE, fond 2324, opis 33, delo 741, ll. 172–74, 179.

40. RGANI, fond 2, opis 5, delo 403, l. 3.

41. GARF, fond 5446, opis 162, delo 268, ll. 109, 116.

42. Ibid., fond 5446, opis 150, delo 288, l. 113.

43. Interview with Liudmila N., Moscow, 2007.

44. Dridze, *Pereraspredelenie dokhodov vnutri*, 25.

45. "Otnoshenie naseleniia, 8.

46. "O gosudarstvennom plane."

47. Pleshakov, "Ne delit'," 2.

48. Ryzhkov, *Desiat' let*, 225–26.

49. Sokolova, "Stali li my zhit' luchshe?," 20–21.

50. Report VTsIOM of May 22, 1990, "Otnosheniie naselelniia k vozmozhnosti uskorennogo perekhoda k rynochnoi ekonomike," GARF, fond 5446, opis 162, delo 2, l. 225.

51. Kostomarskii, Khakhulina, and Shpil'ko, "Obshchestvennoe mnenie," 8.

52. White, *Gorbachev and After*, 239, 247.

53. Ryzhkov, *Desiat' let*, 225–26.

54. Numerous works attest to the deep sociocultural transformation that was required of Soviet people in order to accept, morally and socially, the culture of private enterprise and trading; see Borisov, "Transformatsiia sotsio-kul'turnykh tsennostei."

55. Sokolova, "Stali li my zhit' luchshe?," 20–21.

56. Hohnen, *Market Out of Place?*, 23; see also Fische-Ruge, *Survival in Russia*.

57. See also Wallace, Bedzir, and Chmouliar, "Spending, Saving," 15.

58. Grigorieva, *Okhrana materinstva*, 116.

59. Interview with Tatiana O., Moscow, 2007.

60. Nenashev, *Poslednee pravitel'stvo*, 53–54; Gorbachev, *Zhizn' i reformy*, 575–76.

61. Gruzdeva, *Zhenskaia bezrabotitsa*, 29–30, 36.

2: The "Golden Age" of the Shuttle Trade and Its Structure

1. Elena, age 42, from an interview conducted in Khabarovsk in 2008. Elena currently works as an interior designer but used to "shuttle" in the 1990s, selling fur coats in Khabarovsk.

2. See chapter 1 for more data on gender inequality in the shuttle trade.

3. *Narodnoe khoziaistvo RSFSR. 1922–1972*; *Narodnoe khoziaistvo v RSFSR v 1987*; *Narodnoe khoziaistvo v RSFSR v 1993 g.*

4. *Itogi Vsesoiuznoi perepisi*, 13; *Vestnik statistiki* 12 (1974): 90; Gruzdeva, *Zhenskaia bezrabotitsa*, 9–10.

5. *Vestnik statistiki* 8 (1991): 56.

6. *Vestnik statistiki* 2 (1991): 53.

7. Balibalova, "Zhenshchina," 32.

8. *Vestnik statistiki* 2 (1991): 54.

9. Ibid., 58.

10. See, for example, "Russia" (Human Rights Watch report); Khotkina, *Sexual Harassment*.

11. "Russia."

12. Ibid.

13. Busee, "Embeddedness of Tax Evasion," 142.

14. *Gendernye problemy*, 88, 90, 92.

15. Gruzdeva, *Zhenskaia bezrabotitsa*, 29–30, 36. Overall, there is an abundance of research on the feminization of unemployment and poverty in post-Soviet Russia.

16. Research on this topic is exhaustive; see, for example, Tartakovskaia, *Gendernaia sotsiologiia*, 171–89; Buckley, *Post-Soviet Women*; Peterson, "Traditional Economic Theories."

17. Historians have also identified the specific gender setup of Soviet families as contributing to women's exodus from official employment into "dishonorable" businesses like trade. For further discussion, refer to Ashwin, *Gender, State and Society*, 90–105.

18. Samarina, *Polozhenie zhenshchin*, 9–27.

19. Liudmila G., from an interview with the author, Moscow, 2007.

20. *Gendernye problemy*, 83–84.

21. Numbers vary from region to region and from urban to rural locations. For example, the numbers are 21 percent for Moscow and 26 percent for Saratov. Arutiunian, *Transformatsiia postsovetskikh natsii*, 139.

22. For discussions that support this view or argue the contrary, see Iakovlev, Golikova, and Kapralova, "Rossiiskie 'chelnoki'"; Shcherbakova, "Siniia ptitsa"; Il'in and Il'ina, "Torgovtsy gorodskogo rynka."

23. From an interview with the author.

24. Kopylov, "Kupit' po-russki."

25. Volkov, *Violent Entrepreneurs*, 30–31.

26. For some of the underlying reasons for this choice, see Ashwin, *Gender, State and Society.*

27. Ibid.

28. Kiblitskaya, "Once we were Kings."

29. Bruno, "Culture of Entrepreneurship," 69.

30. There is a long and well-documented history of Soviet women using bargaining and petitioning as effective survival strategies; see, for example, Viola, "Bab'i bunty"; Alexopoulos, *Stalin's Outcasts.*

31. [Name suppressed for publication], an interview by the author, 2007.

32. In the interviews, women respondents almost universally complained that they were "real victims" of their life circumstances, whereas males in approximately 60 percent of cases indicated that all it took to solve the problem was to send a woman there (*"da poslat' tuda babu, i vse dela!"*).

33. Interview with Elena Samoilova, Moscow, May 2007; see also Yükseker, "Trust and Gender"; G. Charodeev, "Nashi chelnoki pokinuli bazary Stambula," *Izvestiia,* September 5, 1998.

34. Interview with Galina, Krasnodar, February 2008.

35. For further reiteration of this point, refer to Baskakova, "Sovremennye tendentsii"; Rakovskaia, "Osobennosti"; Ashwin and Bowers, "Do Russian Women?"; Peterson, "Traditional Economic Theories."

36. Presidency of the Russian Federation, "O svobode torgovli." Italics are mine.

37. For further information, refer to GATT VII, WTO; Orders of the President of the Russian Federation no. 630, "O vremennom importnom tarife RF," June 4, 1992; no. 856 "Ob utverzhdenie poriadka tamozhennoi stoimosti tovarov," November 5, 1992; GTK resolutions no. 01/12/248, December 18, 1992; no. 557, December 3, 1992; and the final signing of the act "On customs tariff" of July 1, 1993. For subsequent discussion of applicability and shortcomings of the above-mentioned normative acts, see "Tenevaia ekonomika."

38. In addition to sources cited in the previous footnote, please refer to *Vedomosti Soveta narodnykh deputatov i Verkhovnogo Soveta RF,* no. 6 (1992); "Vedomstvennoe prilozhenie," *Rossiiskaia gazeta,* no. 146 (August 3, 1996); *Tamozhennyi kodeks Rossiiskoi Federatsii,* and numerous interviews and published life stories of traders.

39. For a comparative analysis of the examples of Eastern and Central Europe and the lack of and subsequent development of the legal mechanisms of control, refer to Sik and Wallace, "Open-Air Markets"; Wallace, Shmulyar, and Berdiz, "Investing in Social Capital."

40. See note 4; also E. Leontiev, "Chelnok ne professiia, a diagnoz," *Rossiiskaia Federatsiia* 11 (1997): 50–51.

41. L. Nikonova, "Mama ushla na bazar," *Zerkalo nedeli. Chelovek,* June 19–25, 2004.

42. Kapralova and Karaseva, "Neregistriruemyi import potrebitel'skikh tovarov."

43. Eder, "From Suitcase Merchants," fn. 6.

44. "O poriadke peremeshcheniia fizicheskimi litsami," especially Article 2.A; 3–4.

45. It has been argued that the content of the resolution and its implementation were unconstitutional as they vested too much personal authority in individual representatives of the government; especially problematic was its correlation with Article 15 of Section 3. For further discussions, refer to *Kostitutsionnoe pravo.*

46. Kopylov, "Kupit' po-russki."

47. An anonymous letter from a reader, "Melkooptovaia izmena gosudarstvu s velikim budushchem," to the *News of Central Asia and the World* (Novosti Srednei i Tsentral'noi Azii i vsego mira, Informatsionnoe agenstvo Fergana), August 15, 2003.

48. *Torgovat' po-russki.*

49. Zhilkin, "Chelnochestvo v Rossii."

50. Glushkin, "Peresechenie granitsy."

51. "Istoriia chelnochnogo predprinematel'stva."

52. "O peremeshchenie tovarov."

53. *Rossiiskaia gazeta (Vedomstvennoe prilozhenie)* no. 1469, August 3, 1996; *Rossiiskaia gazeta* no. 148, August 7, 1996; *Sobranie zakonodatel'stva Rosskiiskoi Federatsii.*

54. *Tamozhennyi kodeks Rossiiskoi Federatsii.*

55. The ECU, or European currency unit, was worth 5,269 rubles as of June 15, 1996, or approximately 1.05 times more than 1 USD ($1 = 5,053 rubles).

56. For a discussion on the post-1998 trade, refer to Yakovlev, Golikova, and Kapralova, "Rossiiskie chelnoki."

57. See also Holtom, "Small-Scale Cross-Border Trading."

58. There were also some indirect players in the trade. For example, in 1989, Bobe wholesale clothing market in Bangkok, Thailand, supplied clothing, shoes, children's items, and the infamous padded "Alaska" winter coats to Central European traders. All their goods were later resold in Poland and eventually made their way into the Soviet Union.

59. Interview with Tamara by the author.

60. Chudinovskikh and Zhulin, *Ekonomiko-demografcheskie aspekty,* 20–21.

61. Wallace and Stola, *Patterns of Migration,* 30.

62. Ibid., 17. See also Iglicka, "Economics of Petty Trade."

63. Iglicka, "Economics of Petty Trade," 98.

64. Chudinovskikh and Zhulin, *Ekonomiko-demografcheskie aspekty,* 22.

65. From a personal interview with the author.

66. Eder, Yakovlev, and Carkoglu, "Suitcase Trade," 8.

67. Ibid. See also pertinent discussions above.

68. Ibid., 2–8.

69. Interview with the author.

70. Lan'kov, *Rossiiskie "chelnoki" v Koree.*

71. Interview with the author.

72. Shabaev, *Posobie,* 6.

73. Ibid., 11.

74. 'V Rossii davno est' srednii klass—'chelnoki,'" *Delovaia Pressa* 4, no. 94 (January 26, 2001).

75. Elena Vorobieva, "Chemodan—okzal—istoriia," *Ogoniok* 8 (2006).

76. It should be recognized, however, that the procedure has changed dramatically since the mid-1990s.

77. I interviewed one history professor from Pakistan who saw a trader from Russia and one social scientist who reported that he had heard of several people from the former Soviet Union who had obtained medical treatment in Pakistan and also purchased some items for resale. Neither of these two reports seemed to offer substantial evidence of the existence of trade with Pakistan.

78. After 2000 the remnants of the shuttle trade changed to include, in limited ways, Finland (for refrigerators, computers) and Germany (for used cars).

79. "'Chelnoki'—zalezhalyi tovar?" *Rodnaia Gazeta,* www.turkey-info.ru.

80. Mel'nichenko, Bolonini, and Zavatta, "Rossiiskii chelnochnyi bizness."

81. From an interview.

82. Various press organs and private individuals wrote about the fact that weapons were easily and readily available on the black market, with the average price for an AK-47 ranging from $500 USD (clean) to $150 USD (marked in a police database for a crime). Though the author could not personally interview anyone involved in the sale of more substantial military equipment (e.g., nuclear-weapon launchers), there are numerous references to such instances in personal (published) accounts and the press. See, for example, Daria Luganskaia, "Makarov za 100 dollarov," for *BBC Moscow,* December 1, 2012; *Izvestia,* January 10, 1995; Robert Seely, *Russo–Chechen Conflict, 1800–2000: A Deadly Embrace* (Portland, OR: Frank Cass, 2001); Maxim Kniazkov, "US Certifies Theft of Russian Nuclear Material Has Occurred," *Agence France Presse,* February 23, 2002.

83. Ershov, "Denezhno-kreditnaia sfera," 20.

84. GKRFS, 162, 164. Many sources offer similar statistics; e.g., the Institute of Transition Economies estimated the unofficial shuttle trade in 1995–96 at $2.5–$3 billion USD each quarter; totaling $10–$12 billion annually (in addition to $1.5 billion USD confirmed officially). As cited in Iakovlev, "Nepotopliaemyi chelnok."

85. Eder, "From Suitcase Merchants," 5.

86. "Sotsial'nye izmeneniia."

87. "Denezhnye dokhody naseleniia."

3: Women Traders

1. This is a literary adaptation of a song, "Chelnoki," written by Iakov Kofman, in Russian, in 1994.

2. Similar estimates had been made in the following works and range from 72 to 85 percent: Il'in and Il'ina, "Torgovtsy gorodskogo rynka"; D. Kandioti, "Pol v neformal'noi ekonomike"; Barsukova, "Zhenskoe predprinematel'stvo."

3. From an interview with the author.

4. Note that I use this number as a sample of only one among many field sessions. For a more detailed discussion of the total number of interviews and their analyses, see the introduction.

5. See, for example, Meshcherkina, "Zhiznennyi put'"; Rotkich and Temkina, "Soviet Gender Contracts." All this can also be found in surveys and opinion polls conducted by the National Foundation for Public Opinion.

6. Meshcherkina, *Ustanaia istoriia,* 224–25.

7. For a further discussion of work choices and their close relation to private roles of women, see Turbine and Riach, "Right to Choose."

8. Meshcherkina, *Ustanaia istoriia,* 230–45.

9. Ibid., 249–52.

10. Ibid., 245.

11. The Public Opinion Foundation (VTsIOM), opinion poll conducted in June 2005; also Klimova, "Shuttle Trade."

12. Il'in and I'lina, "Torgovtsy gorodskogo rynka"; Mashkova and Zaitseva, "Praktika zhenskogo predprenimatel'stva."

13. Since traders were not interested in legalizing their enterprises and the recording

patterns were not gender-specific, even in cases when some legalization was sought, only surveys done by sociologists and other fieldwork-trained specialists are available to present a testable social profile of an entrepreneur in the retail and wholesale sector.

14. Welter, "Female Entrepreneurship," 13.

15. E.g., Earle and Sakova, "Business Start-Ups"; Welter and Smallbone, "Distinctiveness of Entrepreneurship."

16. Hisrich and Fulop, "Role of Women Entrepreneurs," 109.

17. Gruzdeva, *Zhenskaia bezrabotitsa*, 34–35.

18. Il'in and I'lina, "Torgovtsy gorodskogo rynka."

19. Yakovlev, Golikova, and Kapralova, "Rossiiskie chelnoki"; Shcherbakova, "Siniaia ptitsa."

20. White, *Russia's New Politics*, 148.

21. Welter, "Female Entrepreneurship," 15.

22. See, for example, Feige, "Underground Activity"; Knaack, "Collapse"; Yeager, *Institutions, Transition Economics*. For the role of social capital in the acquisition of external financing, as well as gender differences in utilizing the capital, see Manolova et al., "Breaking the Family."

23. For a discussion of informal institutions and key definitions, consider Welter and Smallbone, "Entrepreneurship and Enterprise Strategies."

24. From an interview conducted for this project, Khabarovsk, 2007.

25. White, *Russia's New Politics*, 178–81.

26. From an interview with a trader, 2012.

27. From an interview with a trader, Tamara, age 47.

28. Salmenniemi, Karhunen, and Kosonen, "Between Business and *Byt*," 86.

29. Ibid., 87–88.

30. Tamara from Khabarovsk.

31. Interview with Tatiana, Krasnodar, 2008.

32. From an interview with a woman, age 42, officially unemployed, as appeared in Shcherbakova, "Siniaia ptitsa."

33. Ibid.

34. From interviews conducted in Krasnodar in 2007 and 2008.

35. From an interview with a trader.

36. Interview with Elena, Khabarovsk.

37. Similar statements can be found in nearly all works that used oral history and biographical narratives as their core.

38. From an interview with a male respondent, age 44, as published in Shcherbakova, "Siniaia ptitsa."

39. From an interview with a male respondent, age 39, ibid.

40. From interviews conducted in 2005, 2007, and 2008.

41. Paloian, *Chelnoki v Vengrii*, esp. 22–23. It is significant that the novel was written in 1996, but it did not find a publisher until 12 years later. It was considered too mundane and trivial in the mid-1990s, and it took a change in shuttle-trading dynamics to find any interest in the topic.

42. Vladimirov, *Chelnok*.

43. Pilkington, *Looking West?*, xvii.

44. "Chelnoki—dvigatel' kitaisko-rossiiskoi torgovli," *Izvestia*, January 27, 1999, as cited in Chudinovskikh and Zhulin, *Ekonomiko-demograficheskie aspekty*, 25–27.

45. Hohnen, *Market Out of Place?*, 61 (for both).

46. For further discussion, see Pilkington, *Looking West?*, 170–71.

47. Yükseker, "Shuttling Goods," 60.

4: The Price of Success

1. Kopylov, "Kupit' po-russki."

2. "Istoriia chelnochnogo predprinematel'stva."

3. Ibid.

4. Il'ina, "Shtrikhi k portretu 'chelnoka,'" 17.

5. Lan'kov, *Rossiiskie Chelnoki v Koree.*

6. An interview, conducted February 3, 2005.

7. *Biznes-zhurnal*, July 7, 2005; Klimova, "Chelnoki."

8. "Istoriia chelnochnogo predprinematel'stva."

9. Ibid.

10. A. Serafimova, "Chelnochnitsy," *Agenstvo russkoi informatsii*, November 26, 2002.

11. Kopylov, "Kupit' po-russki."

12. V. Koldak, "Odinokoi zhenshchine predostavliaetsia obshchezhitie. Gde nedorogo perenochevat' provintsialu?" *Rossiiskaia gazeta*, January 10, 2007.

13. An anonymous letter from a reader, "Melkooptovaia izmena gosudarstvu s velikim budushchem," to the *News of Central Asia and the World* (Novosti Srednei i Tsentral'noi Azii i vsego mira, Informatsionnoe agenstvo Fergana), August 15, 2003.

14. M. Kucheriavenko, "Poslednii chelnok," *Rossiiskaia gazeta*, September 9, 2003.

15. "Kushat' bol'she hochetsia."

16. Ibid.

17. Ibid.

18. "Istoriia chelnochnogo predprinematel'stva."

19. O. Novgorodtseva, "Banda voznikla stihiino," *Delo. Obshchestvenno-pravovaia gazeta*, January 18, 2006.

20. Mashkova and Zaitseva, "Praktika zhenskogo predprinematel'stva"; see also Tiuriukanova, "Gendernye aspekty."

21. Mashkova and Zaitseva, "Praktika zhenskogo predprinematel'stva."

22. Zhilkin, "Chelnochestvo v Rossii."

23. Kopylov, "Kupit' po-russki."

24. For a lengthier and more nuanced discussion of these issues, see Mukhina and Denisova, *Rural Women.*

25. *Rossiiskii statisticheskii ezhegodnik, 2002*, 127.

26. From an interview.

27. From an interview.

28. Though not all stories were identical among the respondents of the interviews, most women reported that they knew a woman or several women who had followed this path.

29. Zhilkin, "Chelnochestvo v. Rossii."

30. Ibid.

31. Similar stories are also cited in T. Parkhacheva, "Ot nakazaniia osvobozhdena," *Samara informatsionnaia*, January 12, 2001.

32. A. Serafimova, "Chelnochnitsy," *Agenstvo russkoi informatsii*, November 26, 2002.

33. Ibid.

34. An interview conducted by the author with Emma, May 2007.

35. *Rossiiskii statisticheskii ezhegodnik, 2002*, 125, 253–55.

36. Ibid.

37. For an in-depth discussion of the evolution of family law in the Soviet Union, consult "The Politics of Private Life," in Mukhina and Denisova, *Rural Women*.

38. Ibid.

39. *Zhenshchiny v SSSR*, 55.

40. Ibid.

41. Kopylov, "Kupit' po-russki."

42. L. Nikonova, "Mama ushla na bazaar," *Zerkalo nedeli. Chelovek*, June 19–25, 2004.

43. Ibid.

44. Ibid.

45. Ibid.

46. Ibid.

47. Ibid.

48. See, for example, Sclare, "Female Alcoholic"; Ketcham, et al, *Beyond the Influence*.

49. About half of all women discussed their short-term relations in the interviews.

50. A personal interview conducted by the author.

51. E. Karetnikov, "Seks-chelnochnitsy," *Ekspress-gazeta*, January 24, 2003.

52. Ibid.

53. *Rossiiskii statisticheskii ezhegodnik, 2002*, 250.

54. An interview conducted by the author with Nadezhda K., May 2007.

55. *Rossiiskii statisticheskii ezhegodnik, 2002*, 246.

56. Wilke, *Abortion*.

57. *Rossiiskii statisticheskii ezhegodnik, 2002*, 212.

58. Ibid.

59. R. L. Galkin, "Sud'ba chelnoka," *Gazeta "Duel'*," no. 18 (40), September 9, 1997.

60. Zhilkin, "Chelnochestvo v Rossii."

61. Il'ina, "Shtrikhi k portretu 'chelnoka,'" 19.

62. Kopylov, "Kupit' po-russki."

5: Where Did All the Women Go?

1. The statement was widely published in most newspapers and press organs, including *Izvestiia* and *Vecherka*.

2. GKO stands for *Gosudarstvennoe Kratkosrochnoe Obiazatel'stvo*.

3. Goldman, *Petrostate*, 77.

4. Poretskina, "'Chelnochnyi' biznes," 25–26.

5. *Delovaia pressa*, no. 3 (45), February 5, 2001.

6. Cited in "Banki i birzhy," a publication of the Central Bank of the Russian Federation, April 21, 1999.

7. As cited in Poretskina, "'Chelnochnyi' biznes," 24.

8. Thus, in 2006 Moscow was declared the most expensive city in the world. It moved from fourth position, which it had occupied in 2005. *Times (London)*, June 26, 2006.

9. Kapeliushnikov, *Nestandartnye formy*, 19.

10. Ekaterina Shcherbakova, "Regiony Rossii."

11. For example, see Kobzev, "Prigranichnyi Kitaii."

12. For comparable examples, see Lin and Tse, "Flexible Sojourning"; Cheater, "Transcending the State?"; Hannerz, *Transnational Connections*.

13. Schendel, "Spaces of Engagement."

14. Kholtslener, "Eastern Porosity."

15. Public Opinion Foundation, "Shuttle Trade," June 30, 2005.

16. Dmitrii Raichev, "Slavianskii bazaar," *Rossiiskaia gazeta* (August 2, 2011).

17. This case was widely publicized in the media. See, for example, *Ogonek* 42 (2009).

18. This is also a widely discussed topic; the number of articles, TV programs, and forums is endless. See, for example, a parents' forum on the topic "Chinese goods are dangerous," http://www.kid.ru/forum2007/t9209.html.

19. For example, Repetskaia, *Organizovannaia prestupnost'*.

20. Volkov, *Violent Entrepreneurs*.

21. See, for example, Gorodnitskii, "Peredel rynka."

22. See, for example, Mironova, "Rynki smeniat kryshu."

23. The same has been repeatedly asserted in various press organs like *Delovaia gazeta* 3, no. 45 (February 5, 2001).

24. Gansvind, *Bizness est' bizness*; Burkina, *40 sekretov uspeha*.

25. Natalia Radulova, "Ledi chelnok," *Ogonek* 8 (February 26, 2006).

26. Ibid.

27. Gansvind, *Bizness est' bizness*.

28. N. Kopytina, interview with *Business Klass* (October 28, 2011), available in video format from video.mail.ru

29. Kopytina authored *Hochu popast' v Forbes: Put' k milliardu Nadezhdy Kopytinoi*, and produced the highly successful movie *Vanechka*.

30. For more accounts along these lines, see Leonid Kolosov, director of the documentary *Chelnoki. Shkola Vyzhivaniia* (2012).

31. Ivliev, "Stimulirovanie predprinematel'skoi aktivnosti," 35–36.

32. To see the full range of the discussion, consider Federal'noe zakonodatel'stvo Rossiiskoi Federatsii, N 129-FZ, "O gosudarstvennoi registratsii fizicheskikh lits i individual'nykh predprinematelei"; and "Kriterii otneseniia predpriiatii k kategoriiam mikro, malykh i srednikh," TASIS, 1998.

33. Much of this information was collected during my extensive research trip to Romania, Bulgaria, Serbia, Montenegro, Croatia, and Poland in the spring and summer of 2012.

34. The references here are to the two works listed below, but many others shared the general disposition that Russia was on a path to market democracy or had already achieved it. See Aslund, *How Russia Became*; and Layard and Parker, *Coming Russian Boom*.

Bibliography

Archives

Gosudarstvennyi Arkhiv Rossiiskoi Federatsii (GARF, State Archive of the Russian Federation), fond 5446, opis 147, delo 374; opis 148, delo 950; opis 149, dela 1, 1439; opis 150, delo 288; opis 162, dela 2, 268; opis 163, delo 1192.

Rossiiskii Gosudarstvennyi Arkhiv Ekonomiki (RGAE, Russian State Archive of Economics), fond 2324, opis 33, delo 741, ll. 54–58.

Rossiiskii Gosudarstvennyi Arkhiv Noveishei Istorii (RGANI, Russian State Archive of Contemporary History), fond 2, opis 5, dela 45, 403; fond 9, opis 5, delo 33; fond 89, opis 9, delo 23.

Rossiiskii Gosudarstvennyi Arkhiv Sotsialno-Politicheskoi Istorii (RGASPI, Russian State Archive of Socio-Political History), fond 591, opis 1, dela 90, 112.

Financial and Other Reports

"Denezhnye dokhody naseleniia v 1995 g." Goskomstat RF, 1996.

Federal'noe zakonodatel'stvo Rossiiskoi Federatsii, N 129-FZ. "O gosudarstvennoi registratsii fizicheskikh lits i individual'nykh predprinematelei."

Gosudarstvennyi Komitet Rossiiskoi Federatsii po Statistike. *Sotial'no-ekonomicheskoe polozhenie Rossii, 1993–1994 gg.* Moscow, 1994.

Itogi Vsesoiuznoi perepisi naseleniia 1970 g. Vol. 2. Moscow, 1972.

Kostitutsionnoe pravo: vostochnoevropeiskoe obozrenie. Nos. 3–4, 1994.

"Kriterii otneseniia predpriiatii k kategoriiam mikro, malykh i srednikh." TASIS, 1998.

Narodnoe khoziaistvo RSFSR, 1922–1972. Statisticheskii ezhegodnik. Moscow, 1972.

Narodnoe khoziaistvo v RSFSR v 1987. Statisticheskii ezhegodnik. Moscow, 1988.

Narodnoe khoziaistvo v RSFSR v 1993 g. Statisticheskii ezhegodnik. Moscow, 1994.

Narodnoe khoziaistvo v SSSR v 1985–1990 gg. Statisticheskie sborniki. Moscow: Finansy i statistika.

"O gosudarstvennom plane na 1991 god po sferam vedeniia Soiuza SSSR." Decree of the Supreme Soviet of the USSR No. 1897-1. January 12, 1991.

"O peremeshchenie tovarov fizicheskimi litsami cherez tamozhennuiu granitsu Rossiiskoi Federatsii." Gosudarstvennyi tamozhennyi komitet Rossiiskoi Federatsii, Prikaz ot 15 avgusta 1994 g. No. 408.

"O poriadke peremeshcheniia fizicheskimi litsami cherez tamozhennuiu granitsu Rossiiskoi Federatsii tovarov, ne prednaznachennykh dlia proizvodstvennoi ili inoi kommercheskoi deiatel'nosti." Postanovlenie Soveta Ministrov—Pravitel'stva RF ot 23 dekabria 1993, no. 1322, articles 2.A; 3–4.

"Opros naseleniia po reprezentativnoi obshcherossiiskoi vyborke v 100 naselennykh punktakh 44 oblastei, kraev i respublik Rossii." *Dominanty. Pole mneniia,* no. 15, April 9–10, 2005.

Orders of the President of the Russian Federation. No. 630, "O vremennom importnom tarife RF," June 4, 1992; No. 856, "Ob utverzhdenie poriadka tamozhennoi stoimosti tovarov," November 5, 1992.

"Otnoshenie naseleniia k sokrashchenniu chasti rabochikh mest i uvol'neniiu zanimaiushchikh ikh rabotnikov." Report by the All-Russian (formerly All-Soviet) Center for Research of the Public Opinion (VTsIOM), July 12, 1989.

Presidency of the Russian Federation. "O svobode torgovli." *Ukaz ot 29 ianvaria 1992 g.* no 65.

Rossiiskii statisticheskii ezhegodnik, 2002. Moscow: Goskomstat Rossii, 2002.

"Russia: Neither Jobs nor Justice: State Discrimination against Women in Russia." *A Human Rights Watch Report 7,* no. 5 (March 1995).

Sobranie zakonodatel'stva Rosskiiskoi Federatsii, no. 30, article 3660, July 22, 1996.

Strategiia reform v prodool'stvennom i agrarnom sektorakh ekonomiki byvshego SSSR. Washington, D.C.: World Bank Publication, 1993.

"The Suitcase Trade Problems Research Project of the State University–Higher School of Economics" (*Issledovaniia GU-VShE po problemam chelnochnoi torgovli*), within the framework of the project "Razrabotka organizatsionno-metodologicheskikh podhodov k sovershenstvovaniiu metodiki doschetov ob'emov vneshnei torgovli" (co-sponsored by the Rosstat, Bank of Russia, and the Federal Customs and Border Administration), 2003.

Tamozhennyi kodeks Rossiiskoi Federatsii. Moscow: Norma, 1996.

"Tenevaia ekonomika i kontrol' funktsii tamozhennyh organov." *Materialy i predlozhenia MVD RF dlia prorabotki problem tenevoi ekonomiki k doklady Soveta Bezopasnosti RF rukovodstvu strany, ot 1997 g.*

Toplivno-energiticheskii kompleks SSSR v 1990g. Moscow: VNIIKTEP, 1991.

Toplivo i energetika Rossii. Moscow: MTERF, 1999.

Vestnik statistiki, no. 12 (1974), nos. 2 and 8 (1991).

Zhenshchiny v SSSR. Statisticheskie materialy. Moscow: Finansy i statistika, 1990.

Newspapers

Agenstvo russkoi informatsii

Bizness-zhurnal

Delo. Obshchestvenno-pravovaia gazeta

Delovaia gazeta

Delovaia pressa

Ekspress-gazeta

Gazeta "Duel'"

Izvestiia

Izvestiia TsK KPSS

News of Central Asia and the World / Novosti Srednei i Tsentral'noi Azii
Ogoniok
Rodnaia gazeta
Rossiiskaia Federatsiia
Rossiiskaia gazeta
Rossiiskaia gazeta (Vedomstvennoe prilozhenie)
Russkaia zhizn'
Samara informatsionnaia
Svobodnyi kurs
Vedomosti Soveta narodnykh deputatov i Verkhovnogo Soveta RF
Voprosy ekonomiki
Zerkalo nedeli. Chelovek

Articles and Monographs

Aidis, R., and S. Estrin. *Institutions, Networks and Entrepreneurship Development in Russia: An Exploration*. Working paper 833. Ann Arbor, MI: Williams Davidson Institute, 2006.

Alexopoulos, Golfo. *Stalin's Outcasts: Aliens, Citizens, and the Soviet State, 1926–36*. Ithaca, NY: Cornell University Press, 2003.

Arutiunian, Iu. V. *Transformatsiia postsovetskikh natsii: Po materialam etnosotsiologicheskikh issledovanii*. Moscow: Nauka, 2003.

Ashwin, Sarah, ed. *Adapting to Russia's New Labour Market. Gender and Employment Behavior*. London: Routledge, 2006.

———, ed. *Gender, State and Society in Soviet and Post-Soviet Russia*. London: Routledge, 2000.

———. "The Influence of the Soviet Gender Order on Employment Behavior in Contemporary Russia." *Sociological Research* 41, no. 1 (2002): 21–37.

Ashwin, Sarah, and E. Bowers. "Do Russian Women Want to Work?" In *Post-Soviet Women from the Baltic to Central Asia*, edited by M. Buckley, 21–38. Cambridge: Cambridge University Press, 1997.

Aslund, Anders. *How Russia Became a Market Economy*. Washington, D.C.: Brookings, 1995.

Babb, Florence. *Between Field and Cooking Pot: The Political Economy of Market Women in Peru*. Austin: University of Texas Press, 1998.

Babikov, N. K. *Sorok let v pravitel'stve*. Moscow: Respublika, 1993.

Balibalova, D. I. "Zhenshchina v usloviiakh perehoda k rynochnoi ekonomike." In *Feminizm i rossiiskaia kul'tura. Sbornik trudov*, edited by G. A. Tishkin. St. Petersburg: Gosudarstvennaia Akademiia Kul'tury, 1995.

Ball, Alan. "Lenin and the Question of Private Trade in Soviet Russia." *Slavic Review* 43, no. 3 (Fall 1984): 399–412.

Barsukova, S. U. "Zhenskoe predprinematel'stvo." *Sotsiologicheskie issledovania*, no. 9 (1999): 75–84.

Baskakova, M. E. "Sovremennye tendentsii polozjeniia zhenshchin v sfere zaniatosti i na rynke truda." In *Materialy nauchnoi konferentsii "Gendernye issledovaniia v Rossii: problemy vzaimodeistviia i perspektivy razvitiia,"* 65–68. Moscow: RAN, 1996.

Blacker, C. D. *Hostage to Revolution: Gorbachev and Soviet Security Policy, 1985–1991*. New York: Council on Foreign Relations Press, 1993.

Bonnell, Victoria E., and Thomas B. Gold, eds. *The New Entrepreneurs of Europe and Asia: Patterns of Business Development in Russia, Eastern Europe, and China.* New York: M. E. Sharpe, 2002.

Borisov, Vadim. "Transformatsiia sotsio-kul'turnykh tsennostei v khode ekonomicheskikh preobrazovanii v Rossii." Paper delivered at Workshop on the Restructuring of Employment and the Formation of a Labour Market in Russia, sponsored by the Economic and Social Research Council, Dubrovnik, Croatia, September 1998.

Bradshaw, Michael, Alison Stenning, and Douglas Sutherland. "Economic Restructuring and Regional Change in Russia." In *Theorizing Transition: The Political Economy of Post-Communist Transformation,* edited by John Pickles and Adrian Smith. London: Routledge, 1998.

Bridger, Sue, Rebecca Kay, and Kathryn Pinnick. *No More Heroines? Russia, Women and the Market.* New York: Routledge, 1996.

Bridger, Sue, and F. Pine, eds. *Surviving Post-Socialism: Local Strategies and Regional Responses in Eastern Europe and the Former Soviet Union.* London: Routledge, 1998.

Bruni, A., S. Gherardi, and B. Poggio. "Doing Gender, Doing Entrepreneurship: An Ethnographic Account of Intertwined Practices." *Gender, Work and Organization* 11, no. 4 (2004): 406–29.

Bruno, Marta. "Women and the Culture of Entrepreneurship." In *Post-Soviet Women: From the Baltic to Central Asia,* edited by Mary Buckley, 56–75. Cambridge: Cambridge University Press, 1997.

Buckley, Mary, ed. *Perestroika and Soviet Women.* Cambridge: Cambridge University Press, 1992.

———, ed. *Post-Soviet Women: From the Baltic to Central Asia.* Cambridge: Cambridge University Press, 1997.

———. *Women and Ideology in the Soviet Union.* New York: Harvester Wheatsheaf, 1989.

Burawoy, Michael, and Katherine Verdery, eds. *Uncertain Transition: Ethnographies of Change in the Postsocialist World.* Lanham, MD: Rowman and Littlefield, 1999.

Burkina, L. *40 sekretov uspeha.* Moscow: Aplina Business Books, 2006.

Busee, Eva. "The Embeddedness of Tax Evasion in Russia." In *Economic Crime in Russia,* edited by Alena V. Ledeneva and Marina Kurkchiyan. London: Kluwer Law International, 2000.

Cheater, A. P. "Transcending the State? Gender and Borderline Constructions of Citizenship in Zimbabwe." In *Border Identities: Nation and State at International Frontiers,* edited by T. M. Wilson and D. Hastings, 191–214. New York: Cambridge University Press, 1998.

Chudinovskikh, O. S., and A. B. Zhulin. *Ekonomiko-demographicheskie aspekty chelnochnogo biznesa v Rossii.* Moscow: Teis, 2001.

Clark, Garcia. *Onions Are My Husband: Survival and Accumulation by West African Market Women.* Chicago: University of Chicago Press, 1994.

Cooper, Frederick. *Colonialism in Question: Theory, Knowledge, History.* Berkeley, CA: University of California Press, 2005.

Corrin, Chris. *Superwomen and the Double Burden: Women's Experience of Change in Central and Eastern Europe and the Former Soviet Union.* Charlottesville: University of Virginia Press, 1992.

Csaba, L. *The Capitalism Revolution in Eastern Europe: A Contribution to the Economic Theory of Systemic Change.* Aldershot, UK: Edward Elgar, 1995.

Davydov, A. Iu. *Nelegal'noe snabzhenie sovetskogo naseleniia i vlast'*. Moscow: Nauka, 2002.

Dessewffy, T. "Speculators and Travelers: The Political Construction of the Tourist in the Kádár Regime." *Cultural Studies* 16, no. 1 (2002): 44–62.

Dridze, T. *Pereraspredelenie dokhodov vnutri sem'i kak faktor differentsiatsii blagosostoianiia*. Moscow: RAN, 1989.

Earle, John, and Zuzana Sakova. "Business Start-Ups or Disguised Unemployment? Evidence on the Character of Self-Employment from Transition Economies." *Labour Economics* 7 (2000): 575–601.

Eder, M., A. Yakovlev, and A. Carkoglu. "The Suitcase Trade between Turkey and Russia: Microeconomics and Institutional Structure." Series WP4/2003/07, a publication of the State University of the Higher School of Economics (Gosudarstvennyi Universitet Vysshei Shkoly Ekonomiki). Moscow: GU VShE, 2003.

Eder, Mine. "From Suitcase Merchants to Organized Informal Trade? The Case of Laleli District in Istanbul." Unpublished ms.; prepared at Bogazici University, 2003.

Einhorn, Barbara. *Cinderella Goes to Market: Citizenship, Gender and Women's Movements in East Central Europe*. New York: Verso, 1993.

Ershov, Mikhail V. "Denezhno-kreditnaia sfera i ekonomicheskii krizis." *Analiticheskii vestnik Soveta Federatsii SF RF*, no. 113 (2000).

Farnsworth, Beatrice, and Lynne Viola, eds. *Russian Peasant Women*. Oxford, UK: Oxford University Press, 1992.

Feige, Edgar. "Underground Activity and Institutional Change: Productive, Protective, and Predatory Behavior in Transition Economies." In *Transforming Communist Political Economies*, edited by Charles Tilly, Joan Nelson, and Lee Walker, 21–34. Washington, D.C.: National Academy Press, 1997.

Filtzer, D. *Soviet Workers and the Collapse of Perestroika*. Cambridge: Cambridge University Press, 1994.

Fische-Ruge, Lois. *Survival in Russia: Chaos and Hope in Everyday Life*. Boulder, CO: Westview Press, 1993.

Gansvind, I. I., ed., *Bizness est' bizness: 60 pravdivyh istorii o tom, kak prostye liudi nachali svoe delo i preuspeli*. Moscow: Izdatel'stvo "Sekret firmy," 2005.

Gendernye problemy v Rossii: po natsional'nym publikatsiiam, 1993–2003 gg. Moscow: "Aleks," 2004.

Glass, Christy. "Gender and Work during Transition. Job Loss in Bulgaria, Hungary, Poland and Russia." *East European Politics and Societies* 22, no. 4 (Fall 2008): 757–83.

Glushkin, O. "Peresechenie granitsy." *Russkaia zhizn'*, no. 1 (2006).

Goldman, Marshall I. *Petrostate: Putin, Power, and the New Russia*. Oxford: Oxford University Press, 2008.

———. *What Went Wrong with Perestroika?* New York: Norton, 1992.

Gorbachev, Mikhail S. "Ob osnovnykh napravleniiakh vnutrennei i vneshnei politiki SSSR. Doklad na S'ezde narodnykh deputatov SSSR." May 30, 1990. Moscow: Politizdat, 1990.

———. *Zhizn' i reformy. Kniga 1*. Moscow: Novosti, 1995.

Gorodnitskii, Anton. "Peredel rynka: ubita vdova kriminal'nogo avtoriteta Gery Obeziany." *Kriminal*, March 4, 2012.

Grigorieva, N. S., ed. *Okhrana materinstva i detstva v Rossii i Velikobritanii*. Moscow: Meditsina, 2002.

Gruzdeva, E. B. *Zhenskaia bezrabotitsa v Rossii (1991–1994 gg)*. Moscow: Moskovskii institut mirovoi ekonomiki i mezhdunarodnykh otnoshenii RAN, 1995.

Hannerz, U. *Transnational Connections: Culture, People, Places.* London: Routledge, 1996.

Hass, Jeffrey K. "Trials and Tribulations of Learning the Market: Culture and Economic Practice in Russia's Market Transition." *The Carl Beck Papers in Russian and East European Studies,* no. 1706 (October 2005).

Hertz, Noreena. *Russian Business Relationships in the Wake of Reform.* Oxford: Macmillan, 1996.

Hessler, Julie. *A Social History of Soviet Trade: Trade Policy, Retail Practices, and Consumption, 1917–1953.* Princeton, NJ: Princeton University Press, 2004.

Hisrich, Robert D., and Gyula Fulop. "The Role of Women Entrepreneurs in Hungary's Transition Economy." *International Studies of Management and Organization* 24, no. 4 (1994): 100–117.

"Historical Crude Oil Prices, Table." *Financial Trend Forecaster,* a publication of Capital Professional Services. January 16, 2008.

Hohnen, Pernille. *A Market Out of Place? Remaking Economic, Social, and Symbolic Boundaries in Post-Communist Lithuania.* Oxford: Oxford University Press, 2003.

Holtom, Paul. "Shuttle Trade and New Border Regimes." *Russian Regional Perspectives* 1, no. 3 (2006), www.iiss.org.

———. "Small-Scale Cross-Border Trading in Kaliningrad's Borderlands." In *The Kaliningrad Challenge: Options and Recommendations,* edited by Hanne-M. Birckenbach and Christian Wellmann, 152–68. Munster: LIT Verlag, 2003.

Humphrey, Caroline. "Creating a Culture of Disillusionment: Consumption in Moscow, a Chronicle of Changing Times." In *Worlds Apart: Modernity through the Prism of the Local,* edited by Daniel Miller. London: Routledge, 1995.

———. "Traders 'Disorder' and Citizenship Regimes in Provincial Russia." In *Uncertain Transition: Ethnographies of Change in the Postsocialist World,* edited by Michael Burawoy and Katherine Verdery. Lanham, MD: Rowman and Littlefield, 1999.

Hurley, A. E. "Incorporating Feminist Theories into Sociological Theories of Entrepreneurship." *Women in Management Review* 14, no. 2 (1999): 54–62.

Iakovlev, A. A., V. V. Golikova, N. L. Kapralova. "Rossiiskie 'chelnoki'—ot predprinematelei ponevole k integratsii v rynochnoe khoziaistvo." *Mir Rossii,* no. 2 (2007): 84–106.

Iakovlev, Andrei. "Nepotopliaemyi chelnok." *Special Report of the Center of Regional Applied Research* (Tsentr regional'nykh prikladnykh issledovanii). September 2005.

Iglicka, K. "The Economics of Petty Trade on the Eastern Polish Border." In *The Challenge of East-West Migration for Poland,* edited by K. Iglicka and K. Sword. London: Macmillan, 1999.

Il'in, Vladimir, and Marina Il'ina. "Torgovtsy gorodskogo rynka: shtrikhi k sotsial'nomu portretu." *EKO,* no. 5 (1998).

Il'ina, M. A. "Shtrikhi k portretu 'chelnoka': keis-stadi veshchevogo rynka g. Syvtyvkara." In *Sotsial'naia stratifikatsiia: istoriia i sovremennost. Tezisy Vserossiiskoi nauchnoi konferentsii.* Syvtyvkar: Syv GU, 1996.

"Istoriia chelnochnogo predprinematel'stva v Rossii." *Sotsial'naia real'nost'.* April 18, 2007.

Ivliev, A. A. "Stimulirovanie predprinematel'skoi aktivnosti v sfere rossiiskogo malogo biznesa." PhD diss., Moscow, 2004.

Izyumov, A., and I. Razumova. "Women Entrepreneurs in Russia: Learning to Survive the Market." *Journal of Developmental Entrepreneurship* 5, no. 1, (2000): 1–19.

Kandioti, D. "Pol v neformal'noi ekonomike: problemy i napravleniia analiza." In *Neformal'naia ekonomika. Rossiia i mir,* edited by T. M. Shanin. Moscow: Logos, 1999.

Kapeliushnikov, R. *Nestandartnye formy zaniatosti i bezrabotitsy v Rossii.* Moscow: GU-VShE, 2004.

Kapralova, N., and L. Karaseva. "Neregistriruemyi import potrebitel'skikh tovarov: otsenka mashtabov." *Voprosy statistiki,* no. 3 (2006).

Katz, K. *Gender, Work and Wages in the Soviet Union: A Legacy of Discrimination.* London: Palgrave, 2001.

Kay, Rebecca, ed. *Gender, Equality and Difference during and after State Socialism.* Basingstoke, UK: Palgrave Macmillan, 2007.

———. *Men in Contemporary Russia. The Fallen Heroes of Post-Soviet Change?* Burlington, VT: Ashgate, 2006.

Keck-Szajbel, Mark. "Shop Around the Bloc: Trader Tourism and Its Discontent on the East German-Polish Border." In *Communism Unwrapped: Consumption in Cold War Eastern Europe,* edited by Paulina Bren and Mary Nauburger. Oxford: Oxford University Press, 2012.

Ketcham, Katherine, William F. Asbury, Mel Schulstad, Arthur P. Ciaramicoli. *Beyond the Influence: Understanding and Defeating Alcoholism.* New York: Batnam, 2000.

Kholtslener, T. "Eastern Porosity: An Anthropology of Cross-Border Trade and Contact in the Russian Far East." A paper delivered at the international conference "Russkaia Tsivilizatsiia v Severnoi Pasifike," May, 21–22, 2009, Vladivostok, Russia.

Khotkina, Zoya, ed. "Sexual Harassment at the Work Place." *Seminar Material on Women's Rights in Russia.* Moscow, 1996.

———. "Women in the Labour Market: Yesterday, Today and Tomorrow." In *Women in Russia: A New Era in Russian Feminism,* edited by Anastasia Posadskaya. London: Verso Press, 1994.

Kilbitskaya, Marina. "'Once We Were Kings': Male Experiences of Loss of Status at Work in Post-Communist Russia." In *Gender, State and Society in Soviet and Post-Soviet Russia,* edited by Sarah Ashwin, 90–105. New York: Routledge, 2000.

———. "Russia's Female Breadwinners: The Hanging Subjective Experience." In *Gender, State and Society in Soviet and Post-Soviet Russia,* edited by Sarah Ashwin. New York: Routledge, 2000.

Klimova, Svetlana. "Chelnoki: begstvo ot nuzhdy ili pogonia za shansom?" *Sotsial'naia real'nost',* no. 2 (2006).

———. "Shuttle Traders: Escaping Poverty or Pursuing Opportunity." *Social Reality* 2 (2006).

Knaack, Ruud. "The Collapse of the Russian Economy: An Institutional Explanation." In *Economic Institutions, Markets and Competition,* edited by Bruno Dallago and Luigi Mittone. Cheltenham, UK: Edward Elgar, 1995.

Kobzev, Dmitrii. "Prigranichnyi Kita." *Novosti Saratova,* 19 April 2008.

Kochanowski, J. "Pioneers of the Free Market Economy? Unofficial Commercial Exchange between People from the Socialist Bloc Countries (1970s and 1980s)." *Journal of Modern European History* 8, no. 2 (2010): 196–218.

———. *Tylnymi drzwiami. Czarny rynek w Polsce, 1944–1989.* Warsaw: Neriton, 2010.

Kopylov, O. "Kupit' po-russki. Za chem ezdili 'chelnoki' i kuda oni ischezli?" *Svobodniy kurs,* June 8, 2007.

Koriagina, T. I. *Plantye uslugi v SSSR.* Moscow: Ekonomika, 1990.

Kostomarskii, V. L., L. A. Khakhulina, and S. P. Shpil'ko. *Obshchestvennoe mnenie o perehode k rynochnoi ekonomike. Nauchnyi doklad.* Moscow: VTsIOM, 1991.

Koval, Vitalina, ed. *Women in Contemporary Russia.* Oxford, UK: Berghahn Books, 1995.

Kuehnast, Kathleen. "From Pioneers to Entrepreneurs: Young Women, Consumerism, and the 'World Picture' in Kyrgyzstan." *Central Asian Survey* 4 (December 1998): 639–54.

Kuehnast, Kathleen, and Carol Nechemias, eds. *Post-Soviet Women Encountering Transition: Nation Building, Economic Survival, and Civic Activism.* Washington, D.C.: Woodrow Wilson Center, 2004.

"Kushat' bol'she hochetsia, chem rabotat' na chestnom predpriiatii." Interview 6, conducted by the Fond Liberal Mission (*Liberal'naia missiia*), under the auspices of the project Shadow Russia (*Tenevaia Rossiia*).

Lafont, Suzanne, ed. *Women in Transition: Voices from Lithuania.* New York: State University of New York Press, 1998.

Lan'kov, Andrei. *Rossiiskie "chelnoki" v Koree.* Production for Korean State Radio Company KBS, 1996, http://www.lankov.oriental.ru/d30.shtml (accessed in June 2007).

Lapidus, G. "The Interaction of Women's Work and Family Roles in the USSR." *Women and Work: An Annual Review* 3 (1988): 87–121.

Layard, Richard, and John Parker, *The Coming Russian Boom.* New York: Free Press, 1996.

Ledeneva, Alena. *How Russia Really Works.* Ithaca, NY: Cornell University Press, 2006.

———. *Russia's Economy of Favors: Blat, Networking and Informal Exchange.* Cambridge: Cambridge University Press, 1998.

Ledeneva, Alena V., and Marina Kurkchiyan, eds. *Economic Crime in Russia.* London: Kluwer Law International, 2000.

Lin, G., and P. Tse., "Flexible Sojourning in the Era of Globalization: Cross-Border Population Mobility in the Hong Kong–Guangdong Border Region." *International Journal of Urban and Regional Research* 25 (2005): 867–94.

Lo, Bobo. *Soviet Labour Ideology and the Collapse of the State.* New York: St. Martin's Press, 2000.

Mamonova, Tatyana. *Women's Glasnost vs. Naglost. Stopping Russian Backlash.* New York: Praeger, 1993.

Manolova, T. S., R. V. Eunni, and B. S. Gyoshev. "Institutional Environments for Entrepreneurship: Evidence from Emerging Economies in Eastern Europe." *Entrepreneurship: Theory and Practice* 32, no. 1 (2008): 203–18.

Manolova, T. S., I. M. Manev, N. M. Carter, and B. S. Gyoshev. "Breaking the Family and Friends' Circle: Predictors of External Financing Usage among Men and Women Entrepreneurs in a Transition Economy." *Venture Capital* 8, no. 2 (2006): 109–32.

Marangos, John. "Preventive Therapy: The Neoclassical Gradualist Model of Transition from Central Administration to Market Relations." *The Carl Beck Papers in Russian and East European Studies,* no. 1604 (October 2002).

Marsh, R., ed. *Women in Russia and Ukraine.* Cambridge: Cambridge University Press, 1996.

Mashkova, E. V., and I. Zaitseva, "Praktika zhenskogo predprenimatel'stva v monoindustrial'nom gorode." In *Formirovanie gendernoi kul'tury u studencheskoi molodezhi. Sbornik statei i referatov,* 99–122. Naberezhnye chelny: Femina, 1995.

Mel'nichenko, Tatiana, Alberto Bolonini, and Roberto Zavatta. "Rossiiskii chelnochnyi biznes. Obshchaia kharakteristika i zvaimosviaz' s ital'ianskim rynkom." *National'nyi Institut Sistemnykh Issledovanii Problem Predprinematel'stva* (National Institute for Research of Problems of Entrepreneurship), 1997.

Meshcherkina, E. Iu., ed. *Ustanaia istoriia i biografiia: Zhenskii vzgliad.* Moscow: RAN, 2004.

———. "Zhiznennyi put' i biografiia: preemstvennost' sotsiologicheskikh kategorii." *Sotsis,* no. 7 (2002): 61–67.

Millard, Frances. "Women in Poland: The Impact of Post-Communist Transformation." *Journal of Area Studies,* no. 6 (1995): 60–73.

Mironova, Daria. "Rynki smeniat kryshu." *Moskovskie Novosti* 329, July 27, 2012.

Moghadam, Valentine. *Democratic Reform and the Position of Women in Transitional Economies.* Oxford: Clarendon Press, 1993.

Morawska, Ewa. "The Malleable Homo Sovieticus: Transnational Entrepreneurs in Post-Communist East Central Europe." *Communist and Post-Communist Studies* 32 (1999): 359–78.

Mukhina, I., and L. Denisova. *Rural Women in the Soviet Union and Post-Soviet Russia.* New York, London: Routledge, 2010.

Nenashev, M. *Poslednee pravitel'stvo SSSR. Lichnosti. Svidetel'stva. Dialogi.* Moscow: Krom, 1993.

Ogloblin, Constantin G. "The Gender Earnings Differential in the Russian Transition Economy." *Industrial and Labor Relations Review* 52, no. 4 (July 1999): 602–27.

Olimpieva, Irina, and Olga Pochenkova, eds. *Neformal'nia ekonomika v post-sovetskom prostranstve: Problemy issledovania i regulirovania.* St. Petersburg: TsNSI, 2003.

Osborne, Thomas, and Nikolas Rose. "Do the Social Sciences Create Phenomena?" *British Journal of Sociology* 50, no. 3 (1999): 367–96.

Paloian, Genrikh. *Chelnoki v Vengrii.* Moscow: Izdatel'stvo zhurnala 'Iunost', 2008.

Parry, Jonathan, and Maurice Bloch. *Money and the Morality of Exchange.* Cambridge: Cambridge University Press, 1989.

Peterson, J. "Traditional Economic Theories and Issues of Gender: The Status of Women in the United States and the Former Soviet Union." In *The Economic Status of Women under Capitalism: Institutional Economic and Feminist Theory,* edited by J. Peterson and D. Brown. Cheltenham, UK: Edward Elgar, 1994.

Pickles, John, and Adrian Smith, eds. *Theorizing Transition: The Political Economic of Post-Communist Transformation.* London: Routledge, 1998.

Pilkington, Hilary, ed. *Gender, Generation, and Identity in Contemporary Russia.* New York: Routledge, 1996.

———, ed. *Looking West? Cultural Globalization and Russian Youth Cultures.* University Park: Pennsylvania State University Press, 2002.

Pleshakov, L. "Ne delit', a zarabatyvat'. Interviu s L. I. Abalkinym." *Ogonek,* no. 41 (October 1989): 2.

Ponomarev, S. M., and M. G. Burtseva. *Malyi bizness, ego mesto i rol' v rynochnoi ekonomike.* Khabarovsk: Rossiiskii Universitet Kooperatsii, 2007.

Poretskina, Evgeniia. "'Chelnochnyi' bizness i ego osobennosti v Sankt-Peterburge." *Sotsial'no-ekonomicheskie issledovaniia,* no. 5 (2006): 24–31.

"Rabota za granitsei—kak ne popast' v rabstvo." Report prepared by the Non-Governmental Women's Organization "Modar" in Dushanbe, Tajikistan, Moscow, 2006.

Radaev, Vadim V. "Entrepreneurial Strategies and the Structure of Transaction Costs in Russian Business." In *The New Entrepreneurs of Europe and Asia: Patterns of Business Development in Russia, Eastern Europe, and China,* edited by Victoria E. Bonnell and Thomas B. Gold, 191–213. New York: M. E. Sharpe, 2002.

———. "Evolutsiia organizatsionnyh form v usloviiakh rastushchego rynka (na primere rossiiskoi roznichnoi torgovli)." Gosudarstvennyi universitet Vyskhaia Shkola Ekonomiki. Series WP4: Sotsiologiia rynkov. Moscow: GU VShE, 2006.

Rai, Shirin, ed. *International Perspectives on Gender and Democratization.* London: Macmillan, 2000.

———,ed. *Women in the Face of Change: Soviet Union, Eastern Europe and China.* London: Routledge, 1992.

Rakovskaia, O. A. "Osobennosti stanovleniia professional'noi kar'ery zhenshchin." In *Gendernye aspekty sotsial'noi transformatsii, demografiia i sotsiologiia, Vypusk 15,* 111–28. Moscow: Istitut sotsial'no-ekonomicheskikh problem narodonaseleniia, 1996.

Randall, Amy E. "Legitimizing Soviet Trade: Gender and the Feminization of the Retail Workforce in the Soviet 1930s." *Journal of Social History* 37, no. 4 (Summer 2004): 965–90.

Repetskaia, A. L. *Organizovannaia prestupnost'. Tenevaia ekonomika. Kriminal'nyi rynok Rossii.* Moscow: Iurlitinform, 2010.

Rotkirch, A. *The Man Question. Loves and Lives in Late 20th Century Russia.* Helsinki: University of Helsinki, 2000.

Rotkirch, A., and A. Temkina. "Soviet Gender Contracts and Their Shifts in Contemporary Russia." *Idantutkimus—The Finnish Review of East European Studies,* no. 2 (1997): 6–24.

"Russkii biznes: kooperativy." *Ekspert-Sibir* 7, no. 149, February 19–25, 2007.

Ryzhkov, N. I. *Desiat let velikikh potriasenii.* Moscow: Assotsiatsiia "Kniga Prosveschenie, Miloserdie," 1995.

Salaff, Janet W. *Working Daughters of Hong Kong: Filial Piety or Power in the Family?* New York: Columbia University Press, 1994.

Salmenniemi, Suvi, Paivi Karhunen, and Riitta Kosonen. "Between Business and *Byt:* Experiences of Women Entrepreneurs in Contemporary Russia." *Europe-Asia Studies* 63, no. 1 (January 2011): 77–98.

Samarina, O. V. *Polozhenie zhenshchin na rynke truda. Bibliotechka profsoiuznogo aktivista,* no. 10. Moscow: Profizdat, 1998.

Schendel, Van W. "Spaces of Engagement: How Borderlands, Illegal Flows, and Territorial States Interlock." In *Illicit Flows and Criminal Things: States, Borders, and the Other Side of Globalization,* edited by Van Schendel and I. Abraham, 38–68. Bloomington: Indiana University Press, 2005.

Sclare, A. Balfour. "A Female Alcoholic." *British Journal of Additions* 60 (1970): 99–107.

Seligmann, Linda, ed. *Women Traders in Cross-Cultural Perspective: Mediating Identities, Marketing Wares.* Stanford, CA: Stanford University Press, 2001.

Selm, Bert van. *The Economics of Soviet Break-up.* London: Routledge, 1997.

Shabaev, Aleksandr. *Posobie dlia nachinaiushchego "chelnoka."* Moscow: Argus, 1996.

Shanin, T. M. *Neformal'naia ekonomika. Rossiia i mir.* Moscow: RAN, 1999.

Shcherbakova, Ekaterina. "Regiony Rossii." *Naselenie i obshchestvo, Istitut Demografii Gosudarstvennogo Universiteta—Visshaia Shkola Ekonomiki* 277, 19 February 2007.

Shcherbakova, I. "Siniia ptitsa rossiiskikh chelnokov." *Sotsial'naia real'nost,* no. 10 (2006).

Sik, E., and C. Wallace. "The Development of Open-Air Markets in East-Central Europe." *International Journal of Urban and Regional Research* 23, no. 4 (November 1999): 697–714.

Sinel'nikov, S. G. *Biudzhetnyi krizis v Rossii: 1985–1995.* Moscow: Evrasiia, 1995.

Sokolova, G. N. "Stali li my zhit' luchshe?" *Sotsiologicheskie issledovaniia,* no. 1 (1990).

Solnick, S. *Stealing the State: Control and Collapse in Soviet Institutions.* Cambridge, MA:

Harvard University Press, 1999.

"Sotsial'nye izmeneniia v 1992–1995 godakh." http://www.yabloko.ru.

Sotsial'nye transformatsii i polozhenie zhenshchin v Rossii: Materialy mezhdunarodnoi nauchnoi konferentsii v Ivanovo 3–4 marta 1995 g. Ivanovo: IvGU, 1995.

Sperling, Valerie. *Organizing Women in Contemporary Russia: Engendering Transition.* Cambridge: Cambridge University Press, 1999.

Tartakovskaia, I. N. *Gendernaia sotsiologiia.* Moscow: "Variant," 2005.

Tiuriukanova, E. V. "Gendernye aspekty realizatsii prava na svobodnoe peredvizhenie." In *Prava zhenshchin v Rossii: issledovania real'noi praktiki ikh sobliudenia i massovoe soznanie,* 112–43. Moscow: MTsGI, 1998.

Torgovat' po-russki. Documentary by NTV channel, aired on November 15, 2006.

Turbine, Vikki, and Kathleen Riach. "The Right to Choose or Choosing What's Right? Women's Conceptualization of Work and Life Choices in Contemporary Russia." *Gender, Work and Organization* 19, no. 2 (March 2012): 165–87.

Viola, Lynne. "Bab'i bunty and Peasant Women's Protest during Collectivization." In *Russian Peasant Women,* edited by Beatrice Farnsworth and Lynne Viola, 189–205. Oxford: University Press, 1992.

Vladimirov, Vitalii. *Chelnok.* Moscow: Vest-Konsalting, 2008.

Volkov, Vadim. *Violent Entrepreneurs: The Use of Force in the Making of Russian Capitalism.* Ithaca, NY: Cornell University Press, 2002.

Wallace, Claire, Vasil Bedzir, and Oksana Chmouliar. "Spending, Saving, or Investing Social Capital: The Case of Shuttle Traders in Post-Communist Central Europe." *East European Series,* no. 43. Vienna, 1997.

Wallace, Claire, O. Shmulyar, and B. Berdiz. "Investing in Social Capital: The Case of Small-Scale, Cross-Border Traders in Post-Communist Central Europe." *International Journal of Urban and Regional Research* 23, no. 4 (November 1999): 751–70.

Wallace, Claire, and Dariusz Stola, eds. *Patterns of Migration in Central Europe.* New York: Palgrave, 2001.

Welter, Friederike. "Female Entrepreneurship in Transition Economies: The Case of Lithuania and Ukraine." *Feminist Economics* 13-2 (April 2007): 157–83.

Welter, Friederike, and David Smallbone. "The Distinctiveness of Entrepreneurship in Transition Economies." *Small Business Economics* 16, no. 4 (2001): 249–62.

———. "Entrepreneurship and Enterprise Strategies in Transition Economies: An Institutional Perspective." In *Small Firms and Economic Development in Developed and Transition Economies: A Reader,* edited by David Kirby and Anna Watson, 95–114. Burlington, VT: Ashgate, 2003.

Welter, Friederike, D. Smallbone, and N. B. Isakova, eds. *Enterprising Women in Transition Economies.* Burlington, VT: Ashgate, 2006.

White, Stephen. *Gorbachev and After.* Cambridge: Cambridge University Press, 1991.

———. *Russia's New Politics: The Management of a Postcommunist Society.* Cambridge: Cambridge University Press, 2000.

Wilke, J. C. *Abortion: Questions and Answers.* Cincinnati, OH: Hayes Publishing, 1985.

Wolf, Diane. *Factory Daughters: Gender, Household Dynamics, and Rural Industrialization in Java.* Berkeley: University of California Press, 1992.

Woodruff, David. *Money Unmade: Barter and the Fate of Russian Capitalism.* Ithaca, NY: Cornell University Press, 1999.

Yakovlev, A. A., V. V. Golikova, and N. L. Kapralova. "Rossiiskie chelnoki—ot predprinimatelei ponevole k integratsii v rynochnoe khoziaistvo." *Mir Rossii* 16, no. 2 (2007): 84–106.

Yeager, Timothy. *Institutions, Transition Economics and Economic Development.* Oxford: Westview Press, 1999.

Young, Glennys. "Fetishizing the Soviet Collapse: Historical Rupture and the Historiography of (Early) Soviet Socialism." *Russian Review* 66 (January 2007): 95–122.

Yükseker, Deniz. "Shuttling Goods, Weaving Consumer Tastes: Informal Trade between Turkey and Russia." *International Journal of Urban and Regional Research* 31, no. 1 (March 2007): 60–72.

———. "Trust and Gender in a Transnational Market: The Public Culture of Laleli, Istanbul." *Public Culture* 16, no. 1 (Winter 2004): 45–65.

Zatlin, J. R. "Scarcity and Resentment: Economic Sources of Xenophobia in the GDR, 1971–1989." *Central European History* 40, no. 4 (2007): 683–720.

Zhilkin, O. "Chelnochestvo v Rossii: novaia zhiznennaia strategiia v period ekonomicheskikh reform (na primere Irkutskoi oblasti)." In *Neformal'nia ekonomika v post-sovetskom prostranstve: Problemy issledovania i regulirovania,* edited by Irina Olimpieva and Olga Pochenkova. St. Petersburg: TsNSI, 2003.

Zhurzhenko, Tatiana. "Gender and Identity Formation in Post-Socialist Ukraine: The Case of Women in the Shuttle Business." In *Feminist Fields: Ethnographic Insights,* edited by Rae Anderson, Sally Cole, and Heather Howard-Bobiwash. Orchard Park, NY: Broadview Press, 1999.

Index

abortions, 17, 108, 113, 116, 121
acceleration (economy). *See* perestroika
accommodations during the trade, 60, 63, 68, 102–3, 106–7; *see also* lodging
alcoholism, 24, 108, 116–19
All Russian Center for Public Opinion, 133
America, 68, 82, 90, 92, 94, 96
anti-drinking campaign, 21, 23–25
anxiety among traders, 108; *see also* health problems
Armani, 68, 96
Armenia, 38, 129, 136
Asian financial crisis of 1997, 125

Bagrationovsk, 104
banking system (incl. lack of), 84
Bari, 69
Barnaul, 99, 102
barter, as part of the shuttle trade, 21, 30, 32, 37, 60–61, 139
Belorussia, 38, 105, 106
biographical trajectories of traders, 139–42
Birobidzhan, 66–67
birth rates, *also* birth rates among traders, 74–75, 109, 113–14, 121
black market, 6, 37, 93–95
Black Monday of 1998, the, 125–26
boarding schools, 108
Bologna, 69
border controls, 10–11, 56, 66, 97, 103, 131, 144
border-crossing centers, 58, 118
border regions (incl. "frontier"), 132–33

brands, and brand names, 16, 48, 93–95, 116; *see also* Armani; Gucci; Versace
bribes. *See* corruption
Bulgaria, 53, 59, 60, 63, 94, 115, 139, 143

"camels," 129, 131–32; *see also* shuttle trade, helpers
Central Europe, 7, 30, 36, 59, 60–61
Central European traders, 61, 143
Central Organization for the Customs Control, the, 56–57
charter flights. *See* transportation
cheating (also *kidok*), 46, 64, 68
chelnochestvo. See shuttle trade
Cherkizov market in Moscow, 103, 112–13
Childbirth, 74–75, 109, 113, 121
child care, 42, 46, 114–16, 122
children, 10, 39, 42–43, 4, 74–75, 76, 79, 81, 86, 89–90, 99, 103, 108, 111, 113–16, 118, 121–22, 130; and after-school programs, 42, 114, 115; and child-support payments, 44–45, 116; and custody of, 44
China, 8, 16, 51, 53, 57, 59, 61, 64–65, 83, 85, 88, 92, ,96, 102, 104, 107, 110, 120, 124, 129, 130–33, 139; and border crossing, 57, 132–33; and illegal factories in, 64–66; immigration to Russia ("yellow danger"), 133; and quality control in, 66, 83, 135; and visa regulations, 66, 85, 132
Clothing, 4, 19, 26, 30, 37, 45, 47–48, 57, 68, 69, 91, 94–97, 130, 132, 135, 143; and poor quality of, 50–52, 66

confiscation of goods, 49, 104; and personal use of confiscated items, 54–55
consignment shops (*komissionki*), 37
cooperatives, 16, 26–30, 35–36
corruption, 11, 14, 17, 37, 54–56, 58, 85, 136, 141
Council of Ministers, 20, 28, 32, 52
crime, 56, 64, 68, 73, 141; *see also* corruption; racketeering
Criminal Code of the USSR, the, Article 154 of, 48
crisis entrepreneurship, 79–80; *see also* necessity entrepreneurship
customs control, 56; *see also* border controls; confiscation of goods; customs duty
customs duty, 12, 49, 52, 54, 57, 105; and value of goods, 52–54, 57; and valuations, 56; and weight of goods, 12, 57–58, 98, 101, 131
Czechoslovakia, 7, 30, 60, 94

data accumulation, 11, 51–53, 56
deficit items, 21, 24, 25, 32, 37, 60, 61; *see also* shortages, of goods
default of Russian foreign debts, August 1998, 12, 17, 124–27, 128, 133, 136
disability, 71, 108, 113; *see also* abortions; health problems; pensions
discrimination, sex-based in a workplace, 43–44
divorce, *also* divorces among traders, 17, 44–45, 75, 108–9, 110–11, 119, 120
domestic goods, 6, 12, 95, 124, 130–31
double bookkeeping, 35
drunkenness. *See* alcoholism, substance abuse

Eastern Europe, 5, 10, 79, 104, 120
East Germany, 7
economic data, 6, 13, 40, 58; *see also* data accumulation
economy, Soviet, 3–4, 6, 16, 18–26, 31, 33–35
Egypt, 59, 85, 120, 141
Entrepreneur of the Year Award, 140

fakes, 93, 95–96; *see also* valuable fakes
fashions, in clothing, 7, 8, 19, 41, 48, 57, 66, 69, 92–93, 96, 97, 135–36
Federal State Statistics Services, the, 69–70, 71
food, imported, 37, 54, 60, 70, 104; and poor quality and poisoning, 51; and quality control, 135, 140
Freedom of Trade Decree, 49–50, 52

Gangsters. *See* racketeers
gardening plots, private, 80
gender equality propaganda, Soviet, 41–42; *see also* propaganda
gender stereotypes, 39, 40–47
geography of trade, 38, 58–69; *see also individual countries*
glasnost, 4, 18
globalization, 8, 92–93, 97, 132
gold, 31, 36
Gorbachev, Mikhail, 19, 21, 22–24, 31, 38, 92
grain prices, 31
gray market, 9, 13, 17, 132
Great Russian Depression, the (*also* Great Post-Soviet Depression), 42, 69
Greece, 53, 59, 67, 68, 85, 118
Gucci, 68, 95, 96

Harbin, 66, 120
health problems of traders, 51, 88, 98–99, 101, 108, 112–13, 117, 130, 141
hidden unemployment, 42–43; *see also* unemployment
Higher School of Economics, the, 62–63, 70, 82
hoarding, 26, 32
household chores, 74–75, 111
household electronics, 68, 100, 139
housing shortage, 74
Hungary, 7, 30, 59, 60, 63, 79, 91, 94

import-export imbalance, 20, 22–24, 31
import tariffs, 50, 56, 133
India, 16, 53, 59, 68
industrial growth rate, 32, 42

infanticide, 108, 121
inflation, 22, 32, 34, 42, 69, 70, 125
informal institutions, 8, 84, 132, 136; *see
    also* kinship networks
interviews, 13, 16, 41, 51, 56, 73, 82, 91,
    109; and gendered dimensions of,
    74–76; *see also* self-narrative
investment-profit ratio, 69
Italy, 8, 53, 59, 68, 69, 87, 92

Japan, 53, 84–85, 87

Khabarovsk, 13, 65, 66, 133
kinship networks, 84; *see also* informal
    institutions
kolkhoz, 22
Komsomol (Communist Youth League),
    16, 28–29
Komsomolsk-on-Amur, 120
Kopytina, Nadezhda, 139–40
Kosygin reforms, 41
Kunitskaia, Ol'ga, 117–18

Law on Individual Labor Activity, the, 16,
    26
Law of November 1988, the, on Travel
    Abroad, 27–28, 36
lenders, private (*rostovshchiki*), 85, 86
Lithuania, 53, 77, 79, 81
living standards, 4, 7, 18–19, 32, 87, 125
lodging during the trade, 67, 83, 106; *see
    also* accommodations

mafia. *See* racketeering
market assessment, 83
marketplaces and market conditions, 107,
    112–13; *see also* health problems
marriages, 45, 119–20
Mar'ino market, 128–29
Masculinity, 47, 86
maternity benefits (incl. leaves), 43
medical services, 27, 37, 38, 42–43, 99, 113
medication, 37, 31–32, 37–38
melamine, 135
Meshcherkina, Elena, 75–76
Milan, 69

Ministry of Finance, 56
Moscow, 5, 13, 62, 64, 67, 83, 100, 103, 105,
    112, 124, 127, 128–29, 139
Multidisciplinarity, 14–15

Naberezhnye Chelny, 104
Naples, 69
necessity entrepreneurs, 9, 45, 79–80, 81,
    141–42; *see also* crisis entrepreneurship;
    would-be entrepreneurs
New Economic Policy (NEP), 6, 41
Newly Independent States (NIS), 7, 8
Nike, 95–96

oil (*also* oil prices), 21–22, 23, 31–32
orphanages, 108, 122
"outside shock," 22

Pakistan, 53, 59, 68
party elite, 94
patriarchy, 108–9
peddling in non-NIS parts of the world,
    7–8
pensions (*also* state retirement benefits),
    33, 78, 103, 113, 133, 141
people's understanding of new economic
    reality, 33–34
perestroika, 20–21, 111
Persian Gulf, 68
personal narratives, 74–75, 87, 91
Peter the Great, 93
petty crime, 63–64, 141
Poland, 7, 16, 19, 28, 30, 37–38, 53, 58–59,
    60, 61, 63, 94, 104, 105–6, 111, 118, 139
Politburo, 20
Poloian, Genrikh, 91
private trade in Stalin's Russia, 6
propaganda, 41–43, 108–9
prostitution, 84–85, 120–21
pseudo-entrepreneurs, 9; *see also* necessity
    entrepreneurs

racketeering, 3, 37, 38, 47, 56, 60, 63, 66,
    86, 98–99, 105–7, 136, 141, 142
real estate (incl. mortgages), 89, 128
Reebok, 95–96

Resolution No 1322, 52–54
Rimini, 69
Roma, 143
Romania7, 59, 60, 62–63, 115, 143
Roskomstat. See State Committee on Statistics, the
Rospotrebnadzor (Russian State Committee for the Safety and Quality Control of Consumer Goods), 135
Russian Boom, 144
Russian Trade Commission, 51
Russian zones, 66
Ryzhkov, Nikolai, 20, 23, 24–25

Samogon, 24, 25, 118
schools, private, 6, 89, 99, 114, 116, 141
secondhand stores, 37, 96
self-esteem, 42, 75, 90, 91, 110, 122, 139, 142
self-narrative, 74–75, 85, 87, 91
sex slavery, 85
sexually transmitted diseases, 17, 108, 121
Shabaev, Aleksander, 67
shortages, of goods. *See* deficit items
shop tours, 36, 60, 63, 66
shuttle trade: and accumulation of capital, 76, 85–86; and traders' social status, 5, 90, 91, 94–95, 96, 119, 122, 135; economic impact of, 69–71; first wave of, 27–30; geography of, *see* geography of trade; "golden age" of, 37, 38, 40–48; helpers in (*pomogaiki, fonari, kirpichi*), 132–33; origins of, 18–40; people involved in (participation), 4, 6, 8, 43, 46, 50, 110, 126, 127, 133; public opinion of/attitude, 14, 19, 37, 46, 75, 76, 84, 86, 110, 133, 134–35, 143; regional variations, 120, 124, 128–29, 130, 143; second wave of, 28, 30–39; significance, 144–45; statues, 3; "transborder," 104; volume (turnover) of, 5, 11, 12, 17, 22, 24, 32, 51, 56, 59, 62, 65, 72, 101, 126–27
social profile of traders, 45, 72, 79–80
social-welfare system (*also* social services), 5–6, 45
South Korea, 65, 84
Sovetsk, 104

Soviet of Ministers. *See* Council of Ministers
Soviet state budget, 24, 32–33
Soviet Union (USSR), 27–29, 30–34, 37, 41, 43, 45–47, 60, 61, 75, 92, 93, 100, 108, 113–14, 115–16, 121, 141
Spain, 53, 59, 68
speculators (*spekulianty*), 37, 48, 82, 100, 134
State Committee on Statistics, the (*Roskomstat*), 51, 69–70, 71, 126–27
State Trade Committee, the, 56, 126
substance abuse, 44, 99, 116–17; *see also* alcoholism
suitcase trade. *See* shuttle trade
sugar, 24, 25, 32, 52, 57
Syktyvkar, 79, 123

tax evasion, 5, 14, 17, 43
Thailand, 59
Thessaloniki, 67
Tikhonov, Nikolai, 20
Tongjiang, 66
trade, legalization of, 4, 19, 133
trading tourism. *See* shuttle trade
trains. *See* transportation
transportations, 42, 52, 55, 62, 67, 83, 88, 89, 101, 105, 118, 132; *see also* charter flights; shop tours; trains
Treasury Bills, of Russian Government, 125
Turkey, 8, 16, 51, 52, 53, 57, 59, 61–64, 70, 85, 88, 90, 92, 95, 96, 104, 106, 111, 118–20
Turkish Central Bank, and "self-completion method," 51–52

Ukraine, 38, 63, 79, 81–82, 105
Unemployment, 6, 33, 35, 38–39, 40, 42–44, 49, 75, 111, 115, 127–28
Union of Business Women, 133
United Arab Emirates, 16, 59, 63, 68, 111
Usenkov, Valerii, 118–19

vacations, and passes to spas, resorts, summer camps, 6, 40, 42–43, 87–88, 90, 115, 129

valuable fakes, 93, 95–97; *see also* fakes
Versace, 68, 95
Veshchism, 93
"violent entrepreneurs," 136
Vladimirov, Vitalii, 91
Volkov, Vadim, 136

wages (*also* wage differentiation), 6, 14–15, 21, 32, 34, 35–6, 41, 58, 80, 85, 109, 129
weapons (incl. nuclear-missile launchers, assault rifles), 49, 55, 69
westernization, 8, 16, 92–93, 97
would-be entrepreneurs, 4, 9, 46; *see also* necessity entrepreneurs
World Trade Organization (WTO), 49–50

Yabloko (the Russian Democratic Party), 70
Yeltsin, Boris, 4, 38, 49, 92, 125
Yugoslavia, 61, 63, 143